Bella Levorsen - March 1973 - Lake Tahoe, CA.
Bella finished the race third out of 25 teams.

DEDICATION

To Bella and Bob Levorsen,

Long time members of Sierra Nevada Dog Drivers and two people I am proud to call friends. Thank you for your help, support and faith in me.

Charlene G. LaBelle

C O N T E N T S

MUSH!

A Beginner's Manual of Sled Dog Training

REVISED

Edited By Charlene G. LaBelle
for the Sierra Nevada Dog Drivers Inc.

Fourth Edition - 2007
Sales and Distributions:
Copyright © 2007 Barkleigh Productions, Inc.
970 W. Trindle Rd.,
Mechanicsburg, PA 17055
(717) 691-3388 • Fax (717) 691-3381
E-mail: info@barkleigh.com
www.**barkleigh**.com

ISBN 13: 978-0-9790676-0-0
ISBN 10: 0-9790676-0-X

ON THE COVER: This mix of registered, pure bred Alaskan Malamutes and Siberian Huskies was taken by Ron Kimball, of Ron Kimball Studios, Mountain View CA. "Buddy" is the dog shown running in lead.

MUSH!

A Beginner's Manual of Sled Dog Training

REVISED!

Edited By
Charlene G. LaBelle
for the
Sierra Nevada Dog Drivers, Inc.

PREFACE

MUSH! has been many years in the making. Literally it's been generations in the making. In its current form you have new authors, new contributors, a new editor and publisher.

A lot has gone into making *MUSH!* a book that we hope you as the reader will find easy to read and understand. We have tried to answer your questions. We hope that this opens the door to help you experience more wonderful times with your dogs.

There is a bit of history that may help you to appreciate the efforts that went into this latest *MUSH!*.

In the late 1800s teams of working sled dogs were hauling supplies and performing rescue missions in the Sierra Nevada Mountains. The natural progression was to have races. In the 1920s "Scotty" Allan's son George was driving a team and Jack London was a frequent spectator at these races. Multiple silent movies about dog teams were made in the Truckee area during this period. Since that time, if there was snow, races have been held in the Northern California area every year since.

In 1961, a group of ten local racers got together to form a club they named the Sierra Nevada Dog Drivers. SNDD was formed because it was important for our sport. SNDD cooperated with other sled dog organizations of the time, being a member the early Western Dog Mushers Association and sending a representative, Roger Reitano, to the organizational meeting for the International Sled Dog Racing Association at Niagara Falls in 1966.

Since the early days SNDD and its members have been strong supporters of the International Sled Dog Racing

Association, even providing it with Presidents and Chairmen of the Board. Robert Levorsen served several years as President (1971 to 1974). Bob served as the Chairman of the ISDRA Board (1989 to 1992). SNDD member Ralph Whitten (winner of seven International medals including eight-dog gold) served as President of the Sierra Nevada Dog Drivers for six years and also served as an ISDRA Director for six years. Ralph was Chairman of the ISDRA Board for four years (1997 to 2000). To this day SNDD continues to support ISDRA and sanctions a majority of our races with ISDRA. SNDD has worked hard to promote sled dog sports and assist new events/classes, such as skijor, to qualify for International medal status.

In 1970, Mrs. Mel Fishback, Mrs. Pat Daniels and Mrs. Betty Allen thought it a good idea to write a few mimeographed sheets of instructions to help the increasing number of beginners in the local club get started running their dogs. Questions commonly asked would be answered in writing instead of verbally. Putting those pages together was how the first edition of *MUSH!* came into existence. Since then the written instructions, like the club and the sport in general, have grown in size and scope.

The third edition of *MUSH!* made use of the varied knowledge of many people both within SNDD and from the mushing community all over the country. Contributions of people outside the club are acknowledged in the main text of the book. Within the club, in addition to the 3rd edition editors, members who have contributed are: Thom Ainsworth, Georgene Goodstein, Randy Roe, Lucy Bettis, Nancy Link, Roxie Varvaro, Pat Daniels, Tom and Sylvia Palmer, Dave Walling, Dave Decker, George Ricard and

Daphne Rippon.

Various quotes and references, which have been taken from published works, are given credit adjacent to the excerpts throughout the book. In addition, much information has been taken from *Team and Trail* with the kind permission of Cindy Molburg and "Uncle Elmer". While the drawings in the first edition of *MUSH!* were done by Mel Fishback, many of them were redrawn for the third edition by Georgene Goodstein, who also did all of the new illustrations for the third edition. Many of which are included in this new work.

For this 4th edition we would like to thank the following people for their help and support. Please forgive me if I forget a name or two.

First my dogs and my husband, Steve LaBelle. Bob and Belle Levorsen have been wonderful help. Many folks from SNDD and my Internet friends from all over the world helped with this effort. A few of the SNDD members and friends that I feel need to be mentioned are: Shirley Austin-Peeke, John Harshman, Rob Loveman, Dru Anne Martin, Kathy Miyoshi, Harman v.s. Peeke, Barbara "Dog Drop" Schaffer, Bruce Smith, Denise Visas-Tyng and Ralph Whitten.

I would also like to thank the wonderful staff with our new publisher, Barkleigh Productions (especially Marsha!).

HOW TO USE THIS BOOK

The primary objective of this book is to assist the beginner to turn themselves and their dogs into a first class racing team. As a beginner you need no experience, just the willingness to try.

This book should also be helpful to the person that has a few years of racing experience and is looking for details or to reinforce that they are doing it right.

You will find a few chapters that have nothing to do with racing have been added for suggestions of other activities you and your dogs can enjoy together. These activities are simply suggestions of other means to strengthen the bond between dog and driver.

This book is intended to be a reference material. Each chapter stands on its own.

It is hoped that you, the reader, will enjoy this book and find it useful.

Welcome to the wonderful world of sled dog sports!

1   MUSH!

Chapter One

SLED DOG LORE

History of Sled Dog Lore

Sled dog racing in North America began as a formal sport with the first All-Alaska Sweepstakes race in 1908. The Nome Kennel Club was formed to organize and sponsor the race. Rules and principles of racing established by this club are still being used at races today.

The All-Alaska Sweepstakes races were run in early April, starting on Front Street in Nome. Then across the Seward Peninsula to Candle and back, round trips distance just over 400 miles.

The All-Alaska Sweepstakes was to be a true test of men and teams as the trail went from "sea ice to high mountains, with rivers, tundra, timber, glaciers, and everything else in the way of mental and physical hardships en route... even Old Death Valley, that was nearly always filled with a smoking blizzard, no matter how fine the weather was on both sides." (A. A. "Scotty" Allan, gold, *Men and Dogs*, G. P. Putnam's Sons, New York, Copyright 1931, p.178.)

The dogs that ran in the first Sweepstakes were regular freighting teams. The harnesses and sleds were freighting types. For the second running of the race, "Scotty" Allan designed a 30-pound racing sled for himself that was quite different, with long runners and a curved handle bar. The curved handle bar replaced the upright posts and allowed for pedaling. Scotty also made other equipment changes in the quest for more speed. One such change was he lightened his harnesses and towlines. George Allan, ("Scotty's" son) wrote in a personal letter that each dog's harness and the towline weighed only 14 ounces.

The types of dogs being run were changing too. Huskies were imported from Siberia. In 1910, dog driver "Iron Man" Johnson set a record of 74 hours, 14 minutes and 37 seconds. This record stood throughout the series.

In 1911 "Scotty" Allan won the race with Alaskan cross-breeds (mostly Malamute-Setter crosses) in just over 80 hours through blizzard conditions. Allan raced in eight Sweepstakes; won three, was second in three, and was third twice.

Another early sled dog racing "great" was the Norwegian immigrant Leonard Seppala. He, too, got his start driving a freight team. But for racing, he used only the smaller Siberian Huskies. When the First World War forced cancellation of further Sweepstakes, Seppala had won three victories as well. He went on later to win many shorter races in Alaska and New England. His Siberians became the forerunner of the American Kennel Club registered Siberian Husky breed. And today there are still people racing and breeding to the lines that Leonard race so well.

While in New England, Seppala gave one of his dogs to a young veterinary student named Roland Lombard. Not only did "Doc" Lombard earn his way through college by racing a small sled dog team (four to five dogs), but also he continued racing, training and improving methods until his death in 1990. Doc won eight Anchorage World Championships and contributed greatly to the sport. He was the first president of the International Sled Dog Racing Association, a position he held for five years.

Another "great" in the recent history of sled dog racing is George Attla. George is an Athabascan Indian from Huslia, Alaska. At this publication Attla has won ten Anchorage Fur Rendezvous and eight Open North American Championships, the most of any musher.

Egil Ellis, like Leonard Seppala, is also a Scandinavian native. He now resides in Alaska as well. Egil Ellis successfully races a cross between an Alaskan Husky and a German Shorthaired Pointer. This is the mix being called the Euro Hound. Ellis is setting records for speed on the same tracks and trails made famous by Lombard and Attla and is threatening their records for number of victories on those same trails.

Dog sled races today are frequently put on by communities, sled dog clubs, civic groups or combination of these groups. There is often support of corporate sponsors as well. Races take much time, hard work and money to organize. For this reason some smaller races have a way of coming and going as the enthusiasm of the sponsoring group waxes and wanes over the years. Still some events continue to be run year after year. Races such as The Anchorage Fur Rendezvous, The Open North American Championship and the Tok Race of Champions have been in existence for many years and are considered by many as the premier events in sled dog racing.

Outside the sled dog community and local towns, these three long-standing races may not be well known. In the early 1970s Joe Reddington Sr. had one of his dreams come true. It was 1973 when the race he started was first run. This long distance racing is known as the "Last Great Race". This very race is known around the world as the Iditarod.

Leonard Seppala
Photo from the private collection of Charlene LaBelle with permission by Sigred Seppala.

Each March the Iditarod is a run from Anchorage to Nome. This race of over 1,000 miles was started as a commemoration of the delivery of a life saving diphtheria serum to Nome via dog teams in 1925. No single race or sled dog related activity has so captivated the imagination and fascination as this race. (1,049 is the mileage listed in many publications. The race is over 1000 miles long, run in the 49th state. The 1,049 is not the actual mileage because the trail changes each year due to snow conditions and multiple other factors.)

The Iditarod takes the fastest mushers and his or her team well over a week to complete. Only the most experienced and hardiest qualify to even attempt running this event.

There is currently a similar race, from Fairbanks to Whitehorse (Yukon Territory) called The Yukon Quest. The Quest is considered by some to be as difficult as the Iditarod, but run under somewhat different rules. These two races are the modern premier distance races. Still each year there are many newer, shorter, but nevertheless challenging races that attract large entries of tough mushers with well-trained and conditioned dog teams.

The above short paragraphs only mentions some of the more

famous of the many races run on the North American continent. It should be clearly noted that sled dog racing has a long history in Europe. In Europe, sled dog races were initially confined in some countries to purebred dogs. It was also a challenge to race because transporting dogs between countries was made even more difficult because of laws designed to protect against rabies. As these rules were relaxed, European mushers became more prominent. In 2005 a Scandinavian musher won the Iditarod and it is unlikely he will be the last.

George Attla
Photo by Lisa B.
Fallgren Stevens.

Sled dog racing is not limited to Europe and the North American continent. Sled dog racing has also established itself in Japan, Australia, New Zealand and many other countries. Some of which are not known for having sled dog events. There is even a Jamaican dog sled racing team.

Chapter Two
TEAM MEMBERS

What makes a team?

You with one or more dogs are a team. You and your dogs can have mushing experiences or no mushing experiences. But together you are not a true team until all can work together smoothly as a unit.

The size of the team is only limited by your comfort, training and the number of dogs you have access to. A team of dogs is as large or small as you want. For many a four, six or eight dog team may be in their comfort zone and another can like running a string of 16, 20 or more dogs. Yet someone else might enjoy running a one, two or three dog team. You are the one to determine what works best for you. Conditions should also play a part in the size of a team you choose to run at any given time.

Members of the team

There are three main names given to the dog members that make up the team. They are your leaders, team dogs and wheel dogs.

Starting at the front and working back, the names correspond to the placement along the towline. Many of these names are also hints as to the job. At the very front you will have a leader or pair of leaders. They are followed by the dogs that are between the front and rear dogs, known as the team dogs. Bringing up the rear of the team are the wheel dogs.

Leader or leaders

These are the dogs that are at the head of your team. Leaders guide your team and follow your verbal commands. Their job is to keep the light taut and to turn the rest of the dogs in the direction as you give commands to change direction. Some leaders follow a trail and other dogs are what are called command leaders. If a dog is up front, it's a leader.

Team dogs

The dogs between your leaders and wheelers are the team dogs. The number of team dogs you run as team dogs is up to you. Team dogs are the dogs that are additional pulling power. They are the dogs that have no other job but to pull.

Wheel Dogs

Some say that wheel dogs are the powerhouses of the team. Some people put their largest dogs in wheel. The wheel dogs have a hard job because they pull the sled through the turns. Wheel dogs are also referred to as wheelers.

Last but not least, The Dog Driver or Musher

That's you. You too are a part of the team. Some say you are the brains of the team and the dogs are the brawn. Your job is to be a cheerleader, doctor and protector. If you take care of the other members of your team, they will take care of you. Your dogs will look to you for guidance. You need to work with your dogs and together with training, patience and practice, you will become a team.

Point and Swing Dogs

The three common and basic positions are the leaders, team and wheelers. There are also dogs referred to as point and swing dogs. The point dogs are the pair just behind the leader. The position of swing dogs is one that is still not all that clear. Some say that point dogs and swing dogs are the same position. The term used for the dogs just behind the leaders depends on the region. Others say the swing dogs are the pair in front of the wheel dogs and their job is to help the wheel dogs swing the sled.

In a quick pole of mushers around the world, it was agreed that the swing dogs are not the leaders or the wheelers, but not agreed on the actual placement in the team. We did agree that point dogs are the dogs just behind the lead dog. The point is a position and it is the place many dog drivers will put upcoming leaders, leaders they are resting or leaders they are using to help an inexperienced leader to learn the commands while gaining confidence.

So when hooking up, it's fine to tell a helper, "That dog goes on the right in front of the wheel dogs." or "Put that dog on the left side behind the leader."

Robert Levorsen, Chester, CA, January 11, 1986. *Photo by Tom Watson.*

9   MUSH!

KINDS OF SLEDS DOGS

A common misconception about sled dogs is that they must be large in size. Most first time race spectators or people new to racing expect to see teams of 100-pound Huskies at races and are surprised at the small stature and size of the average sled dog and the lack of thick coats. They are also surprised at the variety of breeds represented at races.

Almost any dog can be taught to pull, and any medium-sized dog can make a satisfactory sled dog. Many mushers new to the sport will use the breed that they already own as a matter of preference and convenience. Over the years it has not been uncommon for Collies, Dalmatians, Doberman Pinschers, German Shepherd Dogs, Pointers, Poodles and an assortment of other non-traditional sled breeds to be seen in harness. Several winning teams consist solely of non-northern breeds and the list of crossbred dogs used to pull sleds today is endless.

Shear or brute strength is not as important in sled dog racing as speed, since the sled load is distributed among many dogs. The large heavily built dogs with great strength are not nearly as fast as the lean wiry dogs and they tend to tire sooner when asked to go fast. For example, human weight lifters don't typically compete in, or do well, competing in marathon races.

The most important requirement for a good sled dog is the desire to run. Fortunately, most dogs enjoy running. Other important requirements are sound body structure, good health, proper nutrition and sufficient training.

NORTHERN BREEDS

Northern breed dogs have been used for thousands of years by Arctic people as working dogs, hunters, reindeer herders, companions, guardians and sled pullers. Through time, separate ethnic groups have developed their own strains of dogs, most of which have been selectively bred and given the English name of the people with whom they were found. The white Samoyed dogs were developed by the Samoyed peoples of east central Siberia as reindeer herders; the Alaskan Malamute was developed by the Malemuit (Mahlemut) Eskimos of northwestern Alaska for hauling heavy loads long distances. Even the Husky breeds were named after the people that developed them, for the early North American explorers called the Eskimos they encountered the "huskies" because of their solid build. Thus, we have the Greenland Husky, the Mackenzie River Husky, and the Siberian Husky.

The Siberian Husky was imported in the early 1900s for racing in the All-Alaska Sweepstakes and did well there and later in New England. These days they are still the most common purebred registered dogs on the sled dog race trails. The Indian or Village Dog of central Alaska has a varied breed background, though the Husky type dog predominates. The Indian or Village Dog was specifically bred for working, hauling game and belongings on sleds and for running trap lines. They make excellent race dogs and can stand either cold or warm weather.

The three most common breeds that most people think of when you say sled dog are Alaskan Malamute, Samoyed and Siberian Husky. These three breeds are registered breeds with written standards. All three breeds are recognized with the major registries around the world.

Breed: Alaskan Malamute
Origin: USA
Weight: 75 lbs. for bitches and 85 lbs. for dogs
Height: 23 in. for bitches and 25 in. for dogs
* These dogs can be taller or shorter, weigh more or less. The weight and height listed are for the "ideal" dog.
Coat: double, short, stand-off
Markings: symmetrical with white or cream legs and underbelly. The only solid color allowed being white. This is technically white with white.
Eye color: brown and shades of brown
A draft or combination draft and hunting dog. They are known for their ability to go long distances with heavy weight. They were used to haul a family's life possessions from one

nomadic camp to the next. For hunting they were used to hunt seals and then haul the meat home. Many of these dogs lived in the communal homes with the families. The more modern dogs are much better behaved than the dogs of the past. The dogs of the past were known to fight at the drop of a hat and seem to find fighting fun. This could be because while they were loved and cared for, if food was scarce or in the summer months the dogs had to fend for themselves. This is a breed that does not need the same volume of food to maintain body weight as their smaller faster cousins. They have very strong prey drive and pack instincts. They need a home with a strong owner that is firm but fair when dealing with discipline.

Paul Martin running a pair of his AKC Champion Samoyeds at the Shaver Lake race.
Photo by John Harschman.

Breed: Samoyed (proper pronunciation is Sahm-yed, although Sam-oid is used in the US)

Origin: Tamiyr Peninsula, Northwestern Siberia, above the Arctic Circle

Weight: Females: 40-50 lbs.; Males: 50-65 lbs.

Height: 19 - 23 1/2 in. at shoulder

Coat: double, long, stand-off with dense undercoat

Markings: white, biscuit, cream or mixed, black points (dark eyes, eye rims, lips, and nose).

The nomadic Samoyede people's dogs were used to herd reindeer, babysit children and pull sleds as they hunted. Reindeer were also employed as draft animals. Occasionally the dogs were used as hunters. These dogs have a strong affinity for humans due to high regard the Samoyede people had for them. Many say they were treated as family. Nansen used Samoyed Dogs to explore the Arctic in the late 19th Century. A Samoyed Dog named *Etah* led Amundsen's team across South Pole in 1911. These were the preferred dogs of some early polar explorers because they didn't fight amongst themselves and were very amiable with humans.

Breed: Siberian Husky
Origin: Siberia
Weight: Males, 45-60 lbs.; Females, 35-50 lbs.
Height: Males 21-23 1/2 in.; Females 20-21 1/2 in.
Coat: thick, pelt like, stand-off; dense undercoat
Markings: Any color or marking acceptable. Anything from solid white to solid black is acceptable and currently the most popular marking is the traditional Irish pattern.
Eye color: Any eye color is acceptable. Brown, blue or one of each are often seen in addition to green, amber, or particolored (the eye has multiple colors which could be part brown and part blue).

Siberian Huskies from Husker Du Kennels. These dogs are owned, bred and run by SNDD members Glen and Sheila Laughton. *Photo by John Harshman.*

About 3000 years ago, the Chukchi people of Siberia adapted a way of life in the cold by creating a culture based on long-distance sled dogs. These people lived in permanent inland settlements and traveled long distances to hunt sea mammals. Their dogs were neither sprinters nor freighters. They were endurance animals and could pull a light load over incredible distances.

OTHER BREEDS

For pure speed, the coursing hounds, known as some of the fastest dogs on earth, would seem to be most desirable. But speed without the stamina to maintain it mile after mile does not count for much, so the Greyhounds, Salukis, Afghans and Borzois are seldom found in purebred form on the race trails. On the other hand, the moderately fast, long distance hounds developed for tracking coons for days on end have won many races, particularly in moderate to warm weather conditions. Many crosses of Husky and Greyhound have been attempted, often with great success, particularly in eastern Canada. These crosses are what ultimately became known as the Alaskan Husky, which is described in more detail below.

Bird dogs have also been tried as sled dogs, with the Irish Setter doing outstandingly well. These long-haired, long-legged dogs are fast and strong and were used to haul mail in the American Northwest in the 1920s and 30s and won races in the 30s and 40s.

Setter crosses were popular for years. In Idaho they made a cross with a Stag hound; these were named the Targhee Hound, after nearby mountains.

The Alaskan Husky is not your average cross. Some may call it a mutt because it is a mixed breed dog. However, the Alaskan Husky used for racing these days is normally a carefully planned combination of dogs and breeds which are bred for their ability to withstand cold temperatures and their sheer speed. As you move between the different regions of the United States and Canada you may notice the Alaskan Huskies look different in different places. This is because they have been bred to conform to the needs of the region within with the musher lives and races.

Some areas have harsher climates and as a result the dogs may have thicker coats and a more Husky appearance. But other areas that have a milder climate may have dogs that have shorter coats and a very "hound-like" appearance. These types of mixes are referred to as an Alaskan Husky.

This Alaskan Husky breed is one that is constantly changing as mushers continue to refine their breeding programs. As of late, the breeds of choice for mixing with Alaskan Huskies seem to favor the Pointer breeds, with the German Short Haired Pointer becoming quite popular in the late 1990's. These dogs bred to a more standard type of Alaskan Husky continue to win the big races in Alaska and the lower 48.

For years the European racers had been using their hunting dogs not only for hunting, but as skijor and pulk races as well as racing in the more traditional sled dog classes. These dogs and then the mixes were doing so well in competition that the term Euro-Hound was used to identify these racing dogs.

There is one more type of dog you need to consider and that

is the dog of unknown origin. This could be a dog you obtained from a shelter, rescue organization or perhaps the dog showed up on your doorstep one morning. Any age dog from young pup to the adult can make a wonderful addition to your sled dog family. There are people such as John Schandelmeier and his kennel partner Zoya DeNure race dogs rescued from the pound. They and others have done well running dogs that someone no longer wanted. Schandelmeier's running rescued dogs have won major races on multiple continents, including the 1000-mile Yukon Quest (twice).

SNDD member Steve LaBelle running a team of Alaskan Huskies for Wildfire Racing Kennel. *Photo by Bruce T. Smith.*

Chapter Four

ACQUIRING A RACING DOG

So you have been bitten by the racing bug and your current couple of dogs aren't fast enough for you or you want more dogs to run longer races. No matter what the reason, you have decided its time to buy a racing dog. Acquiring dogs occurs at every level of the sport.

Buying a quality dog or several dogs is no easy matter. It is especially difficult for the less experienced driver who hasn't learned their way around the "dog scene". Don't feel bad if you think the task is overwhelming. Learn from the mistakes of others. Olaf Swenson shares his experience in *Northwest of the World Forty Years' Trading and Hunting in Northern Siberia*. His story is typical of many new dog drivers.

"When I first went to Siberia and began buying dogs, I decided that I wanted a sporty-looking outfit. I made up my mind that I would have a white team, composed of especially large, fine, well-matched animals, with fine red harnesses and red sleds. I was going to be cock of the trail and show those natives how fine an outfit could look. I could see that the natives were amused, but they hunted up the dogs all right, and I got my white team. It looked like a million dollars... but as a sled team it was no good at all. There were a few good dogs in it, but before long I replaced half of the team with dogs which had stamina and speed and intelligence. For years the natives kidded me about the white team. They'd laugh and say, 'Swenson wants a white dog. He doesn't care whether it's good or bad; he just wants a white dog." (Olaf Swenson, *Northwest of the World*, Dodd, Mead and Co., New York, 1944, page 188).

The best way to buy the right dog the first time is to get advice from experienced drivers with good dogs. Work with someone and think of him or her as your mentor. These drivers should become acquainted with you and your driving abilities in order to be in a fair position to offer their help in the purchase of dogs. Sometimes you may find dogs locally or your mentor may open the door with referrals to other kennels.

Internet sled dog email groups are a means of meeting other drivers. You may have a local sled dog club with a newsletter or website that people list dogs they are selling. International mushing publications often have advertisements of sled dogs for sale. These publications also contain race results that give the prospective buyer a chance to learn how the drivers with dogs for sale have placed in competition.

When purchasing a dog, you need to understand that the perfect lead dog, team, point or wheel dog is not going to show up at your door. Don't expect perfection; it's not for sale. Get to know the person you are wishing to purchase dogs from. Become friends if possible. Dogs from the big name kennels are fine, but don't forget the smaller kennel with the same blood lines. Many times a dog that does not make someone's "A" team might be as close to perfect for your team as they come.

If the kennel you would like to buy a dog from is close, try to make a personal visit to them. Frequently there is a great distance between you and the kennel. And you may end up purchasing a dog sight unseen. The novice buyer need not hesitate to purchase the dog sight unseen if you and the seller have had good communications. You need to clearly communicate your needs and they need to clearly communicate what they have to offer. You are purchasing performance, not looks. So unless you are set on a dog that has a particular kind of appearance, there is no need to see it beforehand. You can neither tell much about a dog's performance by examining him in a kennel nor learn much by driving him yourself only once. You have to take the owner's word for their ability. One thing you can do is to check on the owner's reputation as a driver and as a person. Most drivers will be completely honest with you because they want you to be satisfied with the dog. Their reputation is at stake.

In order to fit the dog to your needs, you need information. You as the buyer should be completely honest with the seller when informing him about the following:

Your Present Kennel
    Breed of dogs
    Sex of dogs, particularly your leader

Size of your team now
How dogs are housed

Your Expectations
From new dog
Position you want new dog to run
The team size/class you will be putting the dog
Where you want to go as far as racing

Your Experience
Your patience limitations
What class you have raced in
Where you placed

Your Training Methods
Type of trail
If you use a cart, sled, scooter, ATV, etc.
Number of miles in your usual training run
The frequency of runs and temperature
while running

If you are looking for a lead dog, basically there are two kinds:
a) the trail leader who stays in front and strings the team out, and
b) the command leader whom both stays out front and takes commands.

Pair of mid-distance teams at a Shaver Lake Race. *Photo by Bruce T. Smith.*

When you find a leader for sale, ask the seller if the dog is a command leader or a trail leader. Check the size of team they led, if it has actually raced, in what races, types of trails and where the team placed. A leader who has placed 10th in front of 16 dogs in a major race may be a better leader than one who once led two other dogs around the neighborhood.

Just because someone is selling or giving a dog away does not mean the dog is a problem dog. Sometimes an older and reliable command leader who is no longer fast enough to stay in front of a big team is just what a small, beginning team needs to keep out of trouble and to give its new dogs experience. These older leaders are less expensive than dogs in their prime and can be worth their weight in gold to the novice dog driver. There can be times the price is low or even free to the right home if the owner is interested in placing their older dogs in good homes.

If you are set on a specific registered purebred of any of the northern breeds, just because it is a purebred, that does not automatically make it a first-class sled dog. As with any performance animal, what counts is the track record, the proven performance of that particular dog and the racing record of its entire life.

When you are buying a puppy you don't have a running record to go by. You can only go by what's behind the puppy. You have heard the saying: "You pay your money and you take your chances." Well buying a puppy is taking your chances.

The buyer of any dog should have the following information furnished by the seller in your bill of sale. The information should include (but not be limited to):

Vital Statistics
    Sex
    Age
    Breeding lines; registration, if any
    Physical appearance; marking, size (height
    and weight)
    Spay/neutered or intact
    Status of rabies and other vaccinations if
    given and when

You will also want the following information in writing so that you have something that you can refer to. Don't trust your memory. Write it down. Better yet, have them write it down. You will want detailed information on each dog you own or buy.

Temperament
> Any behavior peculiarities (i.e. destroys doghouse)
> Do they travel well
> Are they an easy keeper (i.e.: put food down and it's gone)

Medical and Nutritional
> Past serious illness
> Any chronic illness
> Any medications being administered at present time
> Status of rabies and other vaccinations if given and when
> Last worming; for what type worms
> Any feeding problems
> Type and amount of food being used

Training
> Stage of training
> Trained by a man or a woman
> Discipline used and required
> Size of team usually run with
> Position dog runs best
> Side preferred
> Whether runs better alone or with companion
> Type of trail usually run
> Any experience in front of a cart
> Number of miles in recent training runs
> Speed(s) the dog seems to have as a comfort zone
> Approximate miles put on this season
> Approximate miles put on previous season(s)

Racing Experience
 What races
 What class
 Did they go the distance
 Position team usually places (approximate)
 Kennel's first or second string
 Years of racing

OK, so now the talking is done. You have carefully selected what you hope to be the right dog and a purchase is made. You will have to work out shipping details. Are you going to meet at a race? Will they ship the dog air freight? Can you line up someone that is traveling to races in their area and can bring a dog back for you? You as the buyer wait in anticipation for the new addition to the team to arrive.

The day finally arrives.

Don't expect too much when you first see the dog. After all, this dog is bought for performance. And because this dog was purchased for performance he may not be Mr. Sociability or Show Dog of the Century when he arrives. Performance is what you purchased.

It is important to let the dog get used to its new surroundings and you before putting or adding them to your team. It is a rare dog that will go from crate to harness. It is particularly tough on lead dogs because they need to learn about you as well. This is a team activity and to give a peak performance, you must be comfortable together.

To illustrate, another quote from *Northwest of the World*:

"I shall never forget Billkoff (Snowball in English), the finest dog I have ever known...I met him many years ago when he belonged to a native, and I wanted him ten minutes after I had seen him. It was not only for his record as a leader, but his personality, his character and his wisdom... and I found myself wanting him more than I had ever wanted any other dog. I tried to buy him, but his native owner had as much appreciation of a good dog as I had and would not sell him. Completely courteous, however, he would never come out frankly and tell me that he thought too much of the dog himself to let me have him, but always gave me another reason, saying, 'I don't think that dog would be any good for you. He is too used to me. He wouldn't mind anyone else.'"

Several years later, Swenson got Billkoff and continues; "When I started out to work with the dog, I discovered that the native's spoken reason for not selling him had been more than a stall. For six months, he was the worst dog I had ever known. He simply refused to accept me as his boss and constantly took matters in his own hands. Finally, however, he gave up the struggle and from then until the day he died (several years later) he was the best dog I had ever seen in any man's team." (Swenson, op. cit. page 183.)

There are literally a hundred reasons for initial disappointment in the performance of a newly acquired dog. We need to remember this is an animal that lived and loved, elsewhere. It knew its previous owner and the dogs in the kennel. It knew the local trails. Some of the many reasons that can effect a new dog's performance are:

1. The dog has never run with some piece of equipment (cart, ATV) and is unsure of said equipment.

2. Running conditions vary from area to area, and the dog may never have experienced these conditions.

3. The dog is just plain scared and needs time to settle in to get over it.

4. The dog doesn't understand your commands, is frightened by your motions, voice, correction or training methods.

5. The dog's condition may need to be improved, it may have lost weight or muscle mass from the sudden change in: food, stress, altitude, climate, water, etc.

6. The harness you are using is not quite right in fit, or the dog ran in a different style harness.

7. The dog is not used to a male (or female) driver... you know... you.

And so on.

Please resist the temptation to put your new dog immediately in any position of stress. Even if the dog was an experienced leader, being in lead is always a position of stress. A new driver, new trails and with new dogs behind. Poor dog might not know if those dogs are following or chasing! You can completely ruin good leaders by asking too much too soon. It's a dog, not a car. A high-priced dog does not react like a high-priced automobile. So for the first few runs, take your time. You may want to put your new leader behind your old one. Try it a few times. If all goes well during those runs, put them in double lead, (preferably with a dog of the opposite sex, it's normally less of a challenge). Wait until the right time to move them up front. Be patient, it may take a long time before you put him in single lead. By taking your time it could be well worth the wait!

Don't second guess yourself. Take your time in passing judgment on your new addition. Don't think of it as making a good or bad deal.

If soon after arrival, your new dog turns out to have some physical illness or disability that your veterinarian says must have been present before the purchase you should inform the seller about it. If the dog, after a reasonable time to become adjusted, shows intolerable aggression in harness towards other dogs, you do have reason to complain if you had been told the dog was non-aggressive. Also, if after a reasonable time to become adjusted, the dog when in harness does nothing but lays down and will not get up and run in any fashion, you should make contact with the seller.

There are other less serious reasons you might be unhappy with a newly purchased dog. The dog may not keep the line tight. They may dart off the trail or duck under the truck at every opportunity. The dog may not even want to come out of their dog box. It's frustrating to pay top dollar for a leader, when the leader may not take commands. If it was a known good dog, then it is reasonable to assume that the dog needs more time to adjust.

Even a good dog needs up to a full season with a new driver to turn in a superb performance. Your judgment should not be passed on your new dog until the second season.

Be open to the idea that you might be a large part of the problem, particularly if you are a new driver. It could be your second or third season and you may be doing something wrong. Many novice dog drivers learn more from a seasoned veteran dog than they will ever know. If the dog initially gives good runs and then deteriorates, it indicates that you might be at fault. Talk to a local person, see if they will work with you and give you some help. More than one dog was passed from kennel to kennel until the right owner and dog combination came about. Then the dog turned into one of the best dogs they ever had.

You should not hesitate to contact the seller to openly and honestly discuss the matter. The former owner, in most instances, should be in a good position to offer helpful hints. You should still seek the advice of experienced local drivers who have observed you and the dog in action. Perhaps they can see something that you did not.

When you are working on the deal for the dog, make sure you understand if it's a purchase or a trial. Unless the dog was sent specifically on trial basis, there are no refunds or exchanges in the dog business. A dog is not merchandise with a "completely satisfied or your money back" guarantee. Your best guarantee is to be honest with yourself and the seller and to not expect a miracle. Then if you don't like the dog after a season's trial, just don't deal with that seller again.

This section is on Acquiring a Racing Dog. To most that means buying or trading for a dog or dogs. Yet there will be times that breeding is the means to enlarging a race kennel.

It's not cheap to breed dogs. And it's not quick either. There are fees and a lot of costs involved in breeding. There is also a considerable risk, that your time, money and energy may not pay off. Breeding involves selection of the animals to be bred. If you start with mediocre, you tend to stay with mediocre. With a higher caliber dog, this can greatly increase the chances of having high caliber pups. Still with breeding you may get only two to three out of six puppies which can make your racing team, if any.

Keep all of this in mind when you gasp at the price that a trained seasoned prime sled dog can fetch. You may be lucky and find someone who, for personal reasons, must sell first-class dogs for a "deal". Outstanding command leaders, if you ever find one for sale, usually come in package deals. Frequently you will need to buy several dogs to get the leader you want. These deals can run into the thousands. You are buying years of experience. You are buying someone's proven training, selective breeding, and in a way, all the dogs who didn't make their team. If you take all these factors into consideration, the price doesn't seem quite so high.

If you do not have the money, but have the time and energy, another way to add dogs to your team is from your local pound. More than one first-class racing dog was been discovered in the pound. Crazy Dog Kennel partners John Schandelmeier and Zoya DeNure have proven that rescued dogs can race and do win ... major races! All over the world, there are rescue groups that routinely pull dogs from the pound. Some deal only with sled breeds and with a little TLC turn them into first-rate sled dogs.

Wherever you get your new dog, be sure to give it love, kindness, respect, understanding, the care deserving of a first class athlete and quality time.

SNDD member Preston Springston running an 8-dog team at Shaver Lake, CA. *Photo by Bruce T. Smith.*

CONFINEMENT AND HOUSING
Of Sled Dogs

Sled dogs are a hearty breed. This is a breed that was developed living in the cold and harsh climate. Many sled dogs would rather sleep in the snow than in a nice dry doghouse. Still some of the newer racing dogs need a little more controlled environment to maintain body weight. Heated dog barns are getting more common.

No matter what breed, sled dogs need some method to confine them. This will keep them from running free and getting into trouble. With confinement of any type, a means of getting out of the weather should be available should they choose.

There are many time proven ways of confining sled dogs. The type you will use will depend upon several factors. The four things that quickly come to mind are: the type/breed of dogs you have, number of dogs, space available, and amount of money you have to spend.

Whichever means you use to confine your dogs, every dog should have a house or a bed of their own AND a means to give them a feeling of security and permanence. These houses should give protection from rain, snowstorms and hot sun, depending on the season.

CONFINING WITH CHAINS

Most of the large kennel owners secure their dogs with chains or tethers. Tethering is actually a good way to keep your dogs friendly and they can interact with their neighbors. Tethering is one of the most inexpensive methods and takes up the minimal space. Each dog needs five or six feet of quality chain with a swivel snap at one end to attach to the collar. The other end is fastened permanently, preferably with another swivel attachment, to a variety of objects. Car axles work quite well. There are people that manufacture systems to safely tether dogs (see supplier section). Tethering is also one of the most misunderstood methods for keeping your dog safe and secure.

Precautions

With all systems, it is important to keep the dogs far enough apart so that they cannot quite reach each other. There have been people that mistakenly thought it would be nice for neighboring dogs to be able to play with each other with disastrous results. By having the dogs too close to each other, this increases the chances of fights, accidental breedings or the dogs' being hurt or strangled by tangled chains.

If you have a large lot of dogs on chains it is also a good idea to have a perimeter fence. This fence will keep other animals out of the dog yard. If you use a perimeter fence and can divide your dog yard into two sections, you can have a boy's side and a girl's side. By having all the boys in one enclosure and the girls on another, you will also cut down on the chances of accidental breedings. Just one loose boy can make a lot of litters if you have multiple bitches in heat.

CABLE RUNS

Cable runs work very well for people with a limited number of dogs that can not use fencing. A cable run is two poles with a piece of cable or stout rope run between the two poles. There is a cable or chain run from the cable to the neck of the dog. Most use a wheel of some sort so the dog section moves freely. The piece the dog is on should be long enough so the dog can safely lie down. If it is too long then the distance the dog can travel may need to be reduced.

You can have multiple dogs on one cable. But you need to have stops so that the dogs can not tangle, fight or breed, like tethered dogs. Cable runs are very much like tethering, but the chain or cable is over head.

Precautions

You need to have either stops on the top cable or some means to keep the dog from tangling around the end poles. The cable needs to be kept free of anything the dog can tangle on. With a cable run the dogs can have visitors you may not want (skunks, other dogs, etc).

An Alaskan Huskey and Eurohound, one in a kennel run, the other in the exercise yard. *Photo by Shirley Austin-Peeke.*

CONFINING WITH RUNS

Some owners often prefer runs for their dogs. If they can afford the price and have the room, they may have runs with multiple dogs in each run. Many will spend the extra money because they don't like the idea of keeping their dogs chained. Kennel owners may have a few runs for special dogs in addition to the chains. Most if not all owners have fenced enclosures for puppies.

Runs vary in size, but all are longer than wide, instead of square so that the dogs can get more exercise. It also cuts down on circling if the runs are not square.

Precautions

If you live in snow country the height of your kennel runs can be greatly decreased if there is a major snowstorm. Sometimes to the point the dog can simply step out and over the fencing that was supposed to be confining them. It's also a good idea to not have the gates open at ground level. Having a six inch or higher section below the gate makes it easier to get the gates open with snow on the ground.

Scooping kennel runs is something to think of. If the runs are very narrow, it's hard to maneuver a shovel full of poop. Don't laugh, because there is nothing fun about flinging poop when you misjudge your turn.

If you have multiple dogs in a run, you need to be careful of fighting and to not have intact males with in-heat females unless you are planning on puppies.

DOG HOUSES

If your dogs are going to spend time outside, they need to have some kind of weatherproof shelter. This is usually a separate house for each dog. Plywood doghouses are easy to make and the dogs like them too. In the colder months straw or some other insulating material is normally added to the doghouse, giving your dogs a nice dry nest they can curl up in. Sometimes in the middle of Alaska a long, low communal lean-to is used. The dogs are chained to the posts that hold it up. On places where wood is scarce, metal and plastic drums are used. The drums make a decent dog shelter.

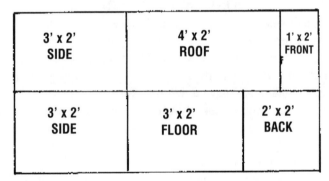

AN INEXPENSIVE DOGHOUSE
MADE FROM ONE SHEET
OF 4' X 8' PLYWOOD
AND APPROXIMATELY
30 LINEAR FEET OF 2 X 4
(OR 2 x 2)

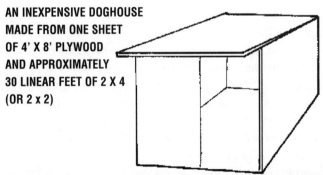

These dogs houses are simple to make, but the addition of a wood frame will make the house sturdier and last longer. The 2 X 4s or even 2 X 2s should be used in all the corners and the plywood screwed to it.

By adding the extra framing (wood) to the door area, this may slow down some dogs in their quest to make the opening larger. Metal edges or strips of metal can be added to the inside and outside edges of the opening and along the top to discourage the hard core chewers. The frame will need five pieces that are 2' long for the sides. One each for the corners and the fifth for the edge of the door. The side, roof and floor pieces will need to be reduced several inches depending on if you use 2 X 4s or 2 X 2s when building the frame. For the floor and roof frame you will want four pieces 2' long and four pieces 3' long.

SHARING YOUR OWN HOUSE

Not all dogs live in kennel runs or on tethers. Some live in the house with their families. Legitimate questions usually asked about dogs living loose in the houses are, "Won't the dogs get spoiled and not want to run? Isn't it necessary to keep them chained so that they will want to run when they are allowed to in harness?" Experience has shown that the answer to both questions is "No". For the record, I still believe it is much easier to live with a 1/2 dozen Siberians or Alaskans in your house than it is with a 1/2 dozen Malamutes. Nothing to do with the breed, more to do with the size. There gets to be a point there is no longer room for you in the bed.

An advantage to having your dogs in the house with you is that you and your dogs will develop better communication when you are living together. The dogs will become more socialized to people if they come in contact with all the people who come visit. When you are living in close contact with your dogs, whether it is the dogs living on tethers, runs or in the house, you can tell immediately when one of them is not feeling well, and you can watch them more carefully. Any illness spotted quickly is much easier to cure, and prompt treatment saves the dog a lot of misery.

On the negative side, if you live with multiple double-coated dogs in the house, it "snows" several months out of the year. So, get used to dog hair in pretty much everything. Care needs to be taken when eating your own meals and each dog needs to be secured for feeding to avoid dog fights and bullies that eat the other's food. If you have boys and girls that are intact/whole, you will require a secure sturdy means to separate dogs from bitches when a bitch is in season. You also need to have a place for safely securing each dog when you are gone from the house. Or when you have company that doesn't understand living with a pack of dogs can be FUN!

Chapter Six

COLLARS

One piece of equipment you will always have on your dog is a collar. There are a variety of collars on the market these days. You should choose the collar you think works best for you.

You may also wish to have collars for racing and collars for at home. The racing collars may have things like quick release buckles that could break or be released in an emergency.

BUCKLE COLLARS

An adjustable buckle collar for sled dog use is one of the easiest collars to fit and use. The basic collar is a piece of webbing with a buckle and some sort of a ring. The ring should be a welded metal ring, preferably a semicircular or a D-ring. The ring is used when attaching a leash, neck line, drop chain or tether. The metal ring should be sewn in the collar towards the buckle end.

Most people use collars made of a sturdy nylon webbing, but some go with the more traditional flat leather collars. An advantage to nylon webbing is that it dries quicker than leather, it does not stretch and is less likely to have stuff grow on it. Collars made of nylon webbing can also be thrown in the washing machine and hung to line dry.

The webbing or collar should be relatively wide. By relatively wide, the webbing should be one-inch wide for most racing dogs. You may choose to use a wider or a narrower collar depending on the size of your dog.

Collars should be worn loosely around the dog's neck, but just tight enough that they cannot be pulled off over his head.

SEMI-SLIP COLLARS

The best collar for sled dog training and racing is the semi-slip type. The regular semi-slip collar barely goes over the dog's head. The adjustable type goes on loosely and then is tightened so that the hand can just go under the collar easily. Both types tighten under tension about 1-1/2 inches so that the collars can neither choke the dog or come off.

Some manufactures will custom make these types of collars for you and at your request will add a *Fastex Fastener*™ , a two piece buckle you squeeze and it releases. There are several pros and cons to adding a quick releasing fastener. One worry is that the fastener will break at the wrong time and another is that the fastener will break at the right time. With the fastener in the collar, you can release the collar without having to slip it over the dog's head, which in a tangle could be an advantage. And having the fastener break in a tangle could also be an advantage.

FULL SLIP OR "CHOKE" COLLARS

If you go to your local pet store you may find rolled leather, nylon or chain collars that have a full choke. You will never want to use a full slip collar made of chain or any other material except in special training situations. (One special training situation is when working with individual dogs, such as when a leader is being trained with the handler on foot).

Too many dogs have been strangled to death because an owner left the full slip collar on when the dog was unattended. Some will hook the snap on the leash to both rings of the collar. This is not a very effective measure because the collar may now be too big/loose and can come off over the dog's head.

Full slip collars are extremely dangerous in a dog team because the dog may become involved in a tangle of such intensity that they cannot be freed before they have been choked to death. Full slip collars are illegal in all sled dog races, as are chain collars of any kind.

WHERE TO BUY

There are many options for collars on the market. You can still make your own but by the time you collect all the components and do the labor, you may as well have purchased collars. With a purchased collar, you know the stitching won't break. Collars come in many colors as well. There is a list of suppliers at the back of the book. Why not order matching collars and harnesses at the same time?

ABOVE: A few choices for collars. The jingle bells are run on our leaders.

LEFT: A close-up of a flat collar (top), a quick release collar (center) and a limited slip collar (bottom). *Photos by Charlene LaBelle.*

ID AND TAGS

With collars you may wish to have a means of identification. If you want to get fancy, you can have a collar made for each dog. Some places you can order your collars with a name and phone number stitched in or dyed in the collar itself (no jangling tags to get tangled). There are brass plates you can pop rivet onto a flat collar and tags the collar is threaded through.

If you choose to put some form of a tag on your dog it is up to you. But if your dog gets loose you have a better chance of getting your dog back if it has some means of identification. Another plus for tags is that the person that finds your dog can call you. And if they call you instead of contacting Animal Control, you will get your dog back quicker and may not have a fine to pay.

If your dog only has a microchip for identification, the dog must still be taken to a place that has a scanner that reads the type of chip your dog has and remembers to scan the dog.

Tags need only have a "If found please call (a phone number)". I list several phone numbers on the tags my dogs wear. I have an answering machine at home in which I can remotely change the message. I can call it from any phone, put in my code and record a new message ... "Yes I am missing a dog. I am in the area, please call my cell phone. The number is 408-767-1234." On each tag I list my cell phone as well with the identifier that it is a cell phone. This way I feel I have a better chance of getting my AWOL dogs returned to me.

I do not put my dogs call names on their tag. I use part of their registered name or a number. If you want, you can have all the tags you order have the same information on them. For a couple of dollars, I think an ID tag is well worth the security.

Chapter Seven 7
HARNESSES

Over the years technology has made major changes to the modern harness. The objective is the same: the harness was designed to give your dog unrestricted movement and to evenly distribute their workload. The objective may have stayed the same, but the harness itself has evolved to the point where you no longer see harnesses that used to be the norm. Many of these old style harnesses you will only see in people's private collections.

A sled dog must have a properly fitting harness to transmit its forward pull to the line attached to the sled, sledge, cart or whatever it is pulling. The activity and the type of pulling can call for different types of harnesses. Harnesses have become as specialized as the events.

Different types of harnesses are used for recreational running, speed racing, carting, weight pulling or freight hauling. Speed racing sled dogs pull comparatively little weight individually, so their harnesses can transmit the pull from their chest along or across their back. When sled dogs are pulling a heavy load, whether by themselves or as a team, they must have the power transmitted back from their chests without downward or sideward pressure on their sides or hind ends.

SPEED RACING HARNESSES
Belly Band Harness

The simplest racing harness was a horizontal padded chest strap held in place by an adjustable neck strap as well as an adjustable belly band. While relatively easy to make and fit, the buckles can irritate a dog with a thin coat or are difficult to adjust on a dog with a lot of coat. This harness has the advantage of not pulling off over the dog's head if they balk or turn around. This is a harness you may see carting. They are rarely if ever on a team of dogs, unless someone is doing a historic presentation.

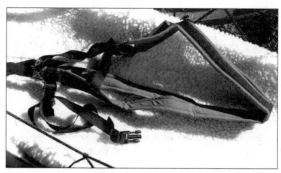

Racing harness with attached belly band. *Photo by Charlene G. LaBelle.*

Siwash Harness or X-Back Harness

The harness most used by modern racing drivers is the Siwash harness or X-back. This harness style was developed by North American Indians for fast trap line runs. It consists of a padded neck loop with a vertical, padded chest strap. There are no buckles so the harness is not adjustable.

You fit each dog's harness individually, and as such may have to fit the dog in different sized harnesses as you progress from training to racing and your dog gains or loses weight, and simply changes body styles from a laid-back dog on vacation to a hardened working dog. With the larger dogs and the thicker coats, there can be quite a difference in the harness size they wear even if the dog has no weight change.

Due to these variations, each dog may eventually wear several harnesses, and you will quickly find that you own double or more the harnesses (and several different styles as well) than you do dogs! For this reason most people end up with a harness selection of varying sizes.

Some color code their harnesses to track the size. Others write the size on the harness. Others may order their harnesses by small, medium, large and extra large and use the manufacturer's marking to track the size.

You quickly learn to know which size each dog takes. The same size may fit a small dog that is stocky and a large dog that is rangy. The size, not the name of the dog, is marked permanently in a conspicuous spot on the harness.

There is also a harness which is a modification to the Siwash harness called the H-back harnesses, and another one harness called a Yukon, or recreational, harness. The H-back is popular with distance mushers whereas the traditional X-back is popular with sprint mushers. This recreational harness or Yukon harness looks like an X-back with no X. There are advantages to the recreational harness for the person that is out having fun with a single dog. It is much easier to fit to your dog. The harness you choose ultimately comes down to which one best fits your dog and you may find that that you need different styles to accommodate different body types in your yard – even if you specialize in one breed of dog.

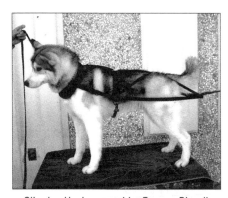

Siberian Husky owned by Denese Bissell wearing a leather horse collar harness (100+ year-old harness) from the collection of Charlene G. LaBelle. *Photo by Charlene G. LaBelle.*

Leather Collar Harness

A leather collar harnesses is a type of harness that is no longer in racing use. Of historic interest is the leather horse collar style. It was extremely popular in the early days of the All-Alaska Sweepstakes. The harness is completely made of leather with a padded leather collar being its main feature. To distribute the pull evenly, the two side straps are attached to a hard leather curved loop set outside the soft padded leather collar. A belly band, side straps, and a singletree complete the harness. In later years, side straps were replaced by a single back strap.

This harness is considerably heavier in weight than the modern nylon Siwash harness.

FREIGHT AND WEIGHT PULL HARNESSES
Buckle Type

The buckle type harness is easily adjusted and is a good beginner's harness. The buckles can irritate a dog with a thin coat. These harnesses are a little more difficult to find if you are looking to purchase one.

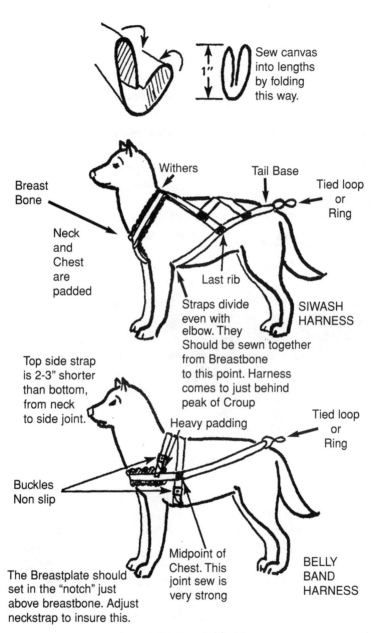

Sew canvas into lengths by folding this way.

1"

Withers

Tail Base

Breast Bone

Tied loop or Ring

Neck and Chest are padded

Last rib

Straps divide even with elbow. They Should be sewn together from Breastbone to this point. Harness comes to just behind peak of Croup

SIWASH HARNESS

Top side strap is 2-3" shorter than bottom, from neck to side joint.

Heavy padding

Tied loop or Ring

Buckles Non slip

Midpoint of Chest. This joint sew is very strong

BELLY BAND HARNESS

The Breastplate should set in the "notch" just above breastbone. Adjust neckstrap to insure this.

RACING HARNESSES

Siwash or X-Back Freight Harness

The Siwash type is more popular with modern freight and weight pullers. A weight pull harness is a little more difficult to fit because it had additional points you need to measure other than the hole for the dog's head. This is a type you have to fit so that it is long enough to have the singletree behind the dogs rear legs but not too far away.

This type of harness the dog pulls with a lowered center of gravity. There is a spreader bar or a singletree that is firmly fastened on either side of the harness webbing just behind the dog's buttocks. The spreader bar should be about 12 to 14 inches long, and can be made of 1/2 inch or 5/8 inch wooden dowel. Wearing the harness, when the dog is stretched, the singletree sets an inch or two behind the buttocks. This is behind the body, not the hair.

If you do not use a singletree and your dog pulls strongly the dog is squeezed by the webbing, which will cause wear on the fur on their hips and sides.

If you put the singletree too far back in the harness, the singletree will hit the dog's rear legs and can make them sore.

Take care in fitting a freight harness. A bad fit will discourage your dog from pulling the heavy loads you want them to pull.

BUYING A HARNESS

Harnesses are available from quite a few sled dog equipment outfitters and suppliers throughout the world. Check the supplier section in the back to see if there are some local suppliers for you.

Many offer harnesses made to your dog's specific measurements and have multiple standard sizes in their inventory. When you order a harness it is wise to send the measurements of your dog so that the outfitter can tell which of their sizes will fit best if you are purchasing a ready made harness. Some will have you send the measurements for a custom harness and once they see what you have, will sell you a lower priced ready made harness at the ready made price.

Measure from the breastbone to the highest point of the shoulder behind the neck, from that point to the base of the tail,

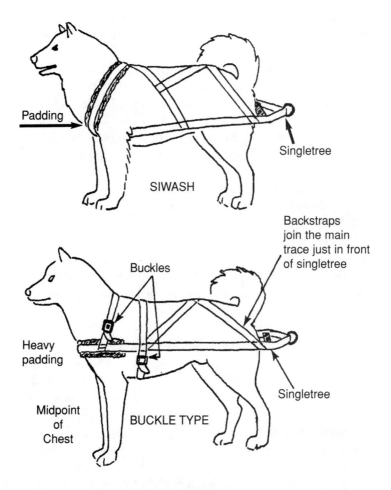

Padding

Singletree

SIWASH

Backstraps
join the main
trace just in front
of singletree

Buckles

Heavy
padding

Singletree

Midpoint
of
Chest

BUCKLE TYPE

FREIGHT HARNESS

and the circumference around the chest. Pull the tape measure tight.

The prices of harnesses vary, depending on many factors. The padding used, the webbing weight, the size (some harnesses use a lot more webbing than others do). Some will charge extra for special colors or if you want reflective tape sewn on the harness.

MATERIALS USED IN HARNESS
Webbing
You want soft webbing that will not irritate the dog. You also want material that will not stretch completely out of shape when wet or shrink too much after drying.

Nylon is the webbing most commonly used because it is strong, durable, and will stretch slightly under tension but recover when the strain is released. It will dry quickly and is easy to sew.

Cotton webbing is satisfactory, but it will shrink the first time you wash it and it takes a long time to dry.

Leather is not recommended because it stretches too much when it gets wet. Leather becomes hardened with steady use unless you spend time caring for it. And the dogs like to chew it. Leather is also heavy, expensive and hard to sew if you need to make repairs. Plus leather will mildew and rot if not cared for properly.

Padding
Padding for harnesses has come a long way as technology changes and mushers experiment with different materials. Padding is something else that can now be color-coded to tell the size of the harness, allowing for the harness itself to be of uniform color on a team.

The materials used for padding vary. Neoprene is used as well as synthetic material with little or no pile. These fabrics with little or no pile look like a fake fur.

The padding is sewn to the harness webbing so that it does not shift. Some people will have padding to protect their dog in places there are buckles. Most padding is in the neck and chest area of the harness, but it can also extend all the way to the back of the harness to the tail.

All Harnesses Have An End Loop Or A Ring

The end loop is used to connect the snap from the tugline to a loop added at the end of the harness. The loop can be made of a small diameter, well-spliced polyethylene. Make sure the snap fits over it easily. An easier method is to make the loop of heavy, well-knotted nylon cord.

The length of the loop depends on the length of each individual harness. Adjust the length of the loop so that the harness fits into the gangline. If the loop must be so long that the snap has too much room to slide back and forth, put another splice or extra knot near the end to confine the snap.

Most weight pull harnesses have a ring in the place of a loop. The ring is securely stitched between a couple layers of webbing and has a couple of inches of play (room it can move/slide). This ring should be a sturdy welded ring.

Fit

No matter which style harness you buy or make, the fit is crucial to both the comfort and the safety of your dog as an improperly fit harness can cause everything from sore spots and rubbed skin to lameness. Harness manufacturers are skilled in telling you exactly how you should fit their harness to your dog and often have diagrams in their catalogs to assist you. Do not be afraid to ask, and do not be afraid to send something back. Better yet, order several sizes at once and try each one to make sure you have it right.

Some things you should be looking for in your fit is to make sure that the collar part of the harness is not choking your dog or pulling down across their forelegs where it will impede their running. This part of the harness should actually be a little difficult to put over the dog's head and fit snugly when on. A harness that is loose fitting in this area will most likely cause rubbing spots on the dog and be too large overall.

Make sure when you put the harness over the dogs' head that you push the collar up on the neck where it belongs so that it is completely out of the way of the harness. A well fitted harness lies comfortably on the dog both at rest and when they pull. To check a fit, ask a couple friends to help stretch your dog out as if your dog was pulling in harness. The loop at the back of the harness should land right at the base of their tail. If the loop begins past the tail, the harness is too long, and vice-versa. This is the back of the harness, not the back of the loop.

HOW TO PUT ON A HARNESS

Buckle type harnesses, should you have one, are quite simple to put on. Head through hole, buckle snugly.

The Siwash, Yukon and weigh pull harnesses, on the other hand, are often put on either backwards, inside out or incompletely upside down the first time you try, or several times when you harness your dog. Don't get frustrated. Just start over and know you are not the first person that put the wrong part in the wrong hole.

For me I found it easiest to harness a dog while straddling it such that you are facing the same direction the dog is facing. Open the harness with the top of the harness on top and put the head through the opening for the head (you can do this while standing in front of the dog as well). No matter which way you are doing it, you then lift one foreleg and carefully fold it and put it through the leg hole (normally there is an unpadded underarm strap).

I then pick up the other leg and then put that foreleg through the other unpadded underarm strap that was lying across the dog's shoulders. From that point, just smooth out the harness along the dogs' back and check the positioning of the rear loop. (If the double center strip ends up down the dog's back instead of down their chest, the harness is upside down, and if the padding shows completely and is not partially covered by the webbing, the harness is inside out.)

If the harness does not lie smoothly along the back, check to make sure you have brought each leg through its correct opening, and then check the size, as the harness could be too small.

HOW TO TAKE OFF A HARNESS

To take off a harness, simply reverse the process of putting on the harness. Slide the back part of the harness up to the shoulders. Bend each foot up, one at a time, almost double. If

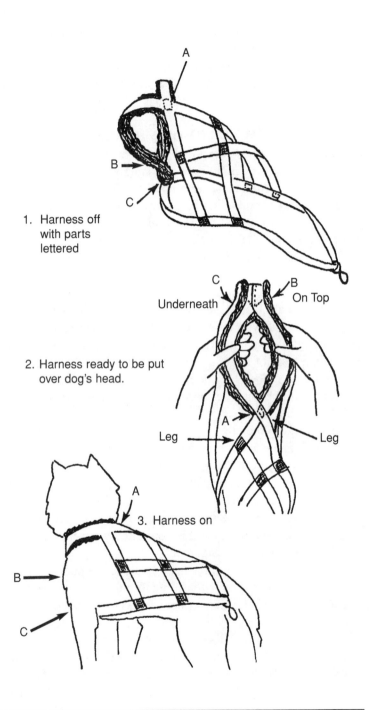

A

B

C

1. Harness off
   with parts
   lettered

C
Underneath

B
On Top

2. Harness ready to be put
   over dog's head.

A

Leg

Leg

A

3. Harness on

B

C

your dog has dewclaws, cover them with your hand so it won't catch. Lift the leg and foot through the strap. When both feet are out, pull the harness back over the head. Make sure to keep one hand on the dog so when you pull the harness off you still have control of them. More than one loose dog has gone happily running the down the trail when their owner took off its harness because they forgot to hold onto its collar and re-attach it to their truck.

PURCHASE OR MAKE YOUR OWN HARNESSES?

It is possible to make your own harness if you are of a creative nature, and it may save you money. Knowing how to sew will certainly help you in making repairs to harnesses so you don't have to buy new ones all the time when they get chewed or frayed. Some people find it is the best way to get that harness that fits their dog perfectly (at least the day they measured their dog it fit perfectly). If you have your mind set on making your own harnesses, the best way to do so is to buy a quality harness and become familiar with how it works. Then look at the construction and use it as a template to make your own.

It takes a special sewing machine to sew on many of the webbing materials. And with harnesses like collars, it might work better for you to simply have one custom made if you have a hard to fit dog.

Chapter Eight — LINES

Your dogs or team will be hooked to you, your sled or some sort of a rig by the means of a line. There are a variety of options and configurations.

FAN HITCH

In the far north, where there are few if any trees and the trails are often blown over by the constant winds, a common configuration for hooking up a group of dogs is called a fan hitch. The name "fan hitch" originated because the way the dogs are hooked to the sled looks like a fan with one line going from each dog's harness to the sled. One dog per line.

The lengths of the lines are not the same. The leaders will have longer lines and the younger dogs will have shorter lines. They are closer to the dog driver and can be corrected if needed. Young dogs that may be insecure tend to follow easier than lead. This system has the advantage of spreading weight when going over thin ice and is convenient in areas that have wide open expanses of land in front of them versus a narrow trail. However, it is inefficient in many ways. For instance, only the leader and one or two other dogs can pull directly ahead. The rest of the dogs pull out towards the sides.

Also, dogfights are harder to prevent since the way the lines are attached gives the dogs more latitude to bunch together and due to the distance they are from the musher, it is more difficult for the driver to get to the dogs. For these same reasons, tangles can happen more frequently.

SINGLE FILE

On narrow trails you may wish to hitch your dogs single file. It is most efficient to run lines on both sides of the dog. Single file has advantages in heavily forested areas with narrow trails or spots. This single-file system evolved in Scandinavia and is still in use today. This system requires lines on both sides of each dog extending from the leader all the way to the sled.

DOUBLE FILE

The system of having a pair of dogs harnessed and pulling side by side, with one pair in front of another, is almost universally used today. There are times when a "paired dog" does not have a partner (a dog is run singly) among the pairs. The pairs, hitched in tandem, use a central towline with separate tuglines extending outward to each dog's harness and a neckline from the towline to each dog's collar. The entire combination of lines is called a gangline.

HOOKUPS - DOUBLE FILE SYSTEM

By having sections of ganglines (towline, tuglines and necklines connected) you can put together the number of sections you require for the number of dogs you will be running.

At the very front you will need one or two tuglines for your leader or leaders. If you run a pair of leaders, they will be connected with a short line, also called a neckline, that goes from collar to collar.

By having modular sections you can quickly configure lines to accommodate the number of dogs you wish to run, and the individual pieces are also easy to replace while on the trail if one should break or get chewed through. Some people build the section (or module) for four dogs. Others may have a section for six dogs. If you are running an eight-dog team you may configure a four-dog section with a two-dog section and add tugs for the leaders.

An important measurement to check when hooking up is the distance from your wheel dogs to the brush bow of the sled or the distance from your wheel dogs to the front of the training cart. If you have too great a distance, the sled or cart will not corner well. Too little distance and you can run into your dogs if the line slacked a little. A general rule of thumb with a sled, there should be just space enough for one of your own dogs to fit between your wheel dogs and the sled. If you do not have enough space in your hookup, add an extension to your towline between the gangline and the sled's bridle (the place you connect the towline to the sled). This extension would be a short in length towline with a loop at each end.

BUYING A GANGLINE

Most people purchase their gangline sections because then you can leave the particular measurements up to the equipment vendor who can customize the lines to your needs, or send you a standard size. These days you have a variety of materials, and colors, that ganglines are made of. More and more are a combination of multiple materials and different diameters of lines. Different colors for different pieces of the gangline come in handy. If the towline (the centerline) is a different color from the tuglines (piece connected to the back of the dog's harness) and the neckline (piece hooked to the dog's collar) is multiple colors, it makes it much easier to sort out a tangle. Some mushers running at night can purchase day glo colors that reflects back and make it easier to see their team. There are many options available, and as you go along you may find your truck full of all of them!

MATERIALS

Aircraft cable or a plastic coated cable is also available for those who have dogs that chew. Aircraft cable is virtually unpenetrable by the dogs. Cable is commonly used within a polyethylene rope to add strength to the entire gangline. The cable is run down the hollow center (or hollow core) of the poly line. This configuration developed because cable can be very dangerous if they get wrapped around a dog's leg, and very difficult to cut loose without the proper tools with you, so putting the poly rope around it makes the line more flexible and less apt to cut a dog. Some people do have lines made entirely of aircraft or plastic coated cable, and if you choose to run with all cable, or any cable, in your lines, be sure to ALWAYS have a means of cutting the cable with you.

Most purchased ganglines are made of plastic rope or polyethylene hollow core line. It is a diamond braid and is very easy to work with. Poly lines can easily be repaired out on the trail.

Another material that is making its way into lines is Kevlar. Kevlar is 20 times stronger than steel and is much suppler. This

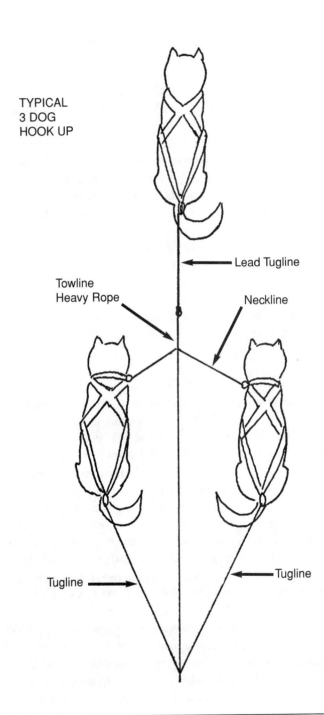

TYPICAL
3 DOG
HOOK UP

Lead Tugline

Towline
Heavy Rope

Neckline

Tugline

Tugline

too is difficult for a dog to chew through, but not 100% fool-proof. There are some chewers that can chew through pretty much anything given the time.

UNDERSTANDING THE COMPONENTS OF A GANGLINE

Towlines

Towlines are generally made from polyethylene (plastic) diamond-braid or hollow core rope. This material is available at marine and other hardware stores. If unavailable in your area, you can substitute diamond-braid nylon rope. The diamond-braid or hollow core rope is preferred over twisted rope because it is easier to splice. The towline is the line that runs down the center of the gangline. The central towline is generally made of a 5/8-inch polyethylene, diamond-braid or hollow core rope. As mentioned earlier, many reinforce the towline with a second line in the center. That line could be more poly rope or a piece of steel cable. The rope used in the towline is typically the thickest in diameter of any of your lines.

Tuglines

Tuglines are also generally made from polyethylene (plastic) diamond-braid or hollow core rope. The tugline is a short piece of rope that is attached to the towline at one end and the dog at the other. A strong and light snap should be used as the means of connecting the tugline to the back of your dog's harness.

Tuglines take less stress than the towline and are typically made of the same size or a smaller diameter material than the towline.

Necklines

Necklines are usually made of the same material as that used for the tugline and are spliced into the towline. Most people use a smaller diameter line for necklines, as well as a smaller snap, because it makes for a lighter arrangement. Some will say that necklines should be made such that they can be broken in case of a problem where you don't want the lead dogs to stay attached (say, going around an obstacle two different ways). A keychain ring will break easily when stressed and can be added

LINES

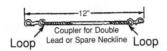

12"
Coupler for Double
Loop   Lead or Spare Neckline   Loop

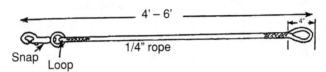

4' – 6'
4"
1/4" rope
Snap   Loop

ONE DOG OR SINGLE LEADER

56"

**TWO DOG OR
DOUBLE LEADER**

Splice

1/4" rope

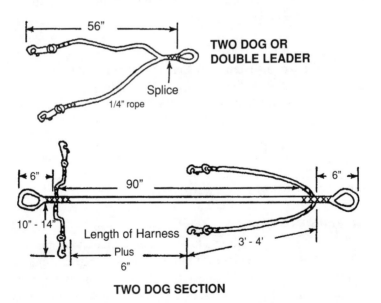

6"   90"   6"

10" - 14"

Length of Harness
Plus
6"

3' - 4'

TWO DOG SECTION

---

as a weak link in a neckline. (Important note: you do not want the rear tuglines to break because that could actually cause injury to your dog.)

Double Leader Necklines

A double leader neckline is a short piece of line or cable with a clip or snap connected at each end. If someone asks you for a neckline, more than likely that want a double leader neckline. Many people connect their double leaders with a coupler called a neckline. Other people choose to not use a neckline between their leaders because they believe it will assist the dogs to make independent decisions rather than one dog following another dogs' lead.

Check the rules at a race if you choose to not connect your leaders because most races do require the use of a double leader neckline to minimize potential problems on the trail. Leaders wandering into other teams are things you wish to avoid.

Necklines are not just for connecting two leaders. They are handy for holding a dog in the basket of the sled, hanging up harnesses, and making a variety of emergency repairs on the gangline. Most drivers always carry a minimum of one (usually more like three or four) extra necklines with them on a run.

Fastenings

Toggles

Toggles are not that common, but can be used to fasten the tugline to the harness. A good way to think of a toggle is something that looks like an elongated button. Some Alaskan natives and others attach a simple wooden toggle to the tugline because the toggle is cheap and will not freeze. Toggles can break unless made of strong hardwood.

Snaps

Tugline snaps are always of the bolt type. They have a piece you slide down with your finger to open. Spring snaps can work loose and are usually neither strong enough nor quick enough to release. All snaps must have a swivel to prevent the line from twisting. For tugline snaps, half-inch Italian brass snaps are a

TUGLINES FASTENED FOR STORAGE

Figure 8 Knot
(before tightening)

Harness Loop

TOGGLE TUGLINE

Toggle

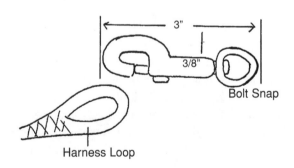

3"

3/8"

Bolt Snap

Harness Loop

Tugline Loop

Pass Loop Through Eye, Then
Over End, Then Snug Down

proven standard. Brass snaps are used most because they do not freeze like steel snaps. Steel snaps are stronger than the brass snaps but need to be oiled frequently. Even when well oiled they will freeze up. Warming them in your ungloved hand will usually thaw them quickly, as will blowing on them in a gloved hand. Just make sure your lips or tongue don't make contact with the steel snap... it's like licking a flagpole.

Neckline snaps can be the same size as your tugline snaps or one size smaller. Even the best snaps can break and springs can wear out. This is a good reason to carry a spare neckline and tugline with you on the trail. Snaps can be woven into the line itself or hooked through a loop. Snaps are easier to replace if hooked into the line, but doing so can cause the line to interfere with the swivel of the snap. Try it both ways and see what works best for you. Pre-made lines that you buy from an equipment supplier will come in the looped format because that is easier to manipulate. Small snaps take a little dexterity to work with a gloved hand but even in the coldest conditions they can work just fine.

Attaching Loops

Gangline sections will have loops at the ends so that the sections can be connected to each other. Tuglines can have loops at the end to connect to the towline. Loops are used at ends because lines with loops at the end are easily attached to each other. Attaching two loops to each other is done by threading one loop through the other and pulling the tail end (other end of the same loop) through. For ganglines the loop should be about two inches in diameter for connecting the modular sections together.

Method of Fastening Two Loops Together.

SPLICING

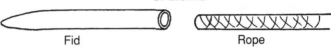

Fid   Rope

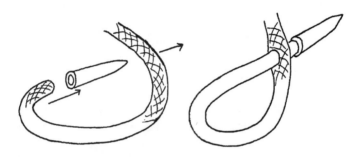

START SPLICING

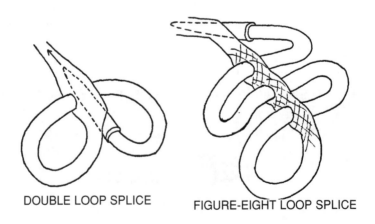

DOUBLE LOOP SPLICE   FIGURE-EIGHT LOOP SPLICE

SPLICING DIAMOND-BRAID ROPE

Fids

When you buy your 1/2-inch, 3/8 and/or 5/8-inch poly line (polyethylene, diamond-braid rope) for the first time you will need to make sure to purchase a fid or several fids. Fids are the tools used to splice the poly line and can be bought at most places that sell sledding equipment, or even sometimes the local hardware store. Fids are made of plastic or metal and come in different sizes. The sizes are to fit each size rope. The end of the line is pushed into the back or opening of the fid. The fid is then woven into or through the poly line. The fid is what you use to make splice with hollow core line.

Old knitting needles that are metal and hollow make excellent fids if you cut them off. And they have a diameter that is large enough for the line you are using. In a bind the plastic cap of a ball point pen can work quite well with small diameter lines. Commercially made fids are easiest to use and some outfitters sell complete sets.

Loop Splices

The basic splice for ganglines is the loop splice. First, seal the end of your plastic rope by melting it with a match. Smooth the melted plastic as it solidifies so that there are no bumps. Next, place the fid over the end of the rope as far as it will go. Force the fid through the rope where you want your splice to start.

For the double loop splice, circle the fid back and insert it into the center of the rope, through the section making the loop, and then down the main part of the rope. For the figure-eight loop splice, weave the fid back and forth a few times before pushing it down inside the center of the main rope. In both splices, hold the original loop at its proper size while the fid is pulled tight. How far the line extends inside the center of the main rope depends on the amount of strain that will be put on the particular loop. The fid is then pulled out, leaving the end of the rope inside the rope. The double loop splice cannot pull out. The figure-eight splice will not pull out if the end inside the rope is at least four inches long. However, to be absolutely sure, sew the splice into place at its end with heavy waxed thread, nylon line, or dental floss.

Please note that in all the illustrations... most of the loops shown need to be pulled tight. Only the loop at the end is to remain.

Splicing to the Towline

Necklines and tuglines are spliced to the towline by any method that involves looping the line through itself and the towline. The method illustrated makes a neat splice that can not pull out or slip.

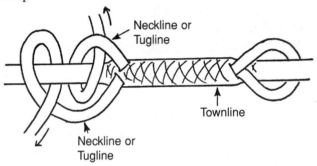

Neckline or Tugline

Townline

Neckline or Tugline

NECKLINE OR TUGLINE SPLICE BEFORE TIGHTENING

TESTING THE GANGLINE

After making your line, hook your dogs up and check carefully how the dogs fit into it. Pairs of dogs should run with heads side by side. Make sure the neckline attached to the towline angles back to the dog's collar, not forward to it. You do not want the dog stretched out tightly, but if the neckline is behind his head, the dog is apt to step over it. To make different sized dogs fit the line, adjust the loops on the rear of their harnesses rather than change the length of the tug. You must allow yourself freedom to move the dogs from one position to another.

If the line from the harness pulls down too much over the wheel dogs' rears, your line is too short. Add an extension to your towline or to the sled's bridle to lessen the angle.

FASTENING THE GANGLINE TO
THE SLED OR TRAINING RIG

Attach the gangline to the loop on the bridle of the sled or rig using a mechanical means such as a carabineer. Use a locking carabineer or a pair of locking carabineers. (Hint: look for ones rated for over 4000 pounds and have a screw collar closure to prevent accidental release of your team.)

FINE TUNING
Shock Cord (Rubber Covered With Fabric aka: Bungee Cord™)

Shock cord is often added to the line system to ease the strain on the dogs when there is a sudden stop. Sometimes shock cord is sewn inside a tug or towline in the area just in front of the sled and behind your wheel dogs. The piece is not that long and a black rubber strap (the kind used to hold cargo in place and come in many lengths, with hooks on both ends) can be used externally. Adding the shock cord in the tug or towline presents a couple of issues.

First, the shock cord shortens the line with a permanent bulge, so this shortening must be allowed for when the line is first measured. Second, the shock cord can cause unnecessary trouble with tangles. If a dog has a line looped around its leg, any easing of tension on a normal line will cause the line to fall to the ground and the dog can untangle himself. If the line has shock cord in it, it must be eased much more before it is loose enough so that the dog can free himself.

Most mushers add their shock cord to the bridle of the sled or put it in a towline extender immediately in front of the bridle.

If you choose not to use a shock cord, you have to be very diligent when starting and stopping your team and remember that there is now no buffer between your rig/sled and your team so they can be jerked if you start or stop too fast.

Storage

To prevent the towlines on the ganglines from tangling during storage, small loops of string are added to the towline to which the tugline snaps are fastened. Keep these loops small so that there is little chance of anything getting caught in them. Use a line that can break if something does get caught. Small loops for the necklines will finish up the package.

CONCLUSION

"Lines" are the very backbone of every dog team. Whether you train with a cart or ATV, skijoring, recreationally driving in the woods or racing full tilt on a track, what kind of lines you have and how they are set up could be difference between safely making it to the end of the trail or not. As such, there are many variations in style and arrangement, and as you become familiar with your needs, you can start making your own lines.

With a little effort you can customize your gangline to the needs of your individual dogs (and probably save a little money as well!) As a new musher to this sport, don't be afraid to ask your friends in the sport, racers at a race or the variety of Internet groups out there for advice. Most folks will be more than happy to tell you what they do and why, and it is a great way to learn.

One final note on lines

It's important to inspect your lines before each run or use. Replace any frayed or components showing wear before they have a chance to fail or break.

Chapter Nine

TRAINING
Carts, Chassis or Wheeled Rigs

There will be times you want to run or train and there is no snow. Some countries basically have no snow and do all their running and racing with a wheeled vehicle of some type.

When it comes to wheeled rigs the sky is the limit. Some have two wheels (scooters and bicycles), some three and many four. I guess if you had something with six wheels you could use that as well. Wheeled rig races are run from the New York City area to California, Japan, Australia, New Zealand. etc and even in Alaska in early fall.

There are many people making training and racing carts. All you need to do is a little shopping and you can find something new or even used that will fit your needs.

Still many people build their own. Since the home built rigs seldom are built alike, examine as many of them as you possibly can before you decide how to build yours. Then don't worry if yours looks different from all the others. Make it so it fits your needs. I added a seat for a passenger to mine. Having a passenger makes it handy when they or I need to correct a dog.

LIGHT CARTS
Design

Most carts for small teams have three or four wheels and are designed so that the driver stands like they are riding a sled. It is much easier to get on and off your cart should you need to make a correction when you are standing.

Weight

You can think of weight as being your friend when it comes to a training cart. Too light and the dogs don't know it's behind them should you get off and they take off. Considerable weight is actually desirable. If you think about it, an adult husky can easily pull a 100-pound rig on level, firm surface with the driver riding.

The lighter rigs are hard to control and often do not stop even with the brakes locked. This is because all the dogs do is drag the cart.

You need to be reasonable. The rig should not be so heavy that the dogs get discouraged trying to pull it. You want them to be able to go fast, the times you want them to. If you ever need to slow them down or to build up their muscles, you can add weight or drag a tire behind the cart.

Weight can be added in the form of a five-gallon water container. A full container weighs over 40 pounds. As you run you can stop and water dogs. When you give the dogs water, they are lightening the load.

SNDD member Selina Topete on a training run with her Siberian Huskies.
Photo by Bruce T. Smith.

Balance

The rear wheels must be located far enough apart to maintain stability. The standing area must be close enough to the axle to keep the front wheel from raising. Don't count on your dogs to hold it down. If you are too far back the front wheel rises easily when going over bumps. And with the front wheel off the ground the little steering you have is gone.

Frame

For the frame itself, probably the best choice is steel pipe, extruded angle or channel, or heavy metal tubing. Welded joints are stronger and preferable. Wooden or aluminum frames don't hold up long enough to be worth building.

Rear Wheels

Large wheels of at least 10 inches diameter are essential. The minimum standard is the heavy wheelbarrow type. Other types that have proven to be good are: go-cart or golf-cart, small trail bike, farm implement, small automobile, boat trailer, and certain types of airplane wheels. Pneumatic tires are more satisfactory than solid rubber. And pneumatic tires can be filled with water for added weight.

Front Wheel

Some carts have a front wheel that is smaller than the rear ones.

There are several pivoting methods that may be employed in the design of the front wheel. Certain types of heavy duty, ball bearing, swiveling caster wheels will work – with minor alterations. Another method is to use a wheel hub from a small vehicle, or a piece of solid rod working inside a close fitting pipe. Regardless of the swivel method used, the axle for the front wheel should trail the swivel point by a 15 to 20 degree angle.

Other carts have front wheels that are the same size. The wheel you use will depend on what you have and the design of the rig.

Four-wheeled training cart with friction brake and locking brake.
Photo by Ron Graft.

Brakes

The type of braking system you use will depend on the type of wheels that are on your cart. The easiest to make is a friction brake. The brake is a paddle that rubs against each rear wheel. The paddle can be a piece of 3/16 inches flat iron bent to the diameter of the tire, a piece of 1-1/2 inch pipe, or a piece of rebar. The paddle for each wheel is connected by a piece of pipe, or solid rod stock, running across the width of the cart. A spring holds the paddles away from the wheels until a foot lever attached to the pipe or rod activates them. The paddles can also have an old piece of tire to make a rubber to rubber friction.

The tires you use and the type of brake you build need to complement each other. If you are using a friction brake, you do not want extremely knobby rear tires. Why? Think about holding something against them and the vibration from the bumps.

Small automobile wheels, along with some golf-cart and go-cart wheels, have the advantage of a drum braking principle.

An emergency or locking brake is useful. But if your cart is too light, its not going to be much more than a nuisance if your dogs take off without you. An easily contrived locking system involves attaching a sliding lever to the deck in front of the brake pedal. While the pedal is held down with one foot, the other foot engages the lever.

Different options for training rigs: Two ATV's and a 4-wheeled cart. *Photo courtesy of Barbara "Dog Drop" Schaefer.*

Steering

Some carts come with steering and others do not. The carts without steering are more like a sled to others. But I like my steering.

Steering is recommended to help avoid rocks and other obstacles and to make it safer to go around corners. Since carts are much more dangerous to dogs than sleds in a passing situation, steering is required in the ISDRA Cart Race Rules.

For a three-wheeled cart, a yoke extended above and to both

sides of the front wheel provides leverage points for lines to be attached. Either two lines or one continuous line can be attached to the handle bar. Crossing the lines in front of the handle bar attains greater turning radius.

My four-wheeled cart had a steering wheel and "rack and pinion steering".

Cart anchored to the front of a dog truck. Note truck parked behind the tree has "outriggers" for their dogs.
Photo courtesy of Barbara "Dog Drop" Schaefer.

Basket

OK, it's not even close to a basket on a sled. It's more like a bottom or a floor for your chart and is needed if you have to carry a dog or a passenger. The floor can be made of plywood, expanded sheet metal, heavy wire or some other sturdy surface. A solid bottom gives you slightly better protection when you go through shallow mud or a puddle.

Safety Features

Like a sled you should have some sort of a "brush bow". And some sort of deflecting guard in front of the rear wheels or paddle brakes to keep any object from getting caught in the wheels. Avoid unnecessary projections. All sharp edges and corners should be ground off.

Bridle For Towline

Weld a ring or a piece of flat iron with a hole to a suitable area on vicinity of or to the forks of the front wheel. With three-wheels it is recommended to hook to the forks rather than the chassis because the front wheel directs the travel of the cart. The cart will stay directly behind the team and not wander. With four-wheels the ring should be in the center of the front of cart and low towards the ground. With the team hooked to the front wheel, in theory the front wheel will not spin or chatter when bumps are hit.

If desired, a permanent heavy polyethylene loop can be attached to the hole or ring to prevent wear on the line. Or use a mechanical means such as a carabineer or quick-link.

SNDD member and ISDRA medalist Cam Byers working with a Siberian Husky, riding a Sacco cart. Sacco is a type and the manufacturer of the cart. *Photo courtesy of Barbara Schaefer.*

MEDIUM CARTS

Drivers training five or more dogs at a time must have a cart with brakes that can be locked if necessary and that weighs so much that locking the brakes prevents the team from dragging it very far, if at all. Three wheeled carts weighing between 200 and 350 pounds are popular. There are several commercial manufacturers. Often used carts of this weight are for sale, and there are a few three and four wheeled vehicles that can be converted, such as motorless golf carts and ATVs without their motor.

HEAVY CARTS

For training ten to twelve dogs at a time, a converted automobile chassis used to be the only kind of vehicle available. These days the car chassis has gone by the way.

The four-wheeled all-terrain-vehicles (ATVs) are now available and are commonly used. ATVs have many advantages, such as getting your dogs to the location because they can be easily carried on a small trailer. Your team is tiring and you want them to finish with a smile on their faces. Put the motor in gear and help your team up a steep hill. It is suggested to have the motor running and ready to put in gear. This way they might not figure out when you are going to help them. An ATV can be backed up slowly if your leader starts to takes the wrong fork in the trail. They also have the advantage of having weight and a braking system that will hold a team if needed. If you have a basket in the front you can carry supplies and a passenger fits behind you quite nicely on some of the bigger ATVs.

Dryland racing rig. *Photo courtesy of Cudos Rigs www.cudosrigs.co.uk*

WORKING CARS

I wouldn't run a team in front of a running car or truck because of the danger of overrunning the team. This is not to say that a car chassis can not make a descent training rig for a large team. In a real bind your car or truck could be used.

WHAT ELSE IS THERE?

There are some mighty fine and highly designed training rigs on the market these days. You may find a riding lawn mower at a garage sale. Who cares if the motor doesn't work? The kids down the street blew up the motor on their go-cart. Or you are out shopping and notice a nice heavy scooter for sale. Don't limit yourself to the cart someone says is best. Get whatever works for you.

If you are working with one dog, your training cart could be a bicycle. A bicycle will work for two dogs as well. Three is pushing it... but it's been done.

ANCHORING THE TRAINING CART

Carts are more of a problem to anchor than sleds. The ones with built-in emergency brakes which simply keep the brake on will slow most teams down. Yet pretty much any team can drag a small cart, even with the wheels locked, faster than you can run. Big team drivers usually use a four-wheel, much heavier type cart to avoid this problem.

Small cart drivers have a couple options. One is to add to the cart itself a two or three-pronged metal fork which the driver forces into the ground after stopping the team. On hard ground this type attachment usually causes the rear wheels to lift off the ground when set.

Racing scooter. *Photo courtesy of Cudos Rigs www.cudosrigs.co.uk*

Another other solution is to attach a sharp, double-pointed snow hook to the cart. It is set in soft ground as it is in hard snow. On hard ground, pulling the cart sideways and resting one wheel on the double-pointed hook helps.

Turning the cart on its side helps with a small and tired team. A strong team that wants to go can pull it along with them and it probably will bounce back on its wheels.

Many drivers avoid the cart anchoring problem by training with teams too small to cause serious problems if the cart can't be anchored. This still results in useful exercise. Another option is to use a snub line. But then you are dependent on there being a stationary immobile object to anchor to.

10 DOG SLEDS

You may have heard a saying "You have come a long way baby." This is very true with dog sleds. The early sled was nothing more than some sort of a flat surface that was pulled by man or animal or a combination of the two. Early sleds didn't have runners you rode. Many had a "gee pole" for steering (a piece of wood pole that was attached at the front of the sled and was used to muscle a sled when direction changes were needed).

These days if not using skis, the usual method of traveling on snow or ice with dog(s) is to use a sled. The basic dog sled consists of two long parallel runners between 19 and 22 inches apart, a frame that holds them in position and a brake for slowing and stopping the team.

From there the designs can change quite drastically. The modern racing sleds evolved from the heavier freight sleds of the early days. Racing sleds are continuing to evolve as more people look for more ways to get additional speed out of their sleds. The progression was to use the best features of the freight sled but eliminate much of the weight and fine tune other features. Early racing sleds are beautiful examples of expert craftsmanship and simple but efficient design. Modern high-tech sleds seem to be using less wood and lighter man made materials. Some with no wood at all.

BEGINNER'S SLED

As a beginner you need not have the latest in hi-tech sleds. Lighter and faster is NOT better for a novice. Nor for someone with a string of big dogs. In many ways starting with a hi-tech sled may do more harm than good. If you can't stay on the runners, you can't have as much fun. When you first start, as a beginner you do not need a proper sled to enjoy having your dogs pull you on the snow.

Crashing and falling is a way of life, but it helps if you have a sled that you can look over your shoulder and your sled does not turn. With some sleds just the shift of your weight looking over your shoulder will initiate a turn. I have a long time mushing friend that has ridden the finest wooden sleds, as well as the most hi-tech sleds. One thing he can say about all of them, he's fallen off every one of them. Some more than others.

When you are first starting you will want to find a sled that works for you and your dogs. For you the ideal sled could be anything that will not fall apart and has at least 1-1/2 inch wide runners so that the sled won't sink too deeply into the snow. It needs a handle bar to hang onto, a brush bar to not injure your dogs and a brake capable of holding the team.

If you are going to put something together, old skis make acceptable runners. While a makeshift sled is fine for the period during which you are deciding whether or not you wish to take up this sport seriously, a regular sled will enable your dogs to perform better if you decide to continue with the sport.

BUYING A SLED

When the time comes that you want a more appropriate sled, you should buy a new or used sled that fits your needs. You should be able to purchase a perfectly functional used sled from another musher as more competitive racers update their racing sleds to lightweight aluminum or composite sleds. They may need to make room and will have an older sled for sale. A good used wooden sled may cost as little as $150.

Board brake (claw brake) still on sled, newer brake added. *Photo by Charlene G. LaBelle.*

Children's sleds and those that are bolted together are probably the least expensive sled you might find. Don't discount either, they may be just what you need at the time.

New sleds come in a variety of styles, materials and prices ranging from $400 – $500 to well over $3000 (then add shipping). There are many manufacturers, now all over the world. If you are interested in a sled, check the suppliers section of *MUSH!*

Pictured on the left is a basket sled with snowmobile track for drag brake. On the right is a toboggan sled with bicycle tire for the driver to stand on.
Photo by Charlene G. LaBelle.

MAKING A SLED

If you are a master craftsman, have the time and the materials, then you might want to build your own sled.

Pouring heart and soul into something is wonderful, but sleds can and do break. Not just when you forget the cover of the bank drive-thru is lower than the height of your truck when the sled is on top, or when your rack breaks driving down the highway, or even when the team zigs and you zag around the same tree.

And let's not forget pulling into the motel in the wee hours of the morning. Overhangs or arches have been responsible for many borrowed sleds on race morning. This is especially true when you first start out, because you are not used to the added height of your vehicle. (I believe it's Ohio, but there is a bank that has a sign "no dog sleds" prominently displayed at the entry to the drive thru teller)

DESIGN

For design, the most important features are lightness, strength and plenty of braking power. A correct amount of flexibility makes the sled easier to ride and keeps it from breaking apart. Too much flexibility makes sleds difficult to control. (See diagram of a wooden basket sled. Please note: the critical parts of the sled that take the strain are marked in the diagram with a star.)

DOG SLED

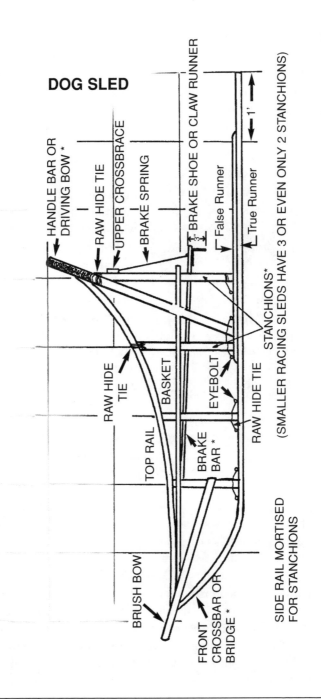

HANDLE BAR OR DRIVING BOW *

RAW HIDE TIE

UPPER CROSSBRACE

BRAKE SPRING

BRAKE SHOE OR CLAW RUNNER

False Runner

True Runner

1'

3"

STANCHIONS*
(SMALLER RACING SLEDS HAVE 3 OR EVEN ONLY 2 STANCHIONS)

RAW HIDE TIE

BASKET

EYEBOLT

RAW HIDE TIE

TOP RAIL

BRAKE BAR *

BRUSH BOW

FRONT CROSSBAR OR BRIDGE *

SIDE RAIL MORTISED FOR STANCHIONS

MATERIALS FOR FRAME
Hardwoods such as ash, oak, birch or maple are used to make wooden basket sleds. Metal tubing has been used, but is generally not suitable because when used, it is too difficult to get the required amount of flexibility.

WEIGHT
An average weight for a wood basket sled is about 30 pounds. A much heavier sled does not have any more stability than the one of average weight. A much lighter one can be difficult to control. If the wood it too thin there is a greater chance of the sled breaking. (Hint: Cut to length all the pieces of wood you plan to use and weigh them before assembly. If they weigh too much they may be too thick. You should look for places you can plane down.)

MEASUREMENTS
A basic dog sled has the approximate measurements of:
Width of the runners (center to center of runners): 19-22 inches
Width of runners: 1 to 1-1/2 inches
Thickness of runner: 1-5/8 inches at front, tapering to 1 inch in the middle and rear
Length of runners: 7-1/2 feet total
Height of basket: 10 inch
Height of handle bar: 32 inch (you can adjust for your height)
Crossbars: 7/8 in. x 1-1/2 inch
Stanchions: 7/8 in. x 1-1/2 inch
Length of basket from front crossbar to rear crossbar: 4 feet
Length of runner behind basket (where driver stands): 3 feet
Brake board: 5/8 inch thick x 3-1/2 in wide x necessary length.

BRAKE
The following are the directions for a brake board with a claw. This is something you will rarely see in use at races. Most people either remove the break board or they add a different

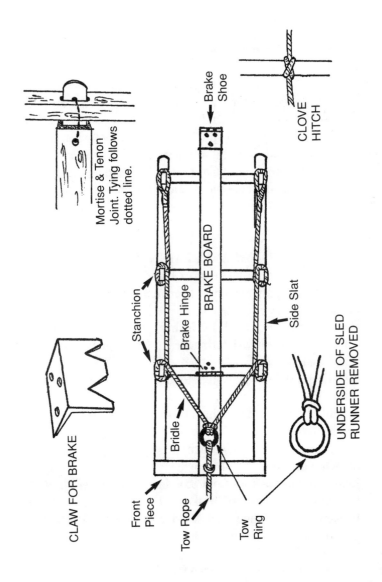

Mortise & Tenon Joint. Tying follows dotted line.

CLOVE HITCH

Brake Shoe

BRAKE BOARD

Stanchion

Brake Hinge

Side Slat

CLAW FOR BRAKE

Bridle

UNDERSIDE OF SLED RUNNER REMOVED

Front Piece

Tow Rope

Tow Ring

brake if their sled came with a brake board. Brake boards work, but are not as efficient as the metal braking systems. If you are making a sled, these are the directions from an earlier copy of *MUSH!*

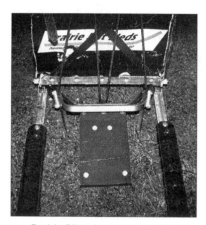

Prairie Bilt toboggan sled with the newer style brake and a high-tech drag brake.
Photo by Charlene G. LaBelle.

The brake board is bolted to one of the forward cross-bars of the sled with a heavy, gate type hinge. The free end at the rear is suspended from the upper cross brace by a length of shock cord (strands of rubber bundled together inside a woven fabric sheath) or by two screen door springs. Fasten the shock cord or springs to the brake in such a way as to not inter-fere with the foot that must use the brake. Sometimes a wide boot gets stuck between springs that are too close together and too close to the end of the brake.

The brake claw is often made from a piece of heavy angle iron of about three or four inches on each side. Cut off a length equal to the width of your brake board. The claw portion should be cut out with a hacksaw. The other side is drilled and bolted onto the brake board.

Most people use a brake that is connected to the rear stan-chions or to a metal bracket bolted to the top of the runner beneath the rear stanchions. This metal brake spans the distance between the runners, making it so you can "catch" the brake with either foot anywhere between the runners. Where a break board is only 3-1/2 inches wide and is centrally located between the runners, this metal brake has two or more points that you press into the snow to slow the team. This allows for much bet-ter stopping power. Some have tips that can be changed if they wear.

Toboggan next to a wooden basket sled. *Photo by Charlene G. LaBelle.*

In addition to these metal brake systems, many mushers also use a mat that can be made to drag between the runners such that foot pressure on the mat can control the amount of drag, controlling the speed of the team more precisely than the brake. The benefit of using a drag brake is that it is kinder to the trail. It does not plow a furrow like using a brake board or the more common metal braking system.

FASTENINGS
A tied racing sled is held together mainly with mortise and tenon joints which are tied with heavy nylon cord (3/16 inch). A real purist will use rawhide.

A sled may be entirely bolted together if it is not expected to receive strenuous use. If it is pulled too fast over too many miles of rough trail, the bolts may work loose and/or the wood may crack. There are some makers that have their designs so dialed that their sleds that are bolted together are just as sturdy as a ties sled. But most people lean towards tied when using wood.

Eyebolts are secured into the runners on both sides of every stanchion to take the rawhide or nylon ties. The ties run through a hole in the stanchion.

Wood screws or ties are used to fasten the basket slats to the crossbars. The slats can also be lashed to the crossbars.

RUNNERS

Runners are one of the parts of the sled that may have evolved the most. Runners can be wood, metal or some type of plastic with most being a combination of two or three.

The runner must be flexible to get through rough spots and around corners. And sturdy enough to not break when being bounced from surface to surface.

A runner before adding "bonus" is simply a piece of some material that goes the entire length of the sled. There are two runners per sled. You stand on the top of the runner and the sled slides on the bottom of the runner. The "bonus" I mention is what you can add to the top and bottom surface.

Runner Bottoms

The runner bottoms can be bolted on, glued on, a "QCR" system, ski-bases or actual skis. (Concern should be taken if these have metal edges. This is still a gray area if metal edges are legal at some races. And as a novice, you may injure a dog easier if you have "knives" AKA: sharp edges).

The runners are generally shod with a material from steel to some form of high-density plastic material to ski-base materials. With the plastics, it's frequently in a form that can be easily replaced on the runner bottom when it is worn or scared. If in the form of a ski-base material it is very durable but not replaceable. Early runners were shod with steel. Cold-rolled steel is durable but sticky on snow. Stainless steel is faster. Spring steel works best if you use metal bottoms for your runners. Metal shod runners work fine for a recreational dog driver that has a lot of rocks, pavement and poor snow conditions to run in. Many people replace steel runners with a form of plastic. There is a time and a place for steel runners, the material of choice on a drag sled.

Racing sleds usually have a plastic material fastened to their runners. There are different types (usually sold and referred to by their color) on the market. If you have bolted on plastic runners you will spend time maintaining the surface. You may notice mushers with a thermometer in the snow next to their dog truck. They are watching the snow temperature and will either wax the runners for the conditions and/or change the plastic.

Dog drivers frequently change the material on the runners of their sleds either because what is on the sled wears out or they want to use something different. A musher by the name of Tim White came up with a system that is quite well used. It's called *QCR* or *Quick Change Runner* system. The *QCR* system used aluminum slide rails, which are screwed to the bottoms of the runners and the plastic runners slide onto the rails. With practice, a plastic runner change takes five minutes or less. Scraping and waxing of plastic runners is now to the point mushers can at least start out with the best wax on the best plastic for the conditions.

Many of the state of the art (or high-tech) sleds do not use a runner system such as the *QCR* system. They have runners made of ski base materials. These too can be waxed, smoothed and polished.

If your first sled has runners that are only wood you can buy runners to bolt and glue on or you can purchase the rails for a *QCR* system. If your sled is shod with metal and it works for you that is fine as well. The bottoms of your runners will effect your speed. Even with the best *QCR* system, a mismatch of the runner plastic and the snow conditions can greatly effect your speed.

Runner Tops

So far this section has covered the bottoms of the runners. The top of the runner is quite important as well. This would be the surface upon which the musher stands. "Finished" wood or smooth metal can be quite slippery. Mushers have used multiple materials in their quest for a place to keep their feet and keep them from sliding off.

Small tacks have been nailed in patterns to give additional traction to wood runners. Strips of carpeting, bicycle tire (tacked down "open/flat"), Astroturf, indoor/outdoor carpet or even metal (with nail holes punched through) have been use.

The surface you use must lay flat and not ice up quickly. If you use brads or nails, the heads are not flush with the wood. You want to leave them 1/8 inch or so above the surface for the added traction and so there is less snow or ice build up.

Carpeting tends to ice up pretty quickly, becoming slippery. It also needs to be replaced if it does not dry quickly. Pieces of bicycle tire work well because it is inexpensive, easy to purchase and flexible. Any snow build-up can easily be knocked off with your foot. The metal with ragged nail holes is hard on shoes and knees.

Three basket sleds with three different types of brakes and different material for the top of the runners. *Photo by Shirley Austin-Peeke.*

BRIDLE

Install a bridle as shown in the diagram. Use a heavier polyethylene rope than that is used for your towline. In the middle of your bridle fasten a large and strong metal ring at least 1-1/2 inch diameter, or make a knotted loop. Remember that both your towline and your snowhook fasten to this ring, so you need room.

The ring, or loop, goes in the center of the sled approximately under the front crossbar. Carry the ends of the bridle back, attaching them with clove hitches to the stanchions as you go. Use a loop splice around the last stanchion involved. To give the dogs a straight pull all the way, attach the bridle lines to the stanchions just below the basket so that they are as level as possible with your main towline.

The ring or bridle loop must be held approximately in position both vertically and horizontally to keep it from getting caught under the runners and to guide the direction of the sled. Running the main towline through a U bolt attached to the front crossbar accomplishes both objectives at once. Otherwise, the ring can be suspended vertically by a line fastened loosely to the front crossbar and positioned horizontally by lines fastened between the ring and both forward stanchions.

Before taking your dog team out, put a practice tension on your towline and check to make sure everything is working smoothly.

HANDLE BAR

Usually handlebars (sometimes called the driving bow) can be at different heights depending on the driver. (I have purchased children's sleds because of my short stature.) My first sled originally had rawhide covering the gripping surface or the driving bow. The rawhide would become very soft in wet weather and I replaced the rawhide with a car steering wheel cover after storing my sled too close to one of my dogs (she ate the rawhide, which happens quite frequently if you have rawhide and leave a dog too close). A more common covering for the grip area is friction tapes (made for bicycle handlebars, hockey sticks). The grip area on the handle bar is covered with friction tape, rawhide or soft leather to make it easier to grab, grip and hang onto.

I did learn something else while working on this book. I loaned a wood sled to a novice. He refinished it and changed the bridle and tape on the driving bow. Everything is a pretty blue. I went to pull my sled down and the driving bow disintegrated in my hands. It seems the only thing holding it together was the tape he used. I will have to do a bit of research, but I think the wood had dry rot because the tape used. I just may tie on a high-density piece of plastic for my driving bow.

BRUSH BOW

The brush bow's purpose is to deflect the sled from anything it might hit, so it is an important safety feature. It is tied in position. It must be able to give a little or it will break easily. Brush bows can be made of bent strips of wood, bent plastic materials or material machined to be part of the structure of the sled as well as a deflector.

STEERING

In another chapter there are details on riding a sled, part of which covers steering (verb) the sled. But in the sled section I felt it important to mention that some sleds actually come with "steering" (noun). Some sleds are manufactured with pulley systems or cable systems that are part of the bridle and depending on the direction the dogs are pulling will actually assist in the sled turning. This hardware will assist in high speed turning and takes some getting used to.

Photo of SNDD member, Lucy Bettis, taken during a training clinic for new dog drivers on sleds. *Photo by Bruce T. Smith.*

TOBOGGAN SLEDS

Toboggan-style sleds are popular for people to take on camping trips, with dog sled tour operators or families with children (passengers) and for long distances races, just to name a few. Toboggans have advantages over a basket sled on trails that may have minimal grooming if any or there are heavy supplies to be carried. Toboggan and freight sleds are essentially a longer version of a sprint or recreational sled and as a result they have a longer basket to carry people and/or more equipment.

Toboggans have a flat smooth bottom that is typically a few inches above the runner base. This smooth lower surface, the bottom, provides flotation in deep snow while keeping the center of gravity of heavy loads closer to the ground. The material used in the flat smooth bottoms has evolved as well. These days toboggans have modern man-made materials for the bottoms. These materials slide easier on the snow than the traditional wood. They need little if any maintenance, since they are not wood.

A toboggan sled is only one type of freight sled. Some freight sleds look the same as a basket sled. The visual difference being the basket is much longer.

This section was on sleds. Here's one of those things I ponder sitting on the trail, waiting for the next team to pass. Is it a sled dog race or is it a dog sled race? The person that is entered is the dog driver but it's not called a musher race. Some day I may figure it out.

While hooking up, resting on the trail, stopping to untangle your team or even to stop and appreciate the view while not on the runners, you will need a method of securing your sled and team. To do this you will need a means of keeping them in place. Especially since very few teams will stay in place without something to remind them to stay put.

During hook up, the team is attached to the towline/gangline, with tuglines and necklines. During this process your sled must be secured or anchored while you connect the individual dogs. Most secure their sled to their truck, post or to a tree. By securing the team they are prevented from heading down the trail without you.

There are four methods that are commonly used: snub rope, quick-release, snow hook, or a combination of all of the above.

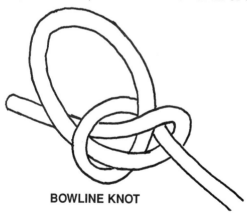

BOWLINE KNOT

A snub rope or snub line is usually a section of soft rope of about 15 feet in length and 1/2-inch diameter rope. The snub line is firmly attached by splice or knot (bowline and figure eight knots work well for these knots) to a loop on the end of the gangline or to the iron ring to which the towline is attached.

Never tie the snub line to the sled itself. Because tying to the sled can reduce a perfectly good sled into kindling depending on the strength of your team.

Secure the snub line's loose end around a stationary object like your truck, post or tree. The loose end is tied with a slip knot that is within easy reach of the dog driver while standing on the runners. As you hook up, check the knot to make sure it is not working its way loose. If it works its way loose before you are ready, you could have a team heading down the trail without you. Be sure to have one hand on the handle bar and at least one foot on a runner prior to release of the slip knot.

Initially the rope will be dragging behind you. Once you are set, you can coil the rope or wrap the dragging line around your handlebars. It's best to not leave the rope dragging behind you. It can tangle on an object on the trail, get under foot, under a runner or interfere with another team.

A quick-release works in the same manner, but the rope and the metal mechanism that is called a quick-release are left attached to the immovable object. An advantage to the quick-release is that it will release under extreme tension. Quick releases are a piece of equipment that was borrowed from another animal sport. They are commonly used by horse folks and can be purchased at many hardware stores or stores that cater to horse people.

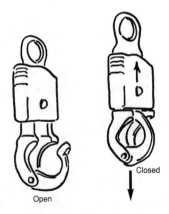

Open

Closed

QUICK RELEASE

There are lots of designs for quick-releases. What you use is personal preference and should be what works best for you. Some people prefer a non-mechanical quick-release. A knot or creative use of screwdriver can do the trick. A quick release with a screw driver requires two lines with permanent loops at their ends. This works as a quick release if the lines are kept under some degree of tension and the surface is firm. The screwdriver acts like a button. It is pulled straight out to release the lines. This is a bit tricky, and you should learn this method from another person who has used this. Still it does work well in a pinch.

Three different snow hooks.
Photo by Shirley Austin-Peeke.

There are also ways to tie slip knots that hold under tension from the snub line but release when pulled. Again, kind of tricky. The screwdriver as a button trick is easier and much more fool-proof if you are in a bind and need to do something.

These days a snow hook or a snow anchor is part of the standard equipment that you have with you when sledding. On the trail they make life a lot easier when you stop. You can use a snow hook as added insurance at hook up as well.

There are multiple methods of securing a snow hook. One is to firmly plant it in the snow. Another is to hook it on an immovable object such as a post or tree. Using a snow hook as the only means of securing a team during hook-up does have a drawback. The drawback being the team must be moved back to release the pressure on the snow hook.

Early snow hooks were modified boat anchors. And they work the same way in snow as they do for boats. As with a boat, tension or the pressure on the line must be released prior to pulling the anchor. The snow hook does not quick-release. With a strong team, the driver, and perhaps his handler, must pull the sled backwards a few inches to reduce the tension on the hook so it can be pulled free.

Snow hooks have come a long way over the years. The use of boat anchors is seldom seen and there are now hooks that will roll and in theory will set themselves if they are being drug behind a team. (More on the hooks in this section.)

SECURING WHILE ON THE TRAIL

There will be times you will need to secure your team on the trail. Most times you will set your snow hook and take care of the reason you needed to stop. You might need to put a bootie on or untangle a dog. Setting your snow hook may be sufficient for your needs.

If you are taking a break to: nap, snack, feed dogs or overnight you will

A stainless steel snow hook. The metal sides have been removed to lessen weight.
Photo by Shirley Austin-Peeke.

want to have a more reliable means of securing your team other than a single snow hook.

Sure your brake may stop the team, but unless you are standing on the brake, it won't hold them. You slow and stop the team and set your snow hook. If you are right handed, set it with your right arm; if you are left handed use your left. If the snow is too hard on the right, then try the left. Whichever side you use…make sure to secure or set the show hook firmly.

Snow hooks come in a variety of sizes and shapes. All hooks should have an angle of 55 to 70 degrees. Although they are easier to build, hooks should never have a 90-degree or right angle, because with this large an angle they pull out of the snow too easily. A snow hook with a 55-70 degree angle hook should dig itself in deeper the harder the team pulls. A good snow hook digs in deeper as the dogs pull against it; a poor one pulls out.

The line on the snow hook is basically an extension of the

gangline/towline. All snow hooks have a line attached to it on one end and the sled tug line on the other. The loops on the ends should be big enough for the hook to go through. This way you can change hooks and/or hooks and line quickly if needed, with or without gloves on. Having a large loop makes it easy to attach the hook to the loop at the end of the towline, or to the ring to which the towline is attached.

The length of this line is different for each sled, and is determined by the requirement that the hook must be set in the snow next to where the driver stands. The driver must be able to pull the hook free while holding onto the sled handle bar and standing on the brake. Standing on a runner, the driver should be able to bend slightly and lift the pull rope, releasing the hook. While it is great to have the snow hook at your feet, the hook should be approximately 6-10" forward of your feet or a hair forward of where the brake is. Having the snow hook even with your feet is a great location for setting and freeing them, but a few inches forward makes them much safer.

Hooks have a 12 to 18 inch line connected to the hook on what you might call the top. It would be towards the back and top of the hook with the eye being the front and the prongs being at the back and bottom. This line, a pull rope, is what is used so the hook can be pulled straight up to free it from the snow.

Snow hooks can also be used to hook on (more like around small) trees, logs, rocks or any other secure thing you can wedge the prongs on when on the trail. Snow hooks do not do well on smooth hard ice and/or dirt.

Snow hooks can actually be quite dangerous if they are bouncing freely on the trail. Dangerous to you because they will bite into flesh as quickly as they can into snow. You need to have a means of safely securing your snow hook when not in use. BUT, it also needs to be easy to get to the snow hook.

SINGLE PRONG HOOK

For hard packed trails that you can not get your hook to set and the trails has trees near enough and small enough to get the hook around, the single-pronged snow hook will work. These hooks set firmly in the hard snow or around the trees. Most

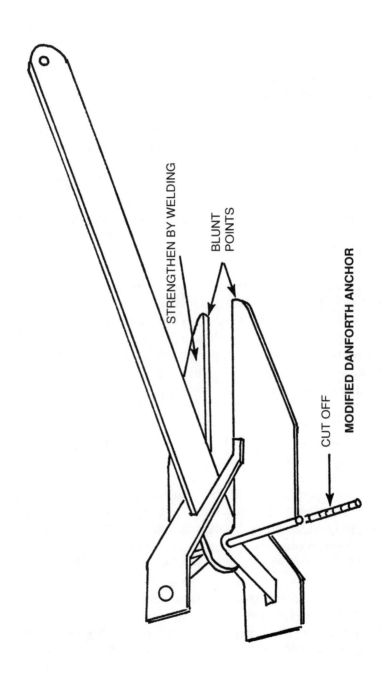

STRENGTHEN BY WELDING

BLUNT POINTS

CUT OFF

MODIFIED DANFORTH ANCHOR

weigh from two to four pounds for a small team and from 10 to 15 pounds for a larger team.

DOUBLE PRONG HOOK
Double-pronged hooks are most popular, as they provide twice the holding power with only a little more weight. They also work very well in soft snow and firm packed snow. These hooks come in many different styles and weights.

MODIFIED DANFORTH ANCHOR
A modified two-pound Danforth sailboat anchor, which can be purchased at almost any boat store, works very well in extremely soft, deep snow. These anchors will hold a 1/2 ton sailboat in soft mud or a 15-dog team in deep powder snow. They dig deeper and deeper as more pull is applied. The pull rope can be three to five feet. The longer pull rope is required because these anchors will go that far down into the snow. A knife should be carried to cut them loose in case they can't be broken free.

With the many different styles and types of snow hooks on the market, you will want to ask around and check what others are using. Then purchase the hook that others recommend will work best for you.

SETTING THE HOOK
Setting the snow hook is critical. Many drivers have lost their teams because the snow hook would not hold.

The procedure for setting a snow hook is as follows:
• Stop the team with the brake.
• Place the hook, point down, into the snow just outside the runner.
• With one foot still on the brake, step on the hook with the other foot.
• Push the snow hook down as far into the snow as you can.
• With your foot still on the snow hook, let up on the brake and urge the team slightly forward.
• The forward movement of the sled will firmly set the hook if you have the proper combination of hook and the snow

conditions. Your hook should hold the team.

If the snow will not hold your hook and a suitable tree or other immovable object is within reach put your hook around it, and push the sled forward to tighten the hook line. The big problem with the tree is that if the tension is taken off of the line, the hook can work free. While if the tension is taken off of a well-planted hook, it will stay in place until "pulled". Trees are preferable only if the snow is bad or thin.

Placement of the Snow Hook

Usually, the snow hook should be placed on the side with the best snow. Sometimes, the side that the snow hook is placed on is based on what is going to happen. For example, if the team is going to be turned around, the snow hook should be placed on the side on which the team is going to pass the sled (left side if they do a *come haw*; right side if they do a *come gee*).

If all things are equal, put the snow hook on the side you have the easiest time setting and removing it. This for a right-handed person may be to their right side.

If you carry multiple hooks, you should set them if the stop is not a brief stop or you want the added insurance. With two hooks, both can be set on one side of the sled, one can be set on either side of the sled or the extra snow hook can be attached to the tow line and used to keep the team in place.

Breaking the Snow Hook Loose

Normally breaking the hook free from the snow is much easier than setting it. You should have a foot on the brake as you pull the last snow hook. This is absolutely critical. There are dogs that will jump forward when they hear the hook pulled and will easily pull the sled out from under your feet if you don't have your foot firmly on the brake to slow them down. Dig the brake in as far as you can, stand on the brake, hold onto the drive bow with one hand and pull the hook with the other. The foot not on the brake is usually on the ground or on the runner to give leverage while pulling the hook. Normally you stand on the runner nearest the hook. Bend slightly to reach the pull rope and pull up on the short rope (pull rope) at the rear of the hook.

Should your snow hook pull out before you are ready if you are at the front of your team, take no chances. Do anything you can to secure your team including grabbing lines or the sled brush bow. If they all go by, belly flop or dive across the sled's basket. Watch out for the snow hook. But it is imperative to stay with your team. Once you are on the sled basket and the "WHOA!" command does not work, then you can climb over or around the handle bar onto the runners.

More teams are lost by improper snow hook setting than by losing the sled on hills or curves. As a new driver, you should practice setting the hook until you have confidence in your ability to make it hold. It should become second nature, part of your routine. Something you do with minimal thought. If your hook won't hold, get a bigger or better designed hook as soon as you can. Preferably before going out again.

Your snow hook is very important, but there will be times a snow hook will not work or you have lost your snow hook. For years people didn't have or use snow hooks. These methods worked for them and they will work for you. Sure snow hooks have now become a piece of equipment that most people use. It's still important to know your options if you can't use or don't have a snow hook.

ANCHORING WITHOUT A SNOW HOOK

If you are carrying a snub line, the sled can be secured by wrapping and tying the line around a tree or post. Another way to anchor a team is to wedge the sled around a fence post or a tree of the sufficient size. (By sufficient size, the tree can't be pulled over by the pull of the team.) To do this, turn the sled on its side. On its side have the brush bow on the opposite side of the tree from the towline. Your team is secure unless one or more of three things happen. Those being: the sled, line or tree break. Wrapping a sled around a post or tree works fine for holding a team, but is likely to present some problems in moving forward again. If the towline is under tension, it's going to be difficult to move the sled back far enough to clear it, especially with a fresh team.

If there are no trees or plenty of soft deep snow, another way to anchor a team without a snow hook or snub line is to carry the sled off the trail, turn it on its side, and push it down into the soft snow.

A fresh or rested team may be harder to secure than a well-trained or tired team. There will be times a single snow hook will hold your team and the same snow hook is ineffective.

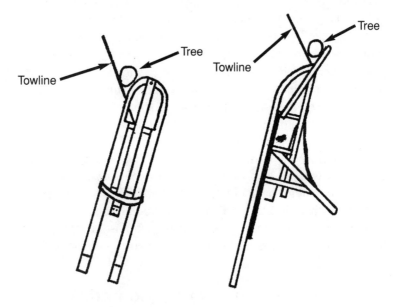

ANCHORING WITHOUT A SNOW HOOK

CARRYING A
DOG IN THE SLED

There may come a time you have to transport a tired, sick or injured dog. If you understand it is the rare dog that likes to ride you are over a big hurtle. Dogs simply do not like to ride in the sled even when they are too tired to run. It may be the bouncing or the jostling or they simply feel out of place. It's normal and they will do their best to get out.

It might be easier on all of us if we trained our dogs to ride nicely in the basket. But the idea of trying to keep a healthy, not tired dog in a basket is not something I want to routinely put myself through.

So you work your hardest and wrestle the dog into the basket. You think you have it secure. Still it escapes. Try to not get frustrated. Dogs are pack animals. Most will simply follow you and the team home. They may stay right with you, but I bet they stay just out of reach. Yet some dogs will run off and get lost if they manage to get loose.

If you are racing a loose dog that cannot be caught, it could cause you and the entire team automatic disqualification. Your loose dog during a race may interfere with other teams, so drivers do their best to keep the riders safely secured in the basket.

The simplest method of securing a dog in a sled is to fasten two double necklines to the sled and snap one to the dog's collar and one to the rear of their harness. The dog is always faced backwards so they can be controlled with the driver's free hand. The lower the dog is kept, the less likely they are to capsize the sled with their weight shifts. Carrying two dogs in the sled at one time is often necessary in a long race and can be quite a feat.

SLED MAT

If the bottom of your sled is not solid, many basket sleds have wooden slats for the "basket." You will need a mat of some sort to prevent the feet of a carried dog from slipping between the slats of the basket of the sled. Covering the slats with a sled mat usually does this. Most mats are made of heavy canvas with grommets in the corners. The corners are tied to the sled with nylon string. Strong nylon netting can be fastened or woven between the side rails and the basket, and across the back to keep dogs and gear from falling out.

A couple of different racing sleds. The left sled has a dog bag folded flat. The right sled has a dog bag ready for the dog. *Photo by Shirley Austin-Peeke.*

DOG BAGS

Most races require a dog bag. You may not notice the sled/dog bag when they are folded flat. But they will secure a dog. Different races have different rules but most now require the entire dog be in a ventilated sled bag. It is easier to keep the dog in the sled bag if its head is inside and the zippers are fastened together.

Ventilated sled bags have reinforced holes or mesh so that the dog is in no danger of suffocation when secured in the bag. The RGOs (Race Giving Organizations) are so firm on this, there are rules to the <u>minimum</u> number of square inches of ventilated material a bag must have. Some bags have a mesh panel in the back so you can see your dog.

A dog bag will help keep an injured dog from further injury, but unless the bag is well designed, any dog who has any strength left will still fight being put into one.

If the dog is put in backwards with some of their head sticking out, they should be faced towards the rear of the sled. They must be within your reach and facing so they can watch you.

Heavy canvas or plastic cloth bags with zippered or draw

string openings work well. Most dog bags are firmly attached to the sled before the run, and serve as a floor mat when not in use.

If ISDRA race rules are being used, dog bags are required. If not, the race entry form should say whether or not dog bags are required.

Dog bags may be purchased from most of the sled dog equipment firms, or they may be made at home. When you buy your sled, ask about a dog bag.

97   MUSH!

Chapter Thirteen

ACCESSORIES

There are many different styles/types/variations of mushing. (Racing vs. recreational and sprint vs. distance are only some of the general dynamics.) It is hard to give a definitive list of what you need to take with you in the sled, but the following offers some guidelines based on how long you intend to be on the runners.

If you are planning on being on the trail for a few hours or more you will definitely want the means of carrying a few items with you that are easily accessed while you are moving down the trail. The items you carry could be a snack or any number of supplies for both you and your dogs. No matter what it is, you may want it in a location you have access to while standing on the runners.

SLED/GEAR BAGS

Most sleds you buy from a commercial outfitter will come with a canvas sled bag custom made for that sled. Again, there are several different sizes and options for these, so telling the outfitter what you are planning on doing will allow them to assist you to get what is best for your needs.

Some of the items carried in the bag are:

Snow hook *
Spare gloves and hat
Spare necklines (the neckline that is a short line with a snap at each end)
Extra harness
High energy snacks (dog and human)
Chemical heating pads
Matches, fire starter
Small first aid kit
Cell phone
Water and bowls
Toilet paper or tissue
A camera may come in handy for recording the beauty of it all.

* Instead of putting the snow hook in the bag, you may want to purchase a snow hook holder or put your hook under a shock cord fastened over your sled mat/dog bag.

If you carry your snow hook on one side of your sled, you can tip your sled to that side in an emergency. BUT, race workers do NOT like snow hooks aimed their way. Attached to the side of your sled would only be for while you are out training, NEVER in a race situation, especially where you could injure a person or a dog.

Sled bags can be purchased or made at home. Fanny packs and small backpacks can be modified to work quite well. Many outdoor stores sell modules that can be added to backpacks. These can work as well. Most of this gear is the same as what you will want with you in your cart or ATV during fall training as well!

Thin coated and older dogs may need protection from extreme cold before and after running. If you have dogs with short coats, you may want to carry a dog coat with you or go ahead and put a coat on a dog that is likely to get stiff. A child's sweatshirt can also be used in a pinch, but dog coats are easy to make or purchase from an outfitter. If you are the creative type, you can make a dog coat or blanket by starting with any heavy material that is preshrunk.

The pattern shown is easy to make. "A" fits across the nape of the dog's neck. Lap "B" and "C" over each other in double thickness. Fasten with anything, even two safety pins. If you make the neck opening large enough to go over the dog's head, you may sew "B" and "C" permanently together. Tape "D" should be long enough to have the ends cross under the dog's belly and tie on top of his back.

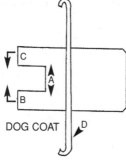

DOG BOOTS (OR BOOTIES)

Dog boots can be helpful during long distance traveling where icy trail conditions exist to prevent feet from getting cut. They will also protect feet already damaged, but be aware that they wear out quickly. You need to be careful when tying or taping booties on your dog. If they are fastened too loosely, they will fall off, and if fastened too tightly, they can impair circulation and injure the dog.

Booties can be used to protect your dog's feet if you are running in snow conditions where there is a chance of foreign matter being in the snow. It is much better to cut a bootie than it is to cut a foot.

Exceptionally bad weather conditions during the 1974 Iditarod Trail race caused a tremendous number of emergency dog boots to be needed. *The Anchorage Daily News* printed an appeal for boots, and in two days 4,500 were donated. The *Daily News'* instructions were:

"Making the dog boots is simple. They can be made of heavy canvas or mattress ticking cut into a 'U' pattern seven inches high and four inches across. Once the simple 'U' pattern is cut, all that needs to be done is to sew a zig-zag stitch around the 'U' and put a hem at the open top of the 'U'." (*Anchorage Daily News,* March 9, 1974.)

Booties made of various materials are widely available through suppliers and are inexpensive. *Velcro* ™ fasteners make them easy to put on and take off. And now there is even a *Velcro*™ stretchy material you can buy.

Don't buy the booties they sell in the designer dog shops. Make your own or buy from a dog sled supplier. Those fancy designer booties may cost you $20 or more dollars for four, when basically the same four booties will cost you less than $10.

101   MUSH!

Chapter **F**ourteen **TRAILS**

For your safety and the safety of your dogs, always have a good idea of what you are getting yourself and your dogs into BEFORE you head out on a trail. Either go over a new trail yourself on a snowmobile, ATV or in a car (if on a dirt road) before you get out there with a team, or get a detailed description from another dog musher who has been over it. Better yet, go with someone that knows the trail and can point out any hidden dangers.

Carry a map of the area or take a GPS. Even if you are familiar with an area in one season, the area can look quite different in another season. And even different yet, depending on the amount of snow.

At races, the Race Giving Organization will frequently hand out a map of the trail system being used for the race and then go over it with the mushers at the Driver's Meeting prior to the start of the race.

TRAIL LAYOUT

As a general rule sled dogs need some sort of a road or trail to follow. If you take them to wide open places like a large field or frozen lake and just tell them to go, they may not know in which direction they should move. If you have taken the time and patience to train a true command leader, then you will have better control, but most teams run best if there is some hint of a trail to follow.

In a perfect world, your team should always go forward. So for a good run the ideal trail would be a big loop. There are variations to the loop trail to add on for additional distance. One option is to split off the main trail, go around a loop, and then join the original trail to come home. Snowmobiles can be very useful tools for putting in these loops!

There are times you have a trail that goes out and back, or

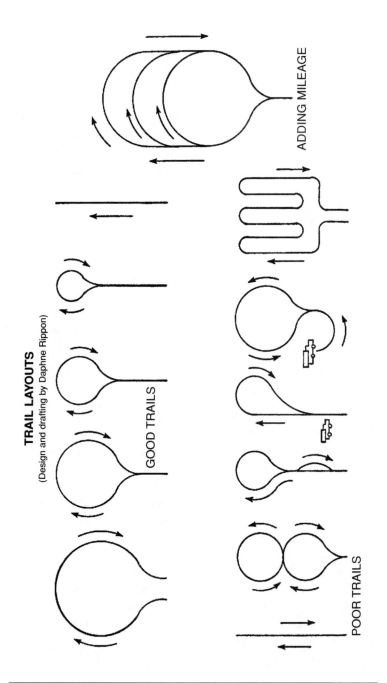

TRAIL LAYOUTS
(Design and drafting by Daphne Rippon)

GOOD TRAILS

POOR TRAILS

ADDING MILEAGE

maybe you will need to turn around sooner than expected. It is helpful when turning around to have a loop, even if small, to follow. The size of this loop depends on the area you have to work with at the end of your trail or at the sides of the trail. (When the loop at the end is rather small in size, these are sometimes called lollipop or needle trails.)

If you don't have a loop, there are four possible scenarios depending on the training of your leader dogs and the situation you are in: 1) hook down your dogs, put snow shoes on and stomp out a loop; 2) you can give your leaders a *Come Haw* or *Come Gee* command which tells them to either swing around and back to the left or the right; 3) you have your trail buddy (who could be on a snowmobile), or nearby stranger, assist you with turning the team by leading the leaders around; or 4) you will have to hook down and manually turn the team yourself.

Manually turning the team yourself is a very risky maneuver, but can be done safely if you are prepared. You will need with you TWO snow hooks. Set one on the "up" side of the trail as you normally would set it, and then set the other on the "down" side of your trail facing backwards. When your team comes around, the sled will then still have a hook facing the correct direction and holding your team. If you do not set a hook facing the opposite direction, when the team turns around the hook it will come out of the snow and release, causing your team to run happily free back at you.

There are different theories on training your leaders to be able to turn around on a trail and head back the way they came. This level of training can certainly come in handy in an emergency or on a trail with no loop to turn around on, but some feel that this practice may teach the dogs to turn around whenever they feel like it, to head home. Training is training, and the key is to always be patient and reinforce the correct behavior. Do not ever go out on the trail with more dogs than you can control by yourself.

Another option is to go only one way down a road for the mileage you want to run and then stop the team and load them into your truck. If you choose to do this, then you will need to have someone move your truck for you. They will either need to drive your truck home or meet you and the dogs at the stopping point.

Some mushers find this type of training particularly effective because dogs running forward down a trail are generally excited to be doing so, whereas if you turn around and come back down the same trail you just went up (whether using a loop or not), dogs tend to know that they are "almost" done with the run and may slow down or lose enthusiasm.

If you can run dogs from your home it may be possible to start the run however many miles that you want to run from your home and then run home, which can make for a very happy finish! (Of course, then you and someone else will have to go back for your truck.)

If trails are close to or parallel to each other you should have a barrier between each trail. If the trails are closer than 50 or 60 feet apart, a barrier should be used. Same goes with a trail that winds back and forth on itself with "fingers". If any of the fingers are within 50 feet of each other, add a physical barrier so the dogs can not cut across or become confused as to whether they are going out or coming back. There are times when "finger" trails are put in. It's usually when someone is trying to get the most mileage they can in a limited area. Or in the case of a race, it's for spectator viewing. Finger trails work well if you have large open space like a large meadow or frozen lake.

There are trails that could be hazardous to you or your dogs. Hazards include hills that are so steep and/or so long you keep your team down to a safe speed. The trail may be narrow with adjacent banks that your sled or cart might go over. Too many rocks, trees, ditches, or sharp curves that could cause you to lose the sled are also hazards to avoid.

Highway crossings or any places where your team could cut from your intended trail to run down a well traveled or paved road is a danger to be aware of. If at any time you might have to deal with motor vehicle traffic such as cars, take someone along with you to help. At right angle road crossings you need a spotter to be able to tell you when it is safe to proceed. Stop your team and have the person walk your leaders across the pavement. You may have to carry the sled to protect the runners, or lift it so that there is not quite so much drag.

Suitable trails can be quite difficult to find. Some people who live in rural areas simply put in their own. Others have to travel many miles for a good trail (dirt or snow). When you do find, or make, a good trail, stick with it. Your dogs won't become bored quickly. And you and the dogs gain confidence from knowing where you are going and what's up ahead.

Eventually your dogs will need a longer trail. When that time comes, either find a new trail or add mileage to the one you are using if possible. You can add mileage by adding an extra loop or extending an existing loop. Being very familiar with the trails you are running on can avoid many pitfalls.

Barb Schaefer with passenger on a dirt trail. *Photo by Bruce T. Smith.*

MULTI-USE AREAS

Most trails on public land are multi use; they are shared by people doing a variety of activities. If you are in the snow, there is a very good chance you will be sharing the trail with cross country skiers, snowshoers and snowmobiliers.

There are many advantages of shared trails. One is that many are groomed and have parking. Another hidden advantage to shared trails is that your team can become accustomed to people doing other activities. They may come in contact with snowmobiles with their sudden appearance, noise and smell. So come race time, they are familiar with them. Should you lose a team, a snowmobile may be the fastest way to catch up to them. And if you train with someone on a snowmobile, that person can put in turn around loops, be extra hands and their snow machine can be a object you can tie off to when taking a break.

TRAIL SURFACE
Frozen Surface

So far we have covered trail layout. Another important part of a trail is the surface of the trail itself.

Firm, hard packed snow. Firm, hard packed snow is the best surface for a sled dog. Dogs enjoy running on snow and it is easy on their feet. A light dusting of snow on top of a nice smooth, hard packed trail is even better because the dusting of snow gives under their feet and doesn't interfere with running.

Punchy snow. Punchy snow is a hard crust on top with soft snow underneath. You want to avoid trails with punchy snow if you are training and working on building up speed for racing. The reason punchy snow is not desired is because it can cause injuries. Your dog's feet can break through the surface at odd intervals. Your dogs can sink down from a few inches to clear out of sight. Some larger dogs have more problems breaking through the surface than some smaller in weight dogs. Dogs with a bigger surface foot tend to not break through as much as dogs with little "cat feet".

Punching through or breaking through is discouraging as well as tiring to the dog that breaks through. It is also hard on the other dogs that have to help drag them out. At the very least, it breaks the rhythm of the whole team. At its worst it will cause injuries to your dog.

Post holing is also a term you may hear when the snow is punchy. Someone may refer to one dog on his or her team post holing on the trail.

Deep snow. Deep snow can be tiring to the dogs and you. At least deep snow doesn't take your dog by surprise the way punchy snow does. Ordinarily if the snow is too deep for good running, mushers will pack the training or race trail with some sort of tracked vehicle before taking the dogs out. This is the reason you see so many dog drivers with snowmobiles. A snowmobile dragging a spare truck tire can put in a mighty fine trail. Especially if the base is nice and firm.

If a team unexpectedly finds itself in snow so deep that the dogs bog down and cannot get through, the musher may need to walk in front of the lead dog to break trail for their team. In areas where this kind of deep snow is expected, the experienced musher has snowshoes on the sled with them.

Photo taken at the 2005 SNDD training clinic. Pictured is SNDD member Laura Crocker with passenger/student Gregory Smith. *Photo by Bruce T. Smith.*

Corn snow. Corn snow is a deceptive kind of surface. This condition occurs when the snow forms in little round pellets that are not noticeable at first. This type of snow is abrasive, and dogs that must run on it for any distance will get sore feet. To visualize corn snow, you can think of it as nothing more than a lot of hail that fell with no rain.

Tagged ice crystals formed by snow that has melted and frozen again, make the worst kind of frozen surface to run on. Smooth ice is all right if gone over slowly, but broken ice will cut the dogs' feet and is to be avoided at all costs.

Open Water. If the weather is very cold, avoid going through any water such as overflow on a frozen river or lake. Your dog's feet will freeze if wet for too long. Should the team go through water by accident, stop immediately and dry the dog's feet with snow. Sled dogs usually don't like water no matter what the weather. Possibly, this dislike comes from an old instinct that tells them that getting wet means freezing to death. Mine sure tell me come bath time.

Dirt

A dirt road or wide path is fine for running dogs with a rig of some kind. A little rounded gravel doesn't seem to bother the dogs' feet too much because it gives. Too much gravel for too long a time can raise blisters on the pads, which are hard to detect. Sharp gravel is to be avoided because it will cut your dog's feet.

One downside for you with dirt roads is that they become muddy when it rains. A few water puddles don't bother the dogs at all. Some dogs go around them and some plow right through. Unfortunately deep mud sticks to wheels and feet. A thick layer of mud can make the going pretty hard if not impossible.

Pavement
Not all pavement is the same. The difference is between a cement road and new asphalt. Pavement is fine if you are road working (bicycling) a single dog. But if your dog starts to dig in and pull, rough pavement can wear down the pads in their feet in an amazingly short distance and cause soreness and even injury. (For this reason, cart races are never held on pavement.) Sometimes crossing a paved road cannot be helped. When doing this be slow and safe. Come to a complete stop, and make sure there is no traffic coming before you cross the pavement.

Pine Needles
Pine needles make an excellent running surface. The dogs enjoy running through pine forests, and the needles are smooth and give under the feet. Pine needles are amazingly slippery. Sap can be an issue in pine forests. To remove sap from a dogs' coat, rub a little vegetable oil in the sappy place and then use a bit of soap to remove the oil.

PRECAUTIONS
Check out a new trail from end to end to see what the conditions are before you run your team over it. If there are hazards that can be removed, do it. By removing broken glass, tin cans and other debris, which will hurt your dog's feet, you won't need to deal with the obstacles next time. For the best training trail you may need to do some work. You may have to move some rocks and fallen logs or fill in gullies. Mushers spend a lot of time working on their trails.

If you run your dogs on a road that has been commercially cleared of snow with the help of chemicals, be sure to clean your dog's feet with fresh snow when you get back to your truck. The chemicals used to melt the snow can be poisonous if licked and introduced into the dog's digestive system. A small pie pan with water can be used to rinse off their feet.

If an otherwise good trail has a few bad spots here and there, don't worry. Just slow down when you come to them. Use those places to practice control. Remember that damage to your dogs' feet is much less when going slowly.

Chapter Fifteen

AGE TO TRAIN

There are many schools of thought on the age to start training. Most agree that younger is better. This it not to say, "you can't teach an old dog new tricks". Quite the contrary, you CAN teach an older dog new activities and behaviors.

When you start training, most people think physical training. Training can be mental training as well. Research by behaviorists Clarence Pfaffenberger and John Paul Scott concludes that a dog is most receptive to new ideas between the ages of three weeks and three months. Scott says that the puppy has an adult brain at seven weeks, and that he will never forget what he has learned between the fourth and sixteenth week.

It is better to teach the puppy desirable traits during this receptive period than to leave them alone and let to pick up undesirable ones. These desirable traits your puppy learns will aid in socialization and mental stability. These traits will be the base for formal training later on. They will also be the base for making your dog a satisfactory pet.

To stress this point I would like to share a personal experience. A friend introduced me to their 15-week-old Labrador Retriever puppy, *Tasha*. *Tasha* had quite the arsenal of tricks. As a 15-week-old pup, *Tasha* was reliable with performing the correct trick when asked. Sit, down, roll over, bang (drop and play dead), speak, catch your tail, shake right paw, shake left paw, kiss me, stand and beg were just a few of the things this cute young pup did when asked.

She was still in the learning process, but she understood which hand signal went with which activity. She was also reliable when given the command verbally. She was not like some dogs, doing all their tricks in hopes of doing the right one for the treat.

Most people start their own sled dog racing careers not with a young puppy but with a grown dog. Any suitably built dog up to the age of about eight years can be trained with varying degrees of success to be a sled dog. The degree of success depends on the physical condition and mental attitude of the particular dog and on the skill and patience of the trainer.

On the average, a sled dog is considered to be in their prime from about four to six years of age. But many have run on competitive teams from just under a year to 12 or 13 years. Much will depend on the breed and size of the dog, as well as the dogs' physical build and mental attitude.

In 1973 George Attla finished fourth in the Iditarod. George had a 13-year-old dog by the name of *Blue* as a leader. Another female, *Tex*, was 10-years-old and on loan as a leader, on George Attla's winning 1972 speed race team. *Tex* was 12 when she ran double lead with 11-year-old *Nugget* on Carl Huntington's winning 1974 Iditarod race team. In 1975, *Nugget*, age 12, again won the Iditarod, this time as leader for Emmitt Peter's team. *Blue, Tex* and *Nugget* all were retired after their long races and later presented their surprised owners with puppies.

Whatever the age of your dog, adapt the training instructions to suit their previous experience, and don't push too hard, too soon. Give the young dog time to physically and mentally mature. Remember that training starts at home. It could be something as simple as to patiently wait for the food bowl to be put down.

Chapter Sixteen 16

TRAINING SCHEDULE

The training schedule you set is the schedule that you believe will work best for you and your dogs. There are many factors to consider when you are putting together the training schedule for your upcoming year. The frequency and level you train your dogs depends on how much time you have. The time of the year is factored in, as is at what stage of training is your team. You must also be realistic in your goal with the degree of proficiency you wish your team to attain.

In the beginning you may start jogging with your dog on a leash near your home. Or you can go short distances on a cart, scooter, bicycle or sled. If you can schedule the time, it's best to take the dogs out four or five times a week.

Your goal at this point is to train them often enough so that they remember what they are learning. Don't train them so often or so hard that you put so much pressure on them that training ceases to be fun. If this happens, they will start to act bored or look for ways to get out of what you want them to do. Even though you don't think you are putting too much pressure on your dogs, try always to think of it from the dogs' point of view. What THEY think is too much pressure.

If the dogs become bored or act up, reduce the number of weekly training sessions for awhile. Their mental attitude is more important than the number of times you take them out. If you diagnose their problem as having insecurity or fear issues, continue to take them out as often as before, but make the lessons shorter and lessen the stress any way you can. Increase the fun of the outing by showing more enthusiasm yourself and by playing with them afterwards.

As your team advances in training, they become stronger physically. You and your team will want to increase the distance. With farther distances, three times a week can be enough training if that is all you can manage. If your situation is such that you can run only on weekends, those two days a week will get results, but not as much as if you could run more often.

The experienced driver ordinarily does not run too many days in a row because the dogs become tired and bored if run too frequently. Yet running two days and then resting for a day or two is good because most races are two day events and your dogs need to be accustomed to running two days in a row. And if you are planning on races that are three days in length, then it is best to have several three days in a row of training with rest between, prior to that first three day race. You don't want your dogs to expect rest on the last day of a race.

For a yearly schedule, established drivers usually start training in the fall as soon as it gets cool enough. The younger dogs need more miles than the older ones to get in condition. As training intensifies the dogs should be running about four times a week with increased mileage at regular intervals. Continue this until the racing season starts.

When your dogs start racing, the training sessions should be cut in number and intensity. If the team is in condition, you will want to train to keep them at that level. George Attla says that when he is racing hard on weekends, he runs only twice midweek. (George Attla, *Everything I Know About Training and Racing Sled Dogs,* Arner Publications, Rome, New York, 1974)

George Attla also mentions in his writings, if during the winter you are not racing the dogs hard but are just going out on easy pleasure jaunts, then you can run the dogs for as many days in a row as you wish and they will enjoy it.

After the racing season is over, your dogs that have been running all season get a rest while you may work with any new puppies for training. When it gets too warm, only the lightest training is done with the pups. Do not train when it is hot or too warm for the conditions your dogs are used to. If you live in a warmer climate, your dogs can run in warmer temperatures than those that live in more arctic conditions. Generally, 50° F is the baseline for the warmest temperature in which it is safe to train your team, but factors such as the humidity of your area as well as wind chill need to be factored into your thinking as well.

Traditionally, dogs are not run year round. They and the driver need some sort of rest to store up enthusiasm for next season.

If the dogs do not get rest from running or are run for too long a time, there is a chance they will become what mushers call sour.

However, if you are in a position during the off season to let your dogs run loose together in safe conditions, you will find it beneficial to do so. The dogs love it and they will stay in better physical condition than if they are kept tied or confined all the time.

The off season is also a time you can try different activities or work on the bond between you and an upcoming leader.

There has been a trend, starting in the late 90s, to add agility work or clicker training to the sled dogs routine as the agility course is great for confidence building and balance, as well as increasing the bond between the musher and dog as the dog must learn to trust handler's instructions and guidance. With clicker training the communication skills are honed.

If you are starting a young pup, you must start training them at the correct age for the pup (taking into consideration the breed and growth process), no matter what time of year it is. And if you are starting with a new dog, starting when you get the dog is best no matter what time of the year.

After your dogs are trained then you can go on the seasonal sequence of building up training before the snow falls, running hard while you have snow, tapering off at the end of the season, and resting for a bit before starting over. For the folks in North America the seasonal sequence is building up training in the fall, running hard in the winter, tapering off in the spring, and resting in the summer.

Robert Levorsen at Bend, Oregon on January 4, 1986. *Photo by Tom Watson.*

Chapter Seventeen
WEATHER

We all watch the weather forecasts. Weather dictates much as to what we do and how we do it. Weather is a huge factor when running dogs. The performance we get out of our dogs depends on the weather. The same dogs can act very differently depending on the weather. On clear, cold days my dogs have more energy that I thought possible. Just looking at them, you can tell they feel like running and will put out their best effort. But when the weather is "icky" (as in too warm, or it is pouring rain, or there is a howling blizzard) my dogs would much rather (and probably should) stay holed up at home.

Just *when is* the temperature is too warm? That answer is "it depends". It depends on where you live. It depends on what the dogs are used to. It depends how thick their coat is at the time. It depends. For example, if you lived in the middle of Alaska or northern Canada and the temperature in January got up to 35 degrees F above zero. You and your dogs would think it was a heat wave. Yet, if you lived in Southern California and it ever got down to 35 degrees F you might think it freezing. I'm willing to bet your dogs would be raring to go. As the temperature drops, the activity levels and amounts my dogs play goes way UP.

Running in temperatures that are too warm for the dogs can be dangerous to their health. Dogs are different than people, they do not sweat. Dogs have a fur coat and do not perspire the way humans do to cool themselves, to lower their body temperature. They pant to try to cool down. If the air temperature is high and they are in direct sunlight and the temperature builds up too much, they can easily die of heat prostration. And too many have. Not just sled dogs, but family pets die every year when left in cars on what people feel are cool days.

Danger from too much heat is not confined to when running the dogs. They have been known to get in trouble due to over-heating while being exhibited in summer parades and even while tied up in their own yard when there was insufficient water and no shade.

To protect dogs from getting overheated when you want to run them in warm weather, it helps to wet them down with water before the run. During a training run, every mile or so, stop the team in the shade and offer each dog a drink of water. In a race, if it is really warm and the Race Marshal does not stop the race, it is much more sensible for you to scratch. Better to protect your dogs from harm, than to learn a hard lesson.

When cooling down a dog, wetting the head is just as important as wetting the body. A wet cloth can be put on their head to cool your dogs. You are trying to keep the brain from becoming overheated as well. There are commercially made blankets that are used to keep dogs cool. Some are made of a material that absorbs water. As the water evaporates the dog is cooled.

The water absorbent pellets are sewn (in tubes) between two pieces of material and shrink as the water evaporates. By submerging the blanket in water, the material will once again absorb water. The blanket will be quite heavy and thick when fully hydrated and will lose volume and weight as the water evaporates.

Any dog that becomes unusually hot during a run should be wet down. If your dog ever becomes overcome with heat, (symptoms: eyes seem glassy, standing stiffly or fall down), your dog is obviously in distress. Wet their whole body completely down to the skin as quickly as possible. Do it NOW! Every minute counts. Don't waste any time trying to take their body temperature.

SNDD member and ISDRA gold medalist Michael Callahan heading out on to the trail. *Photo by Bruce T. Smith.*

If there is a body of water handy, get in. If it's deep, go in together. If it's just a stream, wade in and get your dog to lay down and splash water over their body. If the water is deep enough, submerge their body. Submerge all but their head and hold them there. After you have your dog cooled and you feel no damage had been done keep your dog quiet. Give them a rest and do not run them for several days. If you are not sure, go to your veterinarian. If the same dog gets heat prostration again, go to your veterinarian. Overheating can kill a dog, in temperatures that are not all that warm.

At the other end of the scale, running dogs in temperatures that are too cold can also be dangerous. George Attla says in his book that when it gets to be colder than 30 below zero, he doesn't take his dogs out on a training run. If it is 30 below, he will take them out but will go slowly and for only five or six miles. On the other hand, he says that if you have to take the dogs out to hunt food, you have to go outside no matter how cold it is. (Attla, op. cit. p. 144.)

The danger in cold conditions is that the dogs can freeze their undersides where there is little fur protection. Male dogs have more issues with cold than female dogs. Kenneth Ungermann noted in his book that mushers used rabbit skin covers for their dogs when forced to travel in such extreme temperatures. (Kenneth Ungermann, *The Race to Nome,* Harper & Row, New York 1963, p. 82.) . Even in modern times you can buy clothing for your male or female dog to aid in keeping their underside warm. Rabbit fur may not be used in all the commercially made products. But rabbit fur is still used and it still does the job to protect bellies from the cold.

Another real danger in the very cold is that dogs can also frost their lungs when breathing too heavily in extremely cold weather. It is rare, but it can happen. If it is extremely cold and you don't have to be out in the cold, why not just take the day off and relax or hunker down and enjoy your dogs.

121   MUSH!

Chapter Eighteen 18

ILLNESS
And Mental Attitude

A large part of the success in racing is due to the dog's mental attitude. Many drivers call it heart. A dog that does not enjoy running will not run well. A dog with poor conformation may run like the wind. A dog with the best physical conformation may be slow as a slug. This is where attitude or heart come into play.

Your training, running and racing should only take place when your dogs are in the peak of health. If for any reason they are not feeling well, they cannot and will not be able to give you their best performance. As the driver you need to figure out the difference between their not feeling well physically and if they are mentally out of sorts or just being lazy.

If all of a sudden your dog has a major change in performance, maybe they are not running as well as they have been running, the first thing you should check is for something physical. Be slow and meticulous. Start with an examination for sore or cut feet. Check legs. Check for harness wear. Check for point tenderness. Check their temperature. Have eating habits changed? Still an eager eater? Are there signs of vomiting or diarrhea? Try to think of anything physical that could be wrong with them.

After ruling out physical injury, consider their mental attitude. Have you been asking too much? Have you been trying to make a lead dog out of a dog that seems happier back in the team? Have you been running too many days in a row? Did you run the same trail twice or more in the same day? Did you partner your dog with a partner they don't know, doesn't like, or is afraid of? Was dirt or snow being kicked up excessively in their face? Are any dogs around in season? (This will effect performance in females as well as males.) These are but a few examples of things that could have been wrong.

The learning process for a beginning dog is rarely a smooth

progression. For many their performance will fluctuate, first up, then down a little, then up again. When dogs first start training they are usually enthusiastic because it is something new and they have your complete attention. Then somewhere along the line, this training ceases to be fun and becomes work. Some will become bored. They may go into a slump. Perhaps this is just a natural slump period for your dog.

If you cannot come up with any specific physical or other reason for your dogs not doing well and you think this is just a slump period then give your dog a break and leave the dog at home for a few training sessions. Continue your training runs, but leave the one dog at home, letting them watch the other dogs being loaded up and coming home happy. Frequently that is all it takes to get most dogs out of a slump.

If leaving your dog doesn't do the trick you may have to give your dog more one-on-one time. Take them out and work with them, gently for a few days, or even weeks, with lots of praise and enthusiasm on your part to try to bring your dog out of it.

If you feel the problem is something physically wrong, like a cut foot, take your injured dog along to the training site so that they stay part of the fun. They can watch the other dogs in action. You do not want them to think you are punishing them when they have physical pain. And you do not want them to feel left out. Your dog can still learn by observing. Be sure to give some extra attention. A short walk on a leash or a nice body rub may be enough. It's important for your dog to not feel that they are being punished by not being allowed to run.

Girls in season can still be run, and even can be run with a male partner if you have a well-behaved boy. Girls in heat can get quite crabby, so you may choose to run them as a single dog, or you may choose to leave them at home if they are not per-forming as they normally do. If your girl is performing well, there is no reason to avoid running her, but there are a few things you can do to make life a bit easier on your boys.

At your drug store or a health food store buy chlorophyll tablets. These are given with meals and in theory help to mask some of her body odor from the inside out. If you have a lot of girls this may not work. And it could get quite pricey.

Another helpful product is women's feminine deodorant in a

spray form. This is sprayed in the female's "bloomers" (the fuller parts of her back legs) and on her tail. Do not spray in the anal area or towards the vulva.

The boys may get a dab of *Vicks Vapor Rub* ™ , some *Tiger Balm* ™ , or some other stinky suave. The salve is a VERY small dab and on the nose just above the nose leather. Please be kind and don't use a lot. And don't put too close to the eyes. You do not want to cause discomfort, you want to make it so the boys can't smell too well.

The use of *Vicks* has backfired with some males. There are boys that figured out if the *Vicks* comes out...there is a girl in season... somewhere. Whatever you do may not be foolproof, so be careful to watch your dogs at all times and be aware of how they are behaving.

If you have a female in season and are training with other teams, it is only considerate to advise them of the situation. You would appreciate the same courtesy from them.

The best plans may not work. If you should have a breeding on the trail and they "tie", do not do anything until they are done. They will release when they are ready. Trying to pull them apart can do physical damage to BOTH of them. Should you have a mating on the trail, try to get them off to the side and out of the way of other teams. Don't feel bad, it's happened to others. And sometimes at the wrong time. Anyone that races knows of someone that spent their rest time at a check point only to have a breeding take place as they are ready to go. It happens. Make a note of the date and time. And in 63 days welcome the new additions to your kennel.

One last comment. Even neutered boys will breed with a bitch in heat. The tie will last just as long as one with an intact male. But if the neuter was weeks, months or years earlier you will not have puppies on the way from him. Newly neutered males can make puppies.

COMMANDS

The key to training any animal is patience and consistency. The following should help you to develop better communication skills between you and your dogs.

TONE OF VOICE

The tone of your voice communicates a lot to your dog. The tone you use is just as important as the actual words you use. In *The Pearsall Guide To Successful Dog Training*, Margaret Pearsall identifies voice tones to be divided into four categories:

Coaxing

Happy

Harsh (which she says never to use)

Demanding

She writes you should have a happy ring for your praising and authority for your commands. "Let him know you mean business when you demand something. . .A coaxing or pleading voice will not get the desired response." Further she writes "Also, an unusually loud command is unnecessary, as a dog's normal hearing is so acute that it is one of his outstanding attributes." (Reprinted from *The Pearsall Guide To Successful Dog Training*, By Margaret E. Pearsall, Copyright 1973, Howell Book House Inc., by special permission of the publisher.)

The two of the voice tones you will find most useful are the happy and the demanding. Demanding is a firm command or the command tone in your voice.

A common mistake made by beginning sled dog drivers is yelling at their dogs. Your dogs have acute hearing. You need not yell in a loud voice. If you are in the starting chute with all the noise, they are listening for your command to release them. At home, if you think your dog is asleep in another room, what happens when you open a bag of cookies in the kitchen? Want a fast *COME!*, rattle a food pan. My dogs will come running from the farthest corner of the yard if they think there is a remote chance of an extra meal. There really is no reason to scream at dogs that are only 10 or 15 feet in front of you. Hollering at them or screaming will not get their attention. Sometimes to get them to listen, you need to whisper.

In the midst of the noise of the starting chute, you may feel the need to raise your voice so the dogs hear the command to *GO!* You don't really need to because they are listening for your voice among all the other noises. The key to dealing with your dogs in the chute is making sure you have their attention. And recognizing the commotion is VERY distracting to your dogs. Shouting is especially unnecessary out on the trail, where all is quiet.

Shouting may be a way of relieving your own tensions. But have you considered what it would be like to be in the dogs' place and receive this kind of treatment? Think about it. Constant yelling is nag, nag nag...your dogs stop listening. (You should be aware; yelling at dogs unnecessarily during a race when another team is close by can be called interference. Under the International Sled Dog Racing Association rules, yelling interference can be cause for disqualification.) Practice being nice to your dogs. You don't need to yell at them.

Use a high and happy tone of voice for your turn/trail direction commands and your praise.

Use a low tone and draw out sounds for your slowing down or stopping commands.

TIMING
Snap out your *No!s* , *Gee!s* , *Haw!s* ,*ON-BY!s* etc (see following for more details on what these mean). Give them with authority. Say your leader's name to get their attention before giving the turn commands. Pause briefly between their name and the command. This gives your dog time to react to their name (or get their attention) to listen for the command.

Anytime your dog makes a turn correctly or follows command properly, follow it up with praise immediately afterwards. You want your dog to associate the command with the action and praise so they know that they did the right thing AND you are pleased with them. "Buddy!...*Gee!*...Good Boy!" Be as enthusiastic as you wish after the turning option is complete. Timing is very important.

If you ask your team to slow down, cheerfully praising them may excite them and get them going again. So *EASY!* and *Whooooaaa* might not be best to follow with an upbeat *Good Dog!* Tone is important as well.

WHAT TO SAY
Many of the commands you will want to learn for running sled dogs are commonly used with other species, such as horses. The commands dog drivers use are pretty uniform. Sure you can use any command you want. But if you loan a dog to a friend or you borrow a dog, it's helpful if the dog and you can communicate with that person as well. When they come to an intersection, pointing down the trail they want your dog to go just doesn't cut it.

THE COMMON COMMANDS IN SLED DOG RACING ARE:
To go: A sharp whistle, or, if the driver can't whistle, a sharp sounding word like *HIKE!* or *GET UP!* or *OK* or *LET'S GO!* are the words you hear most.

By the way, *MUSH!*, the traditional command in literature is never used, the title of this book not withstanding. MUSH! is not used because the "sh" is too soft a sound. The word comes from *Marche!,* the familiar imperative form of the French verb Marcher, to walk. (Virginia Daloyan, Alaska Native Language Center, University of Alaska, personal communication.) It was no doubt the command used in the old days by the French voyageurs when they drove their dog teams in Canada.

Right turn: *GEE!* with a soft G as in jelly.
Left turn: *HAW!*
Straight ahead: *ON-BY, STRAIGHT AHEAD!* or *AHEAD*
Speed up: Another whistle, *GET UP!* clapping hands, slapping something against the sled, rattling a jingler, a kissing sound, etc.
Move a little to one side or the other: *GEE OVER!* to get towards the right or *HAW OVER!* to get toward the left
Come: *GEE COME!* or *HAW COME!* Sometimes *COME GEE!* or *COME HAW!*

Slow down: *EASY*

Stop: *WHOA* delivered in a low tone of voice and drawn out.

Stay in one place: *STAY!* or *LINE OUT!*

Anything wrong: *NO!* Used either on or off the trail. *NO!* can be given in a tone that is both command and unhappy.

Praise: *GOOD!, GOOD DOG!* or *GOOD BOY/GIRL!* Praise is sing song (happy tone). Praise should be used either on or off the trail. And used with enthusiasm!!!!!

When training commands, you should work on them in this order of importance:

Good Dog and *NO!* are absolutely critical, but they aren't really commands. This is because they don't require the dog to perform a specific action. But they are a form of verbal communication that is very important to the performance of your team.

The most important commands are *WHOA* and *HIKE* (stop and go).

The second most important set of commands are *Gee, Haw,* and *On-By* (right, left and straight ahead).

Line out (stay) comes next.

Other commands *Gee over, come gee,* etc are nice, but not as important.

All commands should have sounds that are unique. They should not sound like words your dog hears all the time. They should be different from words that the dog knows, such as its own name or the names of its kennel mates or the names of people in the family. Commands are given in command tone, not happy tone.

More Things To Think Of ...

When naming a dog try the name with the different commands. If you can't get the name and the command to roll off your tongue come up with a different name. Some names with command don't quite sound right when said together (they may sound like you are swearing). Try the name and command, out loud, before you stick the pup with the name.

There are commands such as *Whoa* and *No!* that really sound too much alike, but they are in such common usage that instead of changing the commands, we change the way they are said.

Whoa is said low and drawn out.

No! is said high and sharp. (*NO!* can also be given in a tone which is both command and unhappy.)

Go! and *No!* also sound too much alike, so avoid using just the word *Go!* for a command to get moving. *LET'S GO!* sounds differently to the dog when said in one breath. Especially when they are impatiently waiting to *GO!!!!!*.

Teaching your dogs commands that are totally different from those in common use has serious disadvantages. If one of your dogs ever changes owners, they will probably have to be completely reeducated in order to fit in with the new team. Or if someone not in your family helps you out with a team, in the heat of the run, they will probably forget to use the commands that your dogs know. Make life easy on you and your dogs. Teach them the commands that are the standard commands. It will reduce your stress and theirs if they know what you or others are asking of them.

Commands should be short, either one or two words that can be run together. Your dog must be able to pick the sound out and remember it. Avoid commands like, "Let's get moving there old boy!"

When giving and teaching these commands, your dog is learning to associate a specific sound with a specific action. Therefore, use one command and one command only for that specific action. You will only confuse yourself and the dog if you use a variety of commands for the same thing.

Commands are best given by themselves. Please do not give your command in the middle of a sentence so that the sounds are all run together and expect your dog to respond correctly. The dog must be able to pick clearly out the sound/command you are giving.

If you have trouble with *Gee!* and *Haw!* don't feel bad about this either. Many people, even experienced mushers, have difficulty remembering the difference between *Gee!* and *Haw!* It is not unusual to hear a musher who should know better repeatedly give the wrong command to his lead dog. All the while he gets increasingly angry when the dog continues to take the command correctly. When the driver suddenly realizes their error, they sheepishly apologize to their lead dog and wish they could hide in the nearest snow bank!

(Hint: If you are really having a hard time with *Gee!* and *Haw!* you can write G on the right side of your sled and H on the left. If you can write on your gloves, put a G or an H on the back of gloves. I had one friend that even with gloves on could not get it right. She had this big red lead dog named *Tuffy* that would turn and look for her signal (she would point) if she said *Gee!* or *Haw!*)

In our household we use the words *Gee!* and *Haw!* in place of right and left. If I am driving in the car, I may ask my husband which way to turn. He will tell me *Gee!* or *Haw!* We don't use *On-by!* when in the car.

WHEN TO GIVE COMMANDS

Give a command whenever you want the dog to do a specific action for which you have a command. By far the most important concepts for the sled dog are *No!* and *Good!* followed by the turn commands. Teach these to the dog first.

No! and *Good!* will probably have been picked up as a small puppy, so you should concentrate on the turn commands. Other commands will be picked up as you progress if you are consistent about using them. Don't make any specific efforts to teach the dog all the commands at once.

When you start to teach the turn commands, you should repeat the word several times as the turn is being reached. "Buddy!...Gee! ...Gee! ...Gee!...Good!" Although a trained dog should react to one command only, in the beginning they will probably need to hear it several times in order for it to make an impression in their mind.

Be sure to give the command far enough in advance of the turn so that your dog has time to react before the turn is reached. Just how far in advance is this? A good way to find out is to literally put yourself in your dog's place.

Jog at a good clip along a trail that is approaching an intersection. Have a friend jog behind you. Have your friend give either turn command, without your knowing which one it will be, and see how long it takes you to figure it out and react properly. Then remember that you are a human who knows the commands well, that you know what is going to happen, and that you are paying close attention.

Your dog is supposedly not as smart as you are, they will not be paying as much attention as you are, and they certainly will be going a lot faster. This procedure will give you an idea of when to say the command so that your dog can react properly without breaking their pace.

You do not want to give the command so far in advance of the turn that your dog cannot associate the command with the turn. The timing will depend on how far ahead your dog can see the turn and how quickly this particular dog learns to react.

Once you have given a command and your dog has taken it, give a word of praise and then keep quiet. If your team is doing well, there is no need to say anything. A word of encouragement and reassurance during a long, dull stretch is all right, even the quiet whistling of a tune is sometimes good to relieve the monotony.

ON THE TRAIL

Too often beginners keep talking to their dogs the whole time they are on the trail. They keep urging their dogs to do better when they are already doing their best. This is nagging, and it's discouraging to the dogs. The result can be your dogs will tune you out. Then when the driver really wants their dog's attention to give a command, the dog has tuned them out. Your dog will not hear the command. And the noise simply escalates.

As a checker on the trail, when beginner teams are racing, you often hear the teams coming from a mile away. You need to listen more carefully for the more experienced drivers. Normally your only warning is the sounds of the sled, the dogs' feet or the breathing of the dogs. Most will pass you by and give a quick nod of thanks.

I'm a "Chatty Cathy". I have a hard time not talking up my dogs. It's taken a lot of time, but I've gotten pretty good enjoying the moment in silence. In race situations you also need to think about other teams around you. You should refrain from unnecessary talking with other teams or your own handler who may be riding with you.

If you are planning a training run and taking a rider, before you go out, instruct your passenger to keep silent when the team is moving. You are the only one to do any talking. People who have never been on a sled before, in their excitement, always seem to chatter away a mile a minute. Your dogs are taught to pay attention to everything that is said, and they simply cannot do this if there is a stream of conversation going on behind them. You, the driver, are the only person who should to do any talking.

Chapter Twenty

TRAINING THE DRIVER

As a novice you should gather as much information as you can about what you are planning on doing (running dogs). Buying this book is a great first step. It's best for you and your dogs if you have a realistic mental image of what you are about to do before you go out and try it by yourself the first time. Your training begins before the first actual run.

There are easy ways, hard ways and harder ways to learn. By far the easiest way is to find a mentor (or two) and observe the experienced and successful drivers in action. To find a mentor, go to races, offer to help. Look for a local club.

Never take everything your mentor(s) tells you as gospel. Sure there are some things that work basically the same for everyone. But not everything one person does will work for you. You don't have to do everything exactly the way they do it when you are working with your own dogs. If you are helping them, then their way is the only way. Remind yourself, your situation is different from theirs. They may have more dogs to select from. Their dogs may have more experience than you or your dogs.

You should also learn from their dogs. A retired dog from a top-notch team can teach you and your dogs a lot. Still it's fine if both you and all your dogs are novices. You may have house pets and initially have no desire to running to the level your mentor(s) do. You may wish to continue to treat your dogs as the family pets. Your relationship with your dogs does not have to be changed dramatically just because you decide to run them as a sled dog team. Use reason and decide which things your mentor(s) and their dogs do that will work for you and which things won't.

Face to face (person to person) mentors are wonderful...yet they may not work for some people. You can add to your knowledge by reading as many publications as possible. These days the Internet can be a fantastic source of reading material.

There are also several email lists devoted to sled dogs and sled dog sports. Many of the email lists have searchable archives and some question you have may have been discussed at great length. Join a list, introduce yourself and lurk for a while.

Get to know the regular posters on the list. Search the archives and then post your question if you didn't find a satisfactory answer. *A word of warning when listening to advice from people you do not know or on email lists. There are people that may have the same knowledge base as you do that answer your question. On the flip side there may be others that give a suggestion that is far above the level of you and your dogs. Again, some things may be right for you and some may not. You must evaluate what you read, even when reading this book.

So you have set some time aside to harness up your dogs and try sledding for the first time. Have you thought about what may happen? Mentally think through the steps. How are you going to transport your dogs? Do you have an order you will harness them? Do you have an order you will hook them up? What kinds of things might you come across on the trail? How might your dogs react to skiers? Snowmobiles? Before you leave the house to take your dog out, take time to think about what you are going to do and how you will go about it. Try to imagine what situations might occur and decide ahead of time what you will do about them.

If you are serous about running dogs, you will want to start a journal or a training log. Some people have a page for each individual dog and a section they record their runs. Take your training journal with you. In the journal write down which harness fits on which dog when you fitted them at home.

When you get back to the truck from a training session, water your dogs. Take a few minutes to think about what happened. Write down details: *Allie* ran much better on the right. *Corky* was doing a lot of dipping (grabbing mouthfuls of snow). Record the number of miles covered, which position each dog ran, and details on how each dog performed. You may not go into much detail at the truck. But on the drive home, think about the run in more detail. Then try to figure out why each dog did what he did. Think about what you can do differently next time to help each dog who did not perform to your satisfaction.

Happy dogs having a great run at a Shaver Lake race. *Photo by John Harshman.*

Most things go wrong because a dog does not know what you want. Sometimes it's because you may not have had your dog's attention. This is a team effort. You must work with your dog so they understand what you want. Study your literature again to see if you overlooked some suggestion during the first reading. Write down any additional comments from your run when you get home. As George Attla says *(op. cit.* p. 45), "So if a mistake is made in that team, it is you that has made it, not the dog."

When you train or teach your dog a behavior, you need to make sure that it is the behavior you want. If you get it "wrong" and train your dog to do something you can't tell them, "Oops, that was wrong. Let's forget it." They won't forget it. They must unlearn it. As Earnest Barkley, a distinguished dog trainer from New Orleans, always said, "When you let a dog do something wrong, then you have to do it over again right three times: twice to have the dog unlearn it and the third time to teach him the right way." This may be a learning experience for both you and your dog. But your dogs don't know that. They are depending on you to teach them the right way the first time.

One of my friends would push the training cart up hills during training runs. Her dogs got to the point they expected her to push the training cart when they got to a hill. Her first race with hills, her dogs stopped and waited for her to get off and push. Oops! That was wrong. What she should have done was stayed on the cart. Had her dog chug up the hill. And at the race she could have gotten off to help them go up the hill faster.

And they're OFF! ... leaving the starting chute at a race in Chester, CA.
Photo by Bruce T. Smith.

Be consistent in having the dog follow your instructions correctly *every* time. When riding a sled or training cart, never hook up so many dogs that you can't stop to correct a dog when a correction is needed. If you give your leader a *"Gee!"* command, they best go *"Gee!"* and only *"Gee!"* You must be in control, even if you have to stop and haul them to the right trail. Give praise once they are heading the right way.

We all learn new things. A frequent beginner mistake is losing your temper. Losing ones temper happens with experienced drivers as well. We are not perfect, but we should do our best to be firm and fair. Things happen, we are not in control, the dogs aren't listening. Perhaps nothing has gone right at work all week or things have gone wrong around the house. You take your dogs out to train and again nothing goes right there as well. Your inclination may be to take your frustrations out on the dogs. Don't do it!

It's not sled dog related, but it is very training related and sound advice from Margaret Pearsall from her book, saying, "About the most important thing in the beginning is for you to start to school yourself in your voice control, learning not to show your feelings in your voice, no matter what mood you are in." (Page 22, Reprinted from *THE PEARSALL GUIDE TO*

SUCCESSFUL DOG TRAINING, by Margaret E. Pearsall, copyright 1973, HOWELL BOOK HOUSE INC., by special permission of the publisher.)

On this same subject George Attla says, "If you could just keep your cool, even when you are mad, if you don't blow up, then you are in good shape. That is one of the main things – if you could just never lose control of your temper. That could run away with you pretty fast. And when you do that, you are goofing up your whole training program. If you want to be a good dog musher, you keep your temper around your dogs." (Attla, *op. cit.,* p. 55.)

Stop and think about it. In your dogs' eyes, you are the leader of their pack. As pack leader your dogs should give the leader loyalty and respect. This respect must be earned. To earn respect, you as the leader must be wise and always firm, but fair. This is a two way street. You must respect them as well. So to *them* you must always seems wise, firm and fair. Always think of the situation from the dogs' point of view as well as your own.

The following may seem brutal to the modern dog driver, but it does show a valid point, that nothing works for all. Whips and beatings were tools of the drivers from days gone past. The following is from earlier versions of *MUSH!*:

"Scotty" Allan demonstrated this point most graphically in his decisive encounter with Jack McMillan, a dog so undisciplined and vicious that he had once attacked and almost killed a former trainer. Jack McMillan had been whipped constantly, which only made him more defiant. When "Scotty" Allan acquired him, he realized that the dog needed to be conquered in a way that would be more vital but less humiliating than a beating. "Scotty" untied the dog and the two stood facing each other.

"For an instant the man and dog had paused, each seeming to gauge the strength of the other — then the instinct to kill, that heritage from the past, when the timber wolf gave no quarter, rose supreme; and the dog sprang forward, the wide open jaws revealing his sharp, white teeth and the cruelly broken tusks. Suddenly the weight of Allan's body was hurled against him; strong supple fingers closed upon his neck, and with an unexpected wrench Jack McMillan's head was buried in a drift of soft, deep snow. He struggled violently to wrest himself from the iron grasp; madly he fought for freedom, but always there was that slow, deadly tightening at the throat. Panting and choking, he had made one last desperate attempt to break the grip that pinned him down; and then lay spent and inert except for an occasional hoarse gasp, or convulsive movement of his massive frame.

"At length the man had risen, and the dog, feeling himself loosed, and able to get his breath, staggered uncertainly to his feet, turned, and stood bravely facing his foe... "There seemed a sudden comprehension on the part of the dog, like the clearing of a distorting mist. . .and when "Scotty's" hand fell upon his head, and gently stroked the soft sable muzzle, Jack McMillan had not only met a master, but he had made a friend." (Esther Darling, *Baldy of Nome,* The Penn Publishing Co., Philadelphia, 1923, p. 188. printed in the 1997 edition of *MUSH!*, All efforts to contact the person holding the rights to this book were unsuccessful. Ed.)

Jack McMillan turned out to be one of "Scotty" Allan's best and most faithful team dogs. As you and your dogs train, you will get in better physical shape. Dog mushing is **NOT** a matter of just standing on the sled while your dogs pull you over the snow. Dog mushing is a team effort. And you are just as much a part of the team as your dogs. While talking about training a beginning lead dog on a leash, Lee Fishback says, "I am not even discussing how you feel by now. Despite the brevity of the sessions, you probably have aching feet, have started on a diet, and are cutting down your smoking." (Lee Fishback, *Training Lead Dogs My Way,* Zima, Kila, Montana, 1974 p. 17.)

George Attla, in his chapter on riding the sled, *(op. cit.)* talks about both pumping and getting off the runners and running to help the dogs out. And he usually has 16 dogs in front of him! You, with your one or three or five dogs, will find that often you must get off and run, particularly uphill. On occasion you will have to wrestle with several strong dogs all at once. And eventually, if you stick with it long enough, you will have to hang on while dragging behind a fast moving sled and manage to pull yourself up on the runners again. The better physical condition you are in, and the less excess weight you are carrying, the easier it is going to be on you and your dogs.

This chapter would not be complete without some mention of the attitude of the driver toward his sport. The attitude curve for beginning drivers over the country seems to go something like this:

Two teams passing: Note both drivers are off their sleds and helping their teams up the hill.
Photo from Shaver Lake Race by John Harshman.

The first year of running they know that both they and their dogs are beginners, so they don't expect too much. They are happy just to get around the course without trouble.

The second or third year they start taking racing seriously, think they know what it is all about, have bought an expensive dog or two, and are sure they are going to win everything in sight. They get frightfully intense. When things don't work out the way they expect, they get most upset and often take it out on their dogs, other drivers, officials, and particularly their families.

About the fourth or fifth year, they come to realize that you don't get to the top of this sport overnight, and they start to relax. They still want to do well and try their best, but it isn't the end of the world when they don't win.

As George Attla says *(op. cit., p.* 165), "Any time a man can get everything his dogs have got, whether they won the race or came in 15th out of 20 teams, this man should be a happy man."

No matter what the circumstances, sled dog driving is still a sport. There is always something more to learn. In the words of one driver, "At the end of every season, I always say that I wish I had known at the beginning of the season what I know now – and I have been driving dogs for 15 years." Running dogs is a constant leaning process.

141   MUSH!

Chapter Twenty-One

PUPPY TRAINING

The following was printed in the 1980 and 1997 editions of *MUSH!* Harris Dunlap is a respected trainer and I have chosen to leave what he approved in 1980 unmodified. SNDD still has successful dog drivers that follow the suggestions below. Sometimes it is best to leave a good piece of work alone.

Taken from *Do You Train or Break Your Dogs* by Harris Dunlap, published in the Spring, 1973 INFO, quarterly publication of the International Sled Dog Racing Association. Mr. Dunlap was an ISDRA Director, an outstanding editor of INFO for several years, and he has won many major races. Mr. Dunlap has reviewed this chapter for the 1980 edition.

TRAINING BY WEEKS

Three to Four Weeks

According to John Paul Scott's *Animal Behavior* and Clarence Pfaffenberger's *The New Knowledge of Dog Behavior,* the best age to start instilling your puppy with desired associations and behavior patterns is three to four weeks. Therefore, if you have a litter of new puppies, start at three weeks to handle them daily for at least five minutes. Play with the pups and coax them to come to you. Place the bitch, tied, but puppies loose, near the normal flow of family traffic so that the pups will be within easy reach of people. All members of the household, and strangers, too, should handle the puppies. Call them *Puppy, Puppy* so that they associate something you say with something pleasant. This is the very beginning of teaching commands.

Four to Five Weeks

Give each puppy a name and have any person who handles a pup repeat the name while he is playing with him. Still refer to the group as *Puppy Puppy*. This handling and playing will teach each puppy to have confidence in you. The pups will soon wag their tails when you appear and follow you around. They will learn to become socialized with all humans. If you are conscientious about this daily contact, and if you leave the puppies with their mother until the end of the seventh or beginning of the eighth week, you will have well adjusted and emotionally stable puppies.

Scott says that what the puppy learns from the fourth week until the sixteenth week he will never forget. Thus it is important that he learn only good habits at this time. No one needs bad habits that the pup has learned during this time cropping up later.

Six Weeks

At six weeks, during the play period, put a harness on one pup at a time and let him play with it on. Occasionally put a string on the end and let the other pups pull on it. You may wish to put small collars on the pups at this time.

Seven Weeks

About every other day attach a light block of wood to the string. Attach another line to either the front part of the harness or, if the pup has a collar, attach it to the collar. This is a play session. Let the pups lead you around as much as you lead them around.

The session must be fun. Never force any pup to the point of frustration. And never, never strike him. No dog should ever associate pain with training.

(For a training schedule at this age, Thom Ainsworth adds, "Five minutes on, ten minutes off, five minutes on, twice a day. And that's all.")

Eight to Nine Weeks

Take the bitch away from the litter at eight weeks.

During the daily play-training session, carry the pups one at a time a short distance away from their usual play area. Most will run back on their own, dragging the block of wood. If one seems confused, run back to the play area in front of him and coax him to follow. If he stops to investigate some new sight or smell along the route, stop and wait for him to satisfy his curiosity.

Alaskan Malamute puppies, Lucy and Keela. First time in a harness at age four months. *Photo by Lillian Graft.*

When a pup seems stable, take off the block and daily lead and coax him away from his home area. Little by little expose each pup to as many different sights, sounds, smells, and running surfaces as possible. Give him time to explore and smell the new things if he wishes. You are there to give him confidence. If he takes too long with his exploration, coax him to continue his journey. Soon he should be breezing down the road with you running behind hanging on to the end of the harness line for dear life.

Ten to Twelve Weeks

Separate each pup from his littermates at ten weeks. The pups will not be lonely because each one will still be getting his usual daily training-play session. This daily attention from you, now with no more play with the other pups, will strengthen the communication between you even more.

Separating the pups at this time will establish each one's self-importance and individualism. If left together, the group would start to sort out its pecking order. Some would learn to be dominant and some subordinate. Some might even start to be bullies. None of these traits is desirable in a sled dog.

COMMANDS

From the third week when you start calling the group *Puppy, Puppy* you are teaching each dog, by association, to respond to words. Shortly afterwards when you give each pup a name and start calling him by it when you hold him, you are doing the same thing.

From the fourth week start saying *No!* every time the pup does something you don't like. While you are saying it, either push him away gently but firmly, or pull him away by the leash.

When guiding any dog by a leash, do it with a series of small jerk actions rather than a single big dragging motion. If you snap your wrist rather than bend your elbow you will get the desired result. However, if the dog becomes frightened, panics or hangs back, stop the jerking and instead use a steady but firm pull accompanied by a reassuring tone of voice. This is the standard procedure used by all good obedience and other dog handlers.

From the fourth week also start teaching *Good!* by saying the word whenever the pup does something properly. Put enthusiasm in your voice. It is most important that the pup understands when he has pleased you.

When the pup starts running in harness, start saying *Hike!* — or whatever your *Go* command will be every time the pup takes off after a stop.

At the same stage of training start saying *Whoa* every time he stops. Create a few extra stop and go situations to reinforce these commands.

All of the above activities should be done in a play-training atmosphere.

PRELIMINARY LEAD DOG TRAINING
Twelve to Sixteen Weeks

At the age of twelve weeks — usually not before — preliminary lead dog training can be started with any pup that has learned to:

Respond to the above commands

Run in front of you with assurance along familiar trails

Cope with confidence with new situations as they arise

Drag a block of wood without concern

To start your lead dog training, select an area of tall grass. Mow a grid of paths that cross like a four way road crossing.

Run your future lead dog in front of you down a trail. As he approaches a crossing, step off the trail to the right, pull the line to the right, and say *Gee!* If necessary make the right turn yourself. Keep puffing or jerking gently on the line and repeating *Gee!* As the pup starts to make a move in the proper direction, say *Good!* Do only *Gee* turns until the pup understands the command. When he does, then start *Haw* turns.

Teach *Ahead* by at first giving the command several times while the pup is running down a straight stretch. Eventually give the command when he is approaching a crossing. If at any time the pup makes a mistake, stop him and at the same time say *No!* Repeat the proper command while puffing and jerking on the line in the right direction. Move in the proper direction yourself. Don't forget the *Good!* when the pup goes the right way, even if you have maneuvered him there yourself.

RESULTS

If you follow this three to sixteen weeks' routine faithfully from the beginning, by the time you hook all of your pups up as a team you will have a happy, well-adjusted, and confident group of dogs who know only good habits. No bad habits will be there to overcome. No frightened, tangled, bolting six-month-old beginners will have to be coped with. You will have a trained team — maybe even some leaders — and all by the sixteenth week.

Mr. Dunlap kindly gave Mush! this follow-up to his article.

Between the sixteenth week (four months) and the time that the puppies are physically mature enough to be hitched in a team and pull a sled (usually six to eight months), they are put on a schedule of daily socialization. They are played with, taken for walks on a leash, and taken along in the dog truck when the older dogs in the team go someplace. They are not just left on the chain and ignored. But further practice on the drag during this time does not seem to bring significant results.

The six to eight-month variations in age for the time of the first hook-up depends on the stage of maturity of the individual dog. Although none will be completely mature, some will be maturer than others will. The variation in time also allows the first hook-up to take place during good weather and at a time of year when the owner is not completely occupied with the older dogs.

For the first runs, pick a level trail with good footing. If the pups are trained well enough on the flat, they will be able to handle hills with no trouble later on.

Take the pups out in teams of three to five dogs, depending on the experience of the driver. A beginner can take two pups and one leader. An experienced driver can take three pups and two trained leaders or two pups and three leaders, depending on how enthusiastic the pups are. After five or six runs, more pups can be used together because they will settle down.

Nothing special is required for the first runs except that everything must go smoothly. It is the first time the pups have worked together as a unit, and whatever happens will make a great impression on their minds. The pups must never be asked to stand still while being hooked up and there must be no pain whatsoever involved.

The preliminary training should be sufficient to have the dogs run without trouble once they get going. If any problem develops, it may be because the pups got their preliminary training on snow and are now running on dirt with a chassis, or the other way around. With patience, the dogs should adjust after a few runs.

The distance to run depends on the humidity and heat. In the summer the runs should not be more than 1-1/2miles, and with frequent stops. The number of times the pups are taken out is more important than how far they go. Five 10-minute sessions get better results than one 50-minute run. But take the dogs out at least once or twice a week at this stage.

During these runs rotate the positions in which the dogs are hooked. Some dogs have a preference for one side or the other, just as people are right or left handed. Others are ambidextrous.

After eight months, continue the socialization process by exposing the pups to new sights and sounds. Take them to the store or shopping center and stake them out around your truck. Take the shy ones for a walk on a leash around the area. Do as much working on a one to one basis with the pups as you have time for.

Bring each pup into the house on occasion, perhaps even once a day. (Mr. Dunlap is speaking of kennel dogs. Ed.) A dog does not have to be kept on a chain all his life to get him to work. Don't keep him in the house for so long a time, though, that his system becomes adjusted to too much warmth.

In summary, good sled dogs are the result of:

Good breeding

Good health, nutrition and conditioning

The response to sound

In the long run, the dog that is taught to respond to a happy sound like a whistle will turn in a better performance than one that is driven by a pain-fear mechanism. And there are good physiological reasons to support this observation.

149   MUSH!

Chapter
Twenty-Two
TRAINING
AN ADULT DOG

For fine tuning or training your experienced team, read Jim Welch's book, *The Speed Mushing Manual: How to Train Racing Sled Dogs*.

This section is a step-by-step discussion of how to proceed with an untrained dog, from taking your dog out with a vehicle to having them run smoothly in a team. These instructions assume that the dog(s) you are starting out with are one or more adult dogs who are physically mature enough to pull and have never had any sled training. Their physical maturity will depend on the breed, it could be as young as six months of age. With other breeds it can be well over a year. The techniques covered are also applicable to puppy training.

Once again it is important to remember every dog is different and will react in a different manner, so not all situations can be covered. Only typical reactions and the methods to cope with them have been given. Adapt the instructions to suit your dog, training area, the people with whom you are training, and the time you have available.

You can learn what **not** to do by reading *Winterdance*, by Gary Paulsen. If you haven't yet read it, it is a wonderful read and you can learn a lot from some of Gary's (common) mistakes.

The best and easiest way to train a dog is to add them to an experienced team. This should be your preferred method if at all possible. This will allow you to watch experienced dogs handled by an experienced driver. And it will help your dogs to watch an experienced team in action. Finally an inexperienced dog can learn very quickly when running next to an experienced dog.

To do this, contact the sled dog club nearest you by inquiring from the owners of northern breeds or by an Internet search. Watch newspapers for announcements of local races. You will find that "dog people" are typically very friendly and willing to help a newcomer. If you can not find an experienced driver and team to help you out, you can do your training with other beginners. It is good for your morale and good for your dogs to be around other people doing the same thing.

SETTING UP
Taking Dog Out
of Vehicle

Team crossing a bridge during the
Shaver Lake race.
Photo by John Harshman.

It is important to do the little things to avoid injury and undue stress to you and your dog. This starts when taking a dog out of a vehicle. If you have dog boxes or even out of the back of a tall pick-up truck, don't let them jump from a height of more than two or three feet. An uncontrolled jump from this height might strain a shoulder or other joint when landing. Instead, hold the collar with one hand and as your dog comes out of the vehicle, support them with the other hand under their chest. Many dogs will jump out with such vigor that you can be knocked over backwards if you are caught unprepared.

Many people leave the drop chain on their dogs when they are in the box or the chain is in the box and is attached prior to unloading the dog. The advantage of having the chain connected to their collar is that it is another place you can safely grab if needed. And if it's on, you can connect to the vehicle with less fuss.

Walking With The Dog

If your dog is too strong to be walked with all four feet on the ground, lift them by their collar to a vertical position and let them hop along on their hind feet. This position does not hurt the dog, and they are much safer than if they pull you off your feet and get loose. It is wise for you to practice this maneuver before your dog gets too strong and before you must accomplish it on icy footing. This is also a bit more difficult if you have large dogs. If your dog has a harness on, then you grab the harness instead of the collar to hop your dog along.

Securing Dog to Truck

If you must travel to an area beyond your own property to train your dog, don't let them run loose if other people or dogs are around. The easiest way to keep your dog safe while you prepare the equipment is to snap them to a chain attached to your vehicle. Excited dogs will often chew through leashes while your back is turned, so a short piece of chain works the best. If you are working with a group of experienced mushers you will get to see different tethering means that you can adapt for your uses.

Prior to the start of training your dog should be given time to relieve themselves. A beginning dog that has not relieved itself sufficiently before a run will often cause a delay during the run. Your dog may either stop suddenly or may just not run well. So watch your dog before the run to see whether or not they pee or poop. Always pick up the droppings immediately. Training areas should always be kept as clean as possible. If your dog is not used to being tied and won't pee or poop, take them for a walk on a long leash. This may have to be done before reaching the training site to avoid the distractions and excitement at the site.

All dogs need a little time on the chain to look over the new area and any new dogs and people who are there. The sight of other dogs should increase their enthusiasm for the run. Give them a little time to become adjusted to the situation before asking for concentration on their lessons.

Other Dogs in The Area

It's best if you discourage your friends from bringing their pet dogs to watch your dogs practice. If someone does bring a dog, be sure to ask him or her to either keep their dog in their car or on a leash well away from yours. If a loose, ownerless dog arrives on the scene, shoo it away. There can be enough pandemonium associated with training a team without a loose dog making things worse. Sometimes the loose dog will not go away and will have to be tied. Sled dogs must learn to accept the presence of strange dogs in a dignified fashion, but loose dogs excite them more than tied ones do, and right now you would like your dog to focus on pulling rather than loose dogs.

There are numerous ways to teach a dog to pull, however the

most important step is that you (or someone working with you) know how to run a sled dog prior to starting. You must know what you will teach the dog before you begin. You can learn a little by reading this book, a little more by watching an experienced driver or you can learn even more by doing.

When you contact local mushers or local mushing clubs in your area, let them know you are interested in learning and interested in helping. Most clubs and drivers will be happy to help mushers-to-be learn about the sport. However most will want to get to know you a little before letting you help out. If you have the opportunity to join one or more drivers, leave your dog at home or in your vehicle until you are sure you will not cause a problem. It would be a good idea to meet the other drivers first and talk about bringing your dog out before you do. Once the driver gets to know you, he or she will likely let you help out preparing the team. That is great experience that will prepare you to train your own dog(s).

After watching and helping with another team, you will be much more prepared to train your dog. The following sections will provide you with some options for accomplishing this training.

CONTROLLED RUNNING ON FOOT WITH ONE DOG

Whether you will train your dog in an experienced team or not, if you are starting with a dog that you can control on a leash and with whom you can keep up when they are trotting, you can give the first few lessons with you on foot.

If you have your harness, put it on your dog for association. If you do not have a harness yet, you can start with just a strong collar and a line. Fasten the line to their collar and trot alongside. If your dog goes a little in front of you, so much the better. As you are able, drop back behind. You want a steady pace without stopping. If they stop to sniff or lift a leg, say *No!* and urge your dog on. You must be gentle but firm. Your dog must also learn to ignore any loose dog that is in the area.

Whenever you start out, give your *Go* command in a high and happy voice. Say *Whoa* when you want to stop. Give the command in a low-pitched voice and draw the word out. Give words of encouragement now and then but not a steady stream of talking. Give petting and praise if you stop for a breather during your run, but save your most enthusiastic petting until you are finished.

The outing should be training more than play for your dog but must be enough fun so that they look forward to the next time.

If you have a harness, put one lead on the collar and another on the back of the harness. Start out as with a collar only, but when you are able to drop back behind the dog, decrease the tension on the collar line and put the pull on the harness line. Unsnap the collar line when it no longer seems necessary, but be prepared to put it on again quickly if your dog gets out of control and starts to wander off the trail or stops to investigate something.

PROBLEMS

Dog Won't Lead Out: If a dog does not wish to go out in front, fool them into it by doing your training at a time of day when they are feeling their liveliest, and train at a place where they are more interested in the trail than in you.

Timid Dog: Sometimes a dog is so timid and unsure that when he sees the harness and line come out they go off and hide somewhere. Don't be discouraged by this, some of the best sled dogs are timid until they get on the trail. Pull gently but firmly from their hiding place while talking in an encouraging tone. Keep your motions slow and steady and keep your voice calm. Don't reprimand. Your dog would not understand, and the tone of your voice would only upset them more.

When you finally get the harness and line on, the dog may lie down on their stomach or back, or they may just stand there with their feet planted. If the dog is lying down, lift gently to their feet and hold there. Don't jerk the line but use a steady pull. Keep the line low and the pull horizontal so that the dog can keep all four feet on the ground.

Sometimes a little tidbit of food in front of a nose will do wonders to get a timid dog going. Be sure to give the food as a reward, when the dog does move. You will not be spoiling your dog because when they becomes surer of themselves the food can be eliminated.

You can also try running away from the dog, with or without holding the leash, while enticing them to follow you. If they don't move willingly, crouch down in front, with your arms outstretched and again call to come to you. Be sure to give enthusiastic praise for any progress at all.

Hysterical Dog: This dog is afraid and may bite in self-defense. Realize that biting is from fright and not aggressiveness. Wear heavy protection and keep your face away from their face and teeth. While trying to bite, they may jump around in all directions and try to slip their collar. Tread quietly and slowly but firmly. Make sure the collar can't slip off, and use a steady pull on the leash. Do your practicing away from outside noise and confusion until the dog is surer of themselves and settles down.

SPEED VS. LOAD TRAINING

A big question among sled dog trainers is whether it is best to teach a new dog first to pull a load or to go fast. Those who favor teaching load pulling first feel that speed will come easily when the heavy load is removed. They feel that the dog that has been taught to pull a heavy load will never give up when the going gets tough.

On the other hand, those who favor teaching the dog first to go fast feel that teaching the dog to pull a heavy weight accustoms him to going much too slowly. They feel that the dog develops a better attitude toward the sport if they are allowed to run fast because they like to run. And finally, they feel that a dog that knows he or she is supposed to go fast will not slow down any more than necessary when the going gets tough. Learning to pull and gaining confidence to run fast are both important for dog sledding. But running fast can be intimidating to a new dog. It is best to start with moderate speeds and moderate loads and build gradually from there.

LEASH AND LOAD METHOD OF TRAINING

This method stresses pulling first and speed afterwards. It is to be used after the dog has started to learn controlled running on foot.

When the dog has become steady with the leash on the collar and has started to go out in front, attach a load to the back of the harness with about a four to six foot line. Shorter lines place the load too close to the dog, and can make the dog worried about what is behind them. The load should be light enough so that the dog does not get discouraged trying to pull it, but not so light that it bounces around and scares them. A big piece of firewood or a small tire work quite well. Large tires can be tough for the dog to pull. The load should stop when they do and not come up and hit them in the hind legs.

With the load attached, continue trotting with your leash attached to the dog's collar. If they are reluctant to start out, you may try going a few yards away and calling him or her to you. Remember that any dog that is pulling must, by the mechanics of their build, keep their head low; so when you call, crouch down so that they do not have to lift their head to see your face. When they are trotting well, fall back a little way behind. Eventually you must snap the leash to the rear of the harness. As they go faster, you can increase the load until it approximates pulling a person on a wheeled rig.

Things to remember: If the load sticks on anything, do not move it yourself if the dog can. Urge them to pull harder. You do not want to teach them that as soon as the going gets a little tough, they can stop and have someone help.

When your dog is pulling a load at such a speed and for such a distance that you can no longer keep up, now they are ready to run in a team pulling a vehicle.

USING A VEHICLE

Use a vehicle when you can no longer keep up with your dog on foot; or use a vehicle right from the beginning when the dog has no psychological problems and when you want to teach speed before you teach pulling.

Vehicles can be a cart, ATV, sled, scooter or bicycle (for one or maybe two dogs only). All vehicles should have a means of steering and a brake that can be locked if the driver has to get off of the vehicle for any reason. The vehicle should be heavy enough or have a braking system adequate to hold the team stationary while the driver works with the team.

Chassis or Sled Without the Aid of Trained Dogs

Two people known to the dog should be available, if possible, for the dog's first few outings. One must be on the vehicle to prevent its coming up from behind and hitting the dog in case of a sudden stop. The second person starts out controlling the dog with a leash attached to its collar.

The first time a dog is hooked to a chassis or sled, they may do just about anything. Whatever their antics are, they are undoubtedly due to the uncertainty about what is going to happen. Ignore them and go about the business of hooking up as quickly and quietly as possible. The sooner you get going the better.

When all is ready, unfasten the vehicle and give the command to *Go*. The person on the leash should run with the dog a short distance, and if all goes well, they should unsnap the leash while both they and the dog are still running. Once a dog gets going in the right direction it is best not to stop, since the dog may turn around and/or get in a tangle.

If the dog does not run well after being started for a short distance on the leash, alternate methods can be used. The person most known to the dog can run slightly ahead while calling to follow. If the dog is fast, the person may need a good head start, but they must make sure that the dog sees your helper go down the trail and knows where they are. Hopefully, when the dog catches up, they will pass by and keep going.

If the trail is suitable, the person most known to the dog can drive a car well in front of the dog and call to them to follow. In extreme cases, the dog and vehicle can be led away from the holding area, turned around, and then the dog allowed and encouraged to run back. Most dogs will come in better than they will go out. Another method is to let the dog follow another dog team.

Once the dog is going, the person on the vehicle takes over giving all commands and corrects the dog. If it becomes hard for the dog to pull the weight, the driver must either pedal the vehicle or get off and run behind or alongside it. The dog must not have to work so hard that they become discouraged. If there is any choice, the dog should not be trained on a rough or uphill trail that will slow them down.

Bicycle

Using a bicycle is recommended only when no chassis or sled is available and the dog is already partially leash broken. The advantage of using a bicycle is: Most people have one readily available that has a steering mechanism. The disadvantages are: the trainer has little control; the brakes of a bicycle will not hold a strong dog; getting on and off to correct the dog is more difficult than with a chassis, and if the dog suddenly decides to dart sideways, the driver can take a nasty spill. Although training with a bicycle has been successful for some people, it can be hazardous for others.

A harness and two lines are necessary. Fasten one line between the harness and the bicycle. The other line is snapped to the dog's collar. In the beginning, as the dog pulls one person on the bicycle, another runs alongside the dog controlling him with the line attached to their collar. As the dog becomes steady, the line can be removed from the collar.

When only one person is working the dog, the line from the harness is not attached to the bicycle. It is laid across the middle of the handle bar and held with one hand. It should run THROUGH the hand and NOT AROUND it. Care must be taken that the loose end does not get caught in the wheel. In the event of trouble, let the line run through the hand to avoid a violent jerk. An alternative method is to make an extension to the handlebars that will hold a line up about the tire. One way to do this is with a stout wire in a V shape. The two ends of the wire can be fastened to the handlebars and the apex of the V can be attached to the dog's tug line.

Michael Callahan with a pair of dogs, using a scooter for training. *Photo by Bruce T. Smith.*

TRAINING SEVERAL DOGS

If all the dogs being trained are beginners, train them separately at first to minimize tangles and confusion. Start putting them together as soon as they seem to start to know what is happening. Put only two or three dogs together at first. The advantages of putting them together are that they give each other confidence and they can share the pulling load. In the beginning, put together only dogs that know each other well.

If two people with one or two dogs each wish to get together to make up a team, they should do so since such an arrangement can work quite well. The dogs get to know each other and will be kept at the same level of training. It is much easier for two people to train new dogs than one person alone, particularly when the dogs get to the stage of being hooked up together. It is also nice to have sociability and the chance to discuss problems with someone.

Position to Hook Dogs

If you have only two dogs and they know each other and get along well, put them in double lead. If they bother each other or play too much together or one does not seem to like the front position, put one behind the other.

If you have three or more dogs, consider each one's attitude and sex. Put dogs of opposite sex together if possible. If there is any question of one dog that does not like another, put them separately. The only disadvantage of putting a dog separately is that they are more apt to step over the towline than if there is a dog opposite them helping to hold it up.

If you have one dog that is so timid that they won't go out, have a handler walk to the end of the trail and hook the dog in the team for the return trip home.

Try your dogs in different positions to see where they do best. Some like the right side, some like the left, and others do not care.

As a general rule, put the eager dogs at the front of the team and the timid ones behind. Some dogs like to be up front and some are not psychologically suited for that position. Often dogs will change from day to day. One day a dog will do well up front, and the next day they won't go out at all.

It is not uncommon for an experienced driver with a well trained team to observe the attitude of their dogs in the starting chute of a race and at the last minute move their leader back and put up another dog. Likewise, it is not uncommon for drivers to switch leaders out on the trail. Always be alert to your dogs' moods and adjust their positions accordingly. If you can, try to figure out what conditions make the dogs' moods change.

TANGLES

All dogs get into tangles at one time or another with lines, harnesses, other dogs, bushes, or anything else that is within reach. To avoid tangles, first make sure that you never start out unless all lines are straight. If someone is helping you, have him or her hold the lead dog by the tugline. The handler should not stand in front of the dog, so as to block their view of the trail that you want them to take. Neither are they to keep the dog immobile and quiet. Their job is to hold the towline between the dog and the vehicle tight to minimize tangles. If a tangle occurs in any dog's line, your helper/handler is to straighten it out just before the team takes off. If it is convenient and no strain on the dogs, take the handler with you on the run so that they can help when necessary.

When a tangle occurs on the trail, analyze it to see if it will hurt the dog. If it will not, leave it alone and let the dog learn to get out of it by itself. A dog can easily get a leg back on the proper side of the towline. A little pressure taken off the line by increasing the speed of the vehicle sometimes makes it easier for the dog to free a tangle. If the tangle is going to hurt the dog or is of such a nature that they cannot possibly get out of it, such as when a towline gets completely wrapped around a hind leg, then you must stop and straighten it out yourself.

In training there will come a time when you will actually have to take a harness completely off a dog to straighten a tangle. Once in a while a tangle of such intensity occurs that a dog must be cut loose. The experienced drivers carry a knife in case of such an emergency AND cable cutters if they have any cable in their lines. Novice dogs can get themselves into the most awful messes, so be warned. But also take heart; the seasoned sled dog almost never lets anything go wrong.

DISCIPLINE

Do not discourage your dog from getting excited during hitching up time. Discipline at this crucial point for showing their joy of running will only confuse and discourage them. Your dog will be harder for you to cope with when they are jumping around, but will run better for not having their enthusiasm squelched.

Common misdemeanors that do require some degree of reprimand are:

Turning around and coming back to you.

Taking the wrong trail.

Being generally lazy.

Fraternizing with loose dogs or those on another team.

Following small game off the trail.

Stopping to lift a leg. (If you have given the dogs plenty of time to relieve themselves before the run, they should not have to do this. On the other hand, some dogs absolutely must poop on the trail no matter how much time you have given them before the run. It is something about the running. This is not cause for reprimand. Instead, just encourage the dog to keep running while they are performing. If a lead dog stops to perform, you have no choice except to stop and wait until they are finished.)

Picking a fight. Self-defense is legal, as is a female's snapping at a male who is paying her unwanted attention.

Suit the degree of your reprimand to the seriousness of the offense. Never become angry, although sometimes you may wish your dog to think that you are. An Alaskan college professor once said, "A musher is the only person alive who can swear all day at his dogs and never lose his temper."

Never hit a dog. Discipline is by voice only. Even a fight can usually be stopped before it begins if the driver is alert and gives a good shout just as one dog is thinking about jumping another.

Remember that any reprimand must come as close as possible to the very moment of misbehavior so that the dog can associate the reprimand with their act or thought. Do your reprimanding out on the trail, not when you come back from a run. No matter what has happened on the trail, when you come back the dogs must be petted and made to feel happy about the run so that they look forward to the next time.

BREAKING IN A NEW DOG WITH A TRAINED TEAM

Many people decide they would like to try their dog as a sled dog because they have a friend who has a trained team. They would like to have their friend hook up their green dog with his trained team. This is likely to be disastrous. The dogs of the trained team all know each other. The strange dog in their midst is at an immediate disadvantage. The new dog does not like being confined so closely to all those strange dogs and is wondering which one is going to jump him first, though probably none will do so. All the lines and harnesses and the jumping and yelping may confuse them.

Chances are that the novice dog will lie down, start a fight in self-defense, or hold back so much that they are dragged. At best they will certainly not be at the same stage of development as the trained team and could not keep up with them for long. In short, your dog could be mentally ruined before he even starts.

The conditions necessary to have an untrained dog run successfully in a trained team are first that the dog be neither nervous nor aggressive. It helps if the trained team is all of the opposite sex. The trained team must be small and have a reliable leader. The new dog should be hooked up at the back of the team either with a trained dogs of the opposite sex or alone. The team must go slowly and not very far. An experienced musher might arrange such a situation to accommodate a friend, but to ask to do this more than once is an imposition, no matter how polite they may seem.

The tried and true way for an experienced musher to break in a new dog of their own is indeed to hook it up with a few of their trained dogs. Usually they do not have the time to train each new dog separately on lead, and if all conditions are right, it is not necessary to do so. If you ever add another dog to your little team, you may give them some leash training first if you wish; but if you are careful, you may also put the new dog directly into your team.

If the new dog is an adult, give enough time in the dog yard for the established dogs to accept them as one of the group before ever hooking them up. Use a small team with a reliable leader who will hold the line tight and prevent unnecessary tangles. Hook the new dog up either by themselves or with one of the opposite sex. Start him out in wheel position close to the sled or rig so that the established dogs do not feel that they are being robbed of their position at the front of the team. It may be necessary to lengthen the towline so that the noise of the sled or vehicle does not bother the new dog. Go slowly the first few times so they don't get scared, and only gradually allow the team to pick up speed. Do not go far.

If the new dog is a puppy that you have had for awhile, the older dogs will have become used to it. Take the pup to your training sessions so that it can watch. While the pup is still small, let it run loose with the team a few times if possible. Chances are that it will run alongside or behind the team. When you finally hook the pup in the team, make sure the leader is reliable and there are no tangles. Also be sure to go slowly the first four or five times. A dog that has had a bad experience on their first few runs may never get over it.

RESPONDING TO COMMANDS

Give all commands in the manner described in the COMMANDS section. Give them whenever the dogs do that specific action, whether they need the command to do it or not. For example, say *Gee!* when the trail turns sharply to the right. Just hearing the command at the time of the action will help the dog associate the two and learn the meaning of the word.

The *Go* command is easy to learn because the vehicle is released at the same time that the command is given. When the *Stop* command is given, the brake is applied to the vehicle to reinforce the command.

The *Turn* commands are given to the leader. Give them as described in *Chapter 25*. Make all corrections as described in that section.

It is not necessary to give the leader too much special leader training before putting them in front of a small team because a beginning leader of a beginning team can learn the commands right along with everything else. Just do not expect too much of them. The main thing is that if given a command to go a certain direction, that is the direction they must go, even if you must lead them there.

The *Speed-up* commands are the hardest to learn because the ways to reinforce them are the least definite. Before giving the team a command to speed up, make sure the team is capable of speeding up. The dogs must not be too tired and the trail must be good. It helps to give the command when the trail starts to go downhill. When you give your command to speed up, make sure the team does speed up.

You can use your jingler (noise maker) at this time so that the dogs associate the noise of the jingler with speeding up. Pump the sled or chassis to take the strain off the team. If necessary, get off and run. If the team still doesn't speed up, stop and rest it and then try again. If just one dog is slowing down or refuses to speed up, call their name in an annoyed tone of voice just before giving the *Go* command so that all dogs will know that the command is for that dog only.

POINTS TO REMEMBER

1. Give all commands during the run so that your dog can start to learn them. Be careful how you give them.

2. Don't talk to your dog continuously.

3. Don't go too far the first few runs. In the beginning the frequency of the runs is more important than the distance.

4. The distance will be controlled by the condition of the trail, the weather, and your dog itself. Although you must not overdo the distance, keep in mind that a dog with their tongue hanging out is not necessarily any more tired than a person who has just finished one set of tennis.

5. Give your dog enthusiastic praise after returning from a run.

6. Don't repeat a run on the same day unless there is a long time between runs and your dog seems enthusiastic to go.

7. Anytime your dog regresses in their accomplishments, do not hesitate to go back in the training to a place where they feel comfortable. Their forward learning progress the second time around will be quicker than the first.

8. Although repetition is necessary to teach any dog, don't get in a rut. If your dog continually makes the same mistake and gets scolded for it, this is a negative situation. Your dog is probably making the mistake because they do not understand. Try to find some way to change what *you* are doing so that your dog does the right thing and does not have to be scolded. This is positive training. It is a matter of understanding your dog and trying to help them.

You may hear of people using whips to train. They call them signal whips because they do not make contact with the dog, they simply use them to make popping noise in close proximity to the dogs. Forget about this old time "macho" use of whips. Do not use one at all, even for signaling. As of October 1990, ISDRA Race Rules give race organizations the option of prohibiting the use of whips for signaling. More and more race organizations are exercising this option. Whips are completely forbidden in Europe.

Chapter Twenty-Three
CONDITIONING

Definition: **Conditioning** – *A method of controlling or influencing the way people or animals behave or think by using a gradual training process.*

Conditioning your team is working with them to get to a point they can run longer and longer and not be fatigued at the end of your run. Tired yes, but worn out no.

Step one: Identify a short trail to run. Select a trail that is easy on their feet with few obstacles. Don't use a trail that is bad or long. Don't go in weather so hot that they only trot.

Step two: Start with 1/4 to a 1/2-mile trail. Ask your team to run/lope the 1/4 to 1/2 mile at a lope.

Step three: Once they can do the short distances easily, add more distance to get them to one mile. When they can lope the one mile easily, try one and a half miles. Your team should be loping the entire time.

Each time you start a new distance your dogs may slow down. If out on the trail they seem to have slowed down more than normal, it might be time for a break and a bit of praise or a pep talk. Stopping them to rest is better than allowing them to trot on and on. You need to be reasonable with what you are asking. A trotting team will never do well in a speed race. If you are training and conditioning your dogs not to race, but to just enjoy your time on the trail together, then it doesn't matter whether the dogs trot or not. But if racing the shorter distances is your goal then you need to work your dogs and develop the memory in their loping muscles.

Your goal in conditioning your team is to get them physically and mentally ready for the distance and activities you are planning on doing. If you are planning a long distance race, it is completely unreasonable to expect your dog to lope the entire time. If you are entering a three-mile race, well conditioned dogs should have no problem with loping the entire distance.

You will want to train your racing team for the distances you are planning on running. You should vary the distance slightly and never expect a race course to be the exact same mileage as you train. It's best to train with a little excess distance so your dogs don't "hit a wall" and stop at the mileage they are used to. You want your team to cross the finish line with a little bit left, a bit in reserves. You want them to have wagging tails and happy faces.

As the season progresses continue building your dogs up to longer and longer distances until the season is almost over. You should be pleased (and maybe even a little surprised) with how much progress they can make during a single season. Before you know it the season will be over.

The next year when you start training for the season start out on the same short training trails from the year before. If the dogs have no problem loping the trail, quickly add more distance. Run that distance a couple times and add yet more distance. Don't remain at the shorter distances for long. Keep increasing the distance until you find a distance that seems to give the dogs a little trouble. This distance is basically this year's starting point for your serious conditioning. Make sure to note this in your training journal. You will want to be able to look back at these notes next year.

Each succeeding year as you start your race season training, you will find that the same team can start at a longer and longer distance. If you keep the same dogs, the days of the 1/4 or 1/2-mile trail will be long behind you.

To make conditioning more fun for you, there are all sorts of high tech gadgets you can purchase. One is a GPS (Global Positioning System). GPS is an electronic unit that uses a world-wide radio-navigation system, which is formed from a constellation of satellites and their ground stations. GPS uses these "man-made stars" as reference points to calculate positions and speed. A GPS unit and a computer can be a great way to track the progress as well as the speed of your team.

So, with a little work, you can plot the speed your team is going at any part of your trail. When you do your calculations, there is a + or - of 5% when you plot the distance. Which means 10 miles on the GPS can be 9.5 to 10.5 miles. They are still handy pieces of equipment. GPS units are now available in a variety of sizes. The units made and designed to be worn on your wrist have become quite popular with some dog drivers. A noteworthy tidbit on GPS units, some races do NOT allow the dog driver to have a GPS with them during the race. Check with race officials if your GPS becomes part of your normal gear.

169   MUSH!

Chapter Twenty-Four

24

PASSING

When one or more teams share the same trails passing is bound to happen. Passing need not be competitive. It might simply be to pass another team so that team can lead for a while. You and a friend may both be out having a nice run together. Your team may be leading and your dogs could use a mental rest. You can call to the driver of the team behind you and have them overtake your team. And its now your turn to follow merrily along. Get used to it, sled dog teams must pass other teams efficiently and safely, both during training runs and while racing. They need to cleanly pass, both teams they know and teams of dogs they do not know.

Getting your team to make reliable passes takes plenty of practice. So much so that any chance you get to practice, you should take advantage of it. Practicing clean passes develops into good habits. A clean pass during training is no different than a clean pass while racing. A clean pass is a clean pass and deserves praise.

In the following sections there are directions and suggestions as to how to handle different types of passing scenarios. In every different situation remember to always keep a clear head and a calm tone to your voice. Don't get upset if you have a problem. Understand that you have a problem and try to come up with a way to get the behavior you want – a clean pass.

In training be sure and practice everything as best you can so that you can have some expectation of what your dog knows or doesn't know, and what he may have a problem with so you can hopefully prevent it before it occurs. This is one time when repetitions will work to make the behavior one you want, which is a clean pass.

There are two types of passing: head-on and overtaking. Different techniques are used for each one.

Three teams passing. The center team is a team of Alaskan Malamutes. *Photo by Bruce T. Smith.*

HEAD-ON PASSING

When you spot a team heading your way you will need to cleanly continue in the direction of travel in which both of you are traveling. Frequently when two teams spot each other on the trail the dogs tend to get excited and pick up the pace, so be sure and do what you have to do to remain in control of the pass.

If the teams approaching each other are both using the middle of the trail, they will not be able to fit in the same space and therefore both drivers should give their leaders a *Gee Over!* command. It is good to start training your leaders to learn to pass on the right side of the trail in fall training so there will be less confusion when you hit a race or crowded trail. Still passing on the right is not a rule and if both teams are already on different sides of a wide trail, be it left or right, then it is best to let them stay there.

You will want to take care about using the *Gee!* command if the pass occurs at a place where there is also a trail that leads off to the right. Your leader may listen to your *Gee!* command and take the trail to the right.

As the leaders come close together, give a *Straight Ahead!* or *On By!* command, just as you would if you wanted your leader to go across an intersection.

If both teams can keep moving head-on passing is much easier. Partly because the time they are side by side is less. If even one of the teams stops, that team may spread out blocking the trail. There will be times the trail may be so narrow, bumpy or crooked that slowing the team is necessary. And sometimes one driver must get off their sled to lift it out of the way or to hold their team while the other musher passes.

On very narrow trails both teams may wish to stop a short distance apart and the drivers figure out if one team will get off the trail completely. If you are not sure what to do, don't be afraid to communicate with the others on the trail as more experienced drivers will know exactly what they want you to do or not.

PROBLEMS
1. One or more dogs cross over the towline of the other team.
This problem usually occurs when one team slows too much or stops.

Solution: Both drivers stop. If the dogs don't straighten themselves immediately, either one or both drivers must set their snow hooks, go forward, and pull the teams apart.

Sometimes this type of tangle becomes so bad that dogs must be unhooked. If this happens to your team, try not to unsnap both ends of a dog at once lest the dog wiggle free. A loose dog that cannot be caught will cause the team's disqualification in a race. While you may untangle dogs in the other team, do not unsnap them unless specifically requested to do so. To lose someone else's dog is even worse than losing your own.

As with all tangles, move with deliberate speed, but keep calm. Speak quietly to the other driver and keep repeating *Whoa* or *Stay* to your dogs. Watch for other teams arriving on the scene from either direction.

2. Your leader turns around to follow the other team.
Solution: You should be able to see this coming before it actually happens and may be able to keep it from happening with a sharp *No!* as your leader(s) try to watch the other team. However, if it happens too fast or you miss the warning signs, you will have to stop the sled and hook down, and then walk up to your leaders and head them back in the other direction.

This can turn into a terrible game of who is more stubborn as the leaders may turn around again as soon as you head back to your sled. You MUST remain patient and calm and NOT get mad at the dogs. With patience and perseverance, you will get them headed in the right direction, and hopefully this happens in training and not in a race where every second counts.

More experienced drivers can get their team headed in the

right direction without actually setting their snow hook by stopping the sled and jumping off on the side to which the leader(s) are turning. They then will run up and meet the dog(s) head on and grab the collar or harness, turning them in the proper direction, and running down the trail with them until they seem to be going smoothly. At that point, the musher will hop on the sled as it comes along pass them without turning their back on the team.

3. Your dog snaps at a dog in another team. Your dog must be broken of this habit if it is to run on a trail with other dog teams, because this type of behavior will not only disqualify you at a race, but will also make no one want to train with you.

Solution: During a training run, plan a slow pass with another team and ask the other driver to plant a foot hard on the offending dog if they should snap; or, if the dog snaps, immediately stop your team and run up to them. Scream *No!* at your dog and shake the offending dog hard by the scruff of the neck; or, carry a passenger who can run behind the dog during a pass and if the dog snaps, surprise them with a hard slap on their rump, or if you have a specific dog you are having a problem with, you can hook a retractable leash to their collar. The leash can be hooked to the sled and with a gloved hand you can give the line a tug to correct the dog. This can be done with a couple of dogs by using different colored retractable leashes.

In all passes where correction is *not* planned, such as in a race; call the dog's name and give them a firm *No!* or *Leave it!* just before the pass.

We have worked with this so much with our dogs that we have a command the dogs have learned. It's *be nice. Be nice* simply evolved and it works for us.

Knowing which one of these methods to use is sometimes a matter of trial and error to see which one is most effective on that dog. If you have been trying one method again and again with limited results, try another one.

OVERTAKING PASSING

If you plan on racing in speed classes at ISDRA sanctioned races, you should familiarize yourself with the fine points of ISDRA's passing rules. (Complete race rules are available to members and can be downloaded from ISDRA's web site.)

The driver in the front sled is pedaling to help his team of Alaskan Huskies as they pull away after a clean pass. *Photo by Bruce T. Smith.*

When a team driver is ready to pass another team, the passing team driver may demand the right of way when their lead dog(s) comes within fifty (50) feet of the sled of the team being overtaken.

The overtaken team will get out of the way of the passing team by steering the sled to one side of the trail, and slowing their team and, if overtaking team driver requests, stopping their team and keeping the team stationary.

If the passing team becomes tangled or bunched up in the course of the pass, that team's driver may require the overtaken team to remain stopped for up to one (1) minute in Unlimited and Limited Classes involving eight (8) or more dogs, one-half (1/2) minute in all other classes. This time can be used to untangle the dogs.

Once a team has been passed, the team that was passed can not repass the other team as long as the driver in front is making an effort to keep their team moving forward until:

In Unlimited or Limited Classes involving eight (8) or more dogs, after four (4) minutes or one (1) mile the driver of the team in the rear may call for a pass.

In Limited Classes involving fewer than eight (8) dogs, after two (2) minutes or one-half (1/2) mile, the driver of the team in the rear may call for a pass.

OR if both drivers agree the team in the rear may overtake in less time or distance.

EXCEPTION:

If after a pass, the driver need not hold their team if the other team has to do any of the following:

repair broken equipment, or;

stops to move or unhook a dog in their team, or;

leaves the race trail before the above mentioned distance or time interval has elapsed. It should be noted that loading a dog in the sled constitutes changing a dog's position in the team.

If a driver comes upon two or more teams stopped together, they may pass all stopped teams. The teams that are stopped should make every effort to make clear the trail for the moving team(s).

If teams are following each other, they should maintain an interval of not less than one (1) team length between each other, unless they are passing or in the No-right-of way zone.

When a team is passed in the No-right-of-way zone, the team does not have to stop and yield the trail.

Dog drivers should not do anything that might interfere with a competing team.

PROBLEMS

1. The overtaken driver does not hear the *Trail!* call or the request to stop, does not look around, does not slow down or stop, and your team has trouble passing. This can happen when it is windy or very cold and the driver is wearing heavy earmuffs.

Solution: If the problem occurs during a training run, discuss it with the offending driver after the run. If it happens during a race, submit a formal protest to the Race Marshall/ Chief Judge. At the discretion of the Protest Committee, the offending driver can either be given a warning or can be disqualified.

2. The passing leader will not overtake. He stays behind the forward sled, sometimes even stopping when it stops.

Solution: If your leader won't pass because he is tired (it's a long race or he has been chasing) drop back and give your dogs time to get their second wind before trying the pass again.

Wait for a wider part of the trail or a slight downhill, which will encourage your leader to pick up speed. Ask the overtaken team to go very slowly or to stop completely.

A pair of teams making a clean pass. *Photo by Bruce T. Smith.*

Ask the forward driver, as a courtesy, to pull your leader around his sled and as far forward as he can reach.

Run up yourself, and pull your leader past the entire team.

Stay behind the forward team until the end of the race.

Although you could legally keep trying to pass until the no-right-of-way zone, sometimes staying behind will save you more time than passing.

3. The passing team crosses over the towline of the forward team. This happens when the overtaken team is stopped and spread across the trail, usually to turn around to see who is coming.

Solution: Request the overtaken driver to go ahead slightly, as that may separate the teams, or run up and separate the teams yourself.

4. The passing team slows down considerably after the pass. This situation is common.

Solution: The forward driver motivates his team by whistling or other non-interfering sounds and by pedaling or running.

The forward driver may request or agree that the following team re-pass even though the legal time and mileage intervals have not been reached.

Next time, the passing driver should not pressure their team to catch the forward one, rather letting them come up slowly to conserve their strength. Then they will be more physically able to speed up after the pass than if they are completely winded by the chase.

5. The passing team has a tangle that takes more than the

legal time allowed to fix.

Solution: The waiting driver should inform the forward driver that their time is up and then proceed to pass them slowly.

If the forward driver has a safety problem, it is only sportsmanlike for the waiting driver to either continue to wait or to offer to go up and help.

6. A third team comes upon two passing teams with either one or both in a tangle.

Solution: If there is room for the third team to pass either on or off the trail, they have the right to pass both teams.

If either of the teams is in an emergency situation, it is only sportsmanlike for the third driver to stop and either wait on their sled or offer to go up and help.

TRAINING YOUR LEADER TO PASS

The best training is to practice passing every chance you get. On training runs, make arrangements with other drivers to set up passing situations. Owners of large kennels often divide their dogs into two teams, and with a handler driving one of the teams, the two teams practice passing and re-passing each other.

Two teams training and practicing passing. Note passenger is along to help if either team has a dog that needs correction. *Photo courtesy of Barbara "Dog Drop" Schaefer.*

If you can break in your new leader with an experienced one, by all means do so. Always start a new leader on the going-home part of the trail, as in their eagerness to get home, other worries they may have, will be minimized. For the first try, put the new leader on the side away from the team they will be passing. When your dog does not seem afraid of the other teams, move them to the near side.

BEING PASSED

When it is your turn to be passed, practice all right-of-way customs, and help the passing team get by as quickly and as easily as possible.

POINTS TO REMEMBER

1. In a head-on pass, both teams keep moving. Don't push a team to catch one in front.
3. A passing team has all the rights.
4. An overtaken team must slow down, give way, and stop if so asked.
5. Neither driver interferes with the other team by making loud noises before, during or after the pass.
6. The overtaken driver must wait a specific time while the passing driver fixes a tangle that occurred during the pass.
7. The overtaken driver must follow at the correct distance for the correct time or mileage interval.
8. If a leader refuses to pass, lead them by the other team.

Dr. Lombard had to do this with his well-trained leader, *Diamond*, when *Diamond* suddenly refused to pass. He hooked up two seven-dog teams and he drove one and his wife drove the other. The teams passed and repassed each other many times with "Doc" leading *Diamond* each time until *Diamond* regained his confidence.

This technique will also work with small teams of only three dogs. It is nice after a pass for the passing driver to call out "Thank you".

179   MUSH!

Chapter Twenty-Five

TRAINING A
COMMAND LEADER

Every dog on your team should be looked at as one that could be a potential leader and given the opportunity to prove himself or herself. Many a musher has looked at a particular temperament, conformation or size of a dog and made a conclusion that it would, or would not, make a good leader and later were proved wrong. The following chapter should provide you with a guideline for working with your dogs that will maximize your ability to get the most out of your pooch.

Leader training starts with teaching the basic commands as described in an earlier chapter. The basic commands a lead dog will need to know are: *Line Out, Hike!, Gee, Haw* and *On-By.* As your dogs perfect these commands and both them and you become more confident, you can add other interesting ones such as: *Gee Over* (to get the teams over to the right side of the trail where they belong) or *Gee Come* to have them pull the team around and back down the trail you just came up without you having to get off the sled. The more dogs that know multiple commands on your team, the smoother your team will go down the trail. There is no greater feeling than finishing a race and having other mushers tell you what a pleasure it was to run with you because your team was so well behaved.

TRAINING YOUR DOG TO PULL

The only way to tell whether a dog is actually pulling is to look at the tug line and see whether it is pulled tight. Tension on the harness is the key to how hard a dog is pulling. Each dog needs to be taught individually that a tight tug line is what you expect of him or her.

There are a few different methods and philosophies around this, but the current fashion is to use a ground training technique referred to as: "one-on-one" training. What this refers to is simply the act of working with an individual dog, on foot, with either a single leash with clips on either end (which you would have to make yourself) or with the official *Command Training Leash* which can be purchased from outfitters such as Black Ice Dog Sled Equipment (listed in the suppliers section).

Whichever leash you choose, there will be two clips that will get attached to the dog. One clip will get attached to the dog's collar (or a choke chain placed correctly up on the dog's neck behind the ears) and the other to the rear loop on the dog's harness.

If you are right handed, you will start out standing on the right side of the dog and slightly to the rear. Your right hand will hold the part of the lead attached to the collar while your left holds the one attached to the rear harness loop. The left hand's only job is to make sure there is constant tension on the rear of the dog mimicking what it would feel like were they pulling in harness on a team. This is accomplished by bending your left arm at the elbow and keeping approximately a 90 degree angle between your upper and lower arm (see picture above). Once you are set up properly, you can start moving forward.

Give your *Hike!* command, pause, and see if the dog moves ahead. If not, they did not understand what you are asking of them and you need to show them. To show your dog, take your right hand and snap or pop the training collar (similar to giving a correction in obedience training). It is important that this is a quick move, not a pull or a drag. You want to snap, generally in the forward direction to encourage your dog to move forward.

The MOMENT the dog moves (if only one step), give praise so your dog understands forward movement was the right thing to do. It may take awhile, but constant repetition and patience of this maneuver will give you the end result of a dog that moves forward into the harness when you say: *Hike!*

If at any time the tug line becomes slack, then the dog should be corrected in the same manner as above such that it pulls the line tight again. Again, IMMEDIATELY after doing the correct behavior the dog should be praised, and if it took a long time to get there, it may be a good time for a break or even to stop the training session.

Once your dog is moving forward and pulling as you want them too, start to add the other commands one at a time and train in a similar fashion. For example, if you are teaching *Gee,* while walking forward give the command *Gee* (say this in a normal tone of voice, or perhaps a little firm, but not loud), pause a moment and if your dog does not move right, snap the collar generally in the right direction to give them an idea of where you want them to go.

It is best when you are first working with a dog to actually have either a right turn in front of you or an obstacle that you can go around to the right. You want the dog to see the decision point, and learn to listen for a command from you as to which way to go. In this case it's a right turn.

Try to limit your training sessions to approximately ten minutes to keep training interesting and fun. End every training session with plenty of praise and a little play so they look forward to the next time they get to go out and spend time with you.

Most dogs can learn how to pull using this method, as well as learn more specific commands, and thus, most dogs can also become lead dogs with time and patience. However, if you do find that the dog you are working with JUST isn't having fun, you may want to evaluate that dog as you go along and consider whether this is the right dog for you. You will find the occasional dog, even a northern or sledding type of dog, who just doesn't want to pull at all. This could be due to previous experiences or their physical conformation isn't capable of pulling.

Dogs still enjoy a job so you may find that this dog would be better off as your truck dog (the one sitting in the front seat with you keeping it warm) or with another owner. There are dogs that just don't work for some people and work wonderfully with others. If you place a dog because it didn't work for you, that does not mean either of you were failures, it simply means it didn't work out with the two of you.

NEXT STEP: WORKING IN A SMALL TEAM

When your dog(s) are feeling comfortable working commands while on foot, you can start to put them together into a small team attached to a lightweight training cart, Sacco cart, scooter or sled. No matter what you use, you should not hook up more dogs that you can control by yourself. Control means that you can control the speed of the team, stop the team, and keep them stopped.

SNDD's Mike Callahan working one-on-one with one of his dogs using a scooter. *Photo by Bruce T. Smith.*

Hooking up a small three or four-dog team is ideal at this point, ideally one of the dogs already knows what they are doing (even if the trained dog belongs to a friend, although the dog should be one that your dogs know and get along with). Put the trained dog next to a dog in training and then the remaining one or two in the wheel position. Shorten the tug line of the less experienced dog such that the dog is slightly behind the experienced dog. This will help because the new dog can take cues from the experienced dog and won't feel the stress of "being up front" quite as much. Sometimes the trained leader will even forcefully push or pull the untrained dog onto the correct trail.

If this is not possible, hook up the dogs you have been working with (probably not more than three) with a single leader (or less if that is all you have to work with) and just start working from there. It may take a little longer for the new dog to learn, but with patience the results will be the same.

From this point, get positioned on your sled, cart or training rig and when you are ready, give the *Hike!* command as you did in ground training. If the team surges forward like they were taught, great, if not, put your foot on the brake, stop them completely and try again. If they are acting silly, wait for them to settle down first so they are paying attention to YOU.

Get ready again and say your command. If they do not move forward again, stop and this time set your snow hook or lock the break. Walk up to your lead dog(s), grab hold of their collar and gently pull them forward while saying: *Hike*. Do this firmly enough such that the dog(s) actually move forward a step and then praise them.

It can be helpful when training new dogs to keep a short leash or spare neckline hooked to the collar of each leader. If you use an extra neckline, snap both clips to the collar to make a loop that you grab to guide your dog easier. If you use a short leash, the extra portion of leash can be pulled behind and tucked under the dogs' harness. You want something you can quickly grab, but is not flopping around in your dog's face.

Now go back to your sled or cart and start again. Remember that even if the dogs only take ONE step forward, they are doing what you asked and should be praised. Praise in this case is you taking your foot off the brake and allowing them to go forward while giving verbal praise as well. Your verbal praise should not be long or loud, a simple *good dog* will suffice as long as you say it like you mean it. When the team has moved forward nicely for a short bit, apply the brake, stop them, set the brake. Walk up to them and give some good physical petting and *atta-boys* for a minute to let them relax. Then do it again. And once that leader gets it, try another one and go through the

Scooter training an Alaskan Malamute. *Photo by Bruce T. Smith.*

whole routine again with that dog. Pretty soon every dog on your team will be a Command Leader.

As you and your dog(s) gain confidence and experience, you can start adding additional dogs to the team. Make sure and run every dog in every position as a part of your training routine. This affords you the benefit of seeing in which positions each dog naturally excels in, while allowing it to get accustomed to all positions.

Running a dog in only one position may make them a reliable dog there, but were you to run into a problem in the trail and you needed to put them somewhere else (which could be lead!) you could run into problems. Each position is slightly different for the dog as far as how they act or how much they have to think, but that is not to say that most every dog isn't capable of doing each position with the right training and patience. The more you practice, the better they will be, and the more choices you will have when it comes to race day.

USING A HELPER

If you have somebody who is willing help you on your training run, they can be of great assistance to you in training your dogs by stationing them at a junction in the trail. Communicate ahead of time as to which way you are going to go at the junction so your helper is in the right position when you get there and knows what to expect. This person can then assist you should your team not turn the way you want them to by grabbing the leaders and guiding them the correct way or simply standing down the trail a short bit and calling to the team, AFTER you have given the turn command.

Be sure and be clear with regards to what type of a role you want your helper to have as you might just want them off to the side in case of a problem, but don't actually want them to say or do anything. If this is the case, the helper should stand quietly well off the trail as the team goes by so as not to distract them. Or, you may want to be the one handling the dogs and desire the helper to jump on the sled or cart and manage that instead. As training progresses, your dog must learn to take the turns without outside encouragement.

KEEPING THE LINE TIGHT

Your leader(s) has more jobs than making turns at your command. They should also be responsible for keeping the gangline tight while you are hooking up as well as while going down the trail. The cart or sled is anchored and the leaders are put up front before any other dogs are hooked up. At that point give your leader(s) the *Line-Out* command and they should be expected to stay up there and keep tension on the gangline while you hook up the rest of the dogs. This can take a lot of patience on your part, but the end result is definitely worth it!

Sacco carts work very nicely when working on commands and leader training.
Photo by Bruce T. Smith.

After a period you will not have to give a command, they will know their job is to not swing the team until they are off and running. By having your leader keep the line tight, you will have fewer tangles during hook-ups. It's also handy on the trail, if you need to make changes.

You can also use a helper and have them stand and hold the neckline of your leaders. If at hook-up your leaders are very animated, and your handler is a novice, be nice to them and warn them about NOT bending OVER the dogs. This is especially true in the starting chute at races, as broken noses and chipped teeth have been known to occur.

STOPPING THE TEAM

Most race drivers do not specifically train their teams to stop on command because they are more concerned with their team's learning to go forward. However, when you do want to stop you need to communicate with your dogs that you wish to stop. *Whoa* or perhaps *Easy* at the same time as you start to apply the brake cues most dogs that you are going to stop as the dogs learn to associate the command and the sound of the brake with slowing down and stopping.

STAYING STOPPED

The more dogs you run, the more of a challenge it is to keep them stopped out on the trail. Keep in mind that motivated teams can drag a cart, or even an ATV, with the brakes locked. For this reason, another command that is useful to teach is: *Stay!* This command would first be taught on a one-on-one basis before being practiced in a team. Even if you have been

This is the special "leader" training leash and where you should position your hands and body during training. *Photo courtesy of Barbara "Dog Drop" Schaefer.*

working diligently on this command, don't expect them to stay too long, and don't give praise while are staying or they might think you are releasing them from the stay. It will be important to remain calm and move quietly and quickly to get done whatever you need to get done.

TRAINED LEADERS

As a beginning driver you can make training easier both in time and energy by purchasing an older, trained leader. These leaders will teach you and your dogs faster than you can imagine. An older leader with *a few* years of running left is a worthwhile investment for the serious beginner.

EXPERTS HAVE PROBLEMS TOO

Even "Doc" Lombard from Massachusetts had trouble with his well-trained leader on the unfamiliar Anchorage Rendezvous racecourse. Doris Lake tells the story in the *1970 Fur Rendezvous & Dog Musher's Annual*. In 1958, "*Chuckie* tried every Avenue between 4 and 15. (I think that is where Doc's hair started turning grey) and he had to be led across every road crossing." The first two days in 1959 *Chuckie* did the same thing.

"That night he [Doc] sat figuring out a way that might help him, and finally went out to the shed for his towline. He decided to cut his team down to seven dogs for the third day, and he rigged up what can only be called a jerkline. It was snapped to the ring on the lead dog's harness, taped at intervals down the towline, and tied to the handle bar of the sled. That last day he got as far as 6th Avenue when *Chuckie* decided to take the right turn. Doc stepped off his sled to the left, gave a hard jerk on the line to loosen all the tape and brought *Chuckie* to an abrupt halt with the rest of the dogs piled on top of him.

Doc straightened the dogs out and started down Cordova again, but *Chuckie* had to try it one more time. When the same thing happened again the dog decided he had come out second best on that deal and got down to the business of traveling but was unable to get any higher than 9th place in total time. In the 'after-race' talk I commented that I would have liked to have seen the dogs when that jerkline snapped the first time. But Doc said with a chuckle, 'Dogs? I would have given anything to have had a camera to get the expression on the faces of the people standing there, when I stepped off that sled and just had a rope in my hand.'"

189   MUSH!

Chapter Twenty-Six

RIDING THE SLED

Riding or handling a sled is not quite as easy as it looks. It is actually a bit more complicated than most people think. When watching an experienced driver, it actually looks quite easy... that is until it's your turn to try. Going straight is not bad at all, but that first corner can be a real eye opener.

This section will be an attempt to answer questions as to how and why. You will need to polish your method and learn the finer points on your own. But the following text should get you well on your way to riding a sled in the snow.

If you have or know someone with a snow machine, ask then to help you. Learning to ride a sled, with no dogs to worry about, is a great way to figure out what you are doing. It really does help to have someone drag the dog sled with you hanging on. You can concentrate on the feel of gliding, turning and stopping. You will find that some sleds will turn if you are not careful, when all you do is to turn to look if anyone is coming up behind you. Have the person pull you at different speeds. Get accustomed to the reactions of the sled and how it handles at the different speeds and in different terrain.

The most important principle in riding a sled behind a team of dogs is under all circumstances you should be HELPING your team.

What is helping the team? Helping the team is keeping a smooth pull on the gangline. Using your brake or peddling to keep the line from being jerked. It means you use your energy to smooth out the bumps in the trail. It means using the sled to avoid tangles. And it means not turning the sled over.

BALANCE

The sled alone is relatively stable since its center of gravity is quite low. The actual center of gravity is somewhere below the basket. When you stand on the runners this changes the center of gravity nearer to your waist or hips. The combination of sled and rider, with its higher center of gravity, is much more likely to tip over than just the sled alone. Consequently, lowering your body weight to lower the combined center of gravity improves the balance.

A number of ways to lower your body weight and the center of gravity are: a) bend your knees; b) squat down; or c) lean forward over the handle bar. If you are leaning forward, you will want to hold onto the side rail as close to the basket as you can comfortably reach.

Low center of gravity, leaving the starting chute. *Photo by Bruce T. Smith.*

Squatting has the serious disadvantage of allowing tangles to go undetected because you as the driver can't see your team as clearly. This position should be used sparingly, especially when the team is starting up or running at top speed. On the other hand, if you think you are going to turn over, "dragging your butt in the snow" for a few seconds may keep you upright. Occasionally you will see people start races and squat right out of the chute.

Running alongside also lowers the center of gravity back to the sled. You can run holding the handle bar, lowering the center of gravity and dramatically reducing its tendency to tip over. Running holding onto the sled is useful when going over rough or uneven ground since it reduces the strain on the team. Expert drivers with fast teams will run around sharp curves, reducing the strain on the wheel dogs. Unfortunately, if you stumble and fall while running, you have not helped the team at all!

Sled balance is also affected by the stiffness of the sled, the body of the driver, and by the rigidity of the hand hold. If both the sled and driver can give, or flex, when bumps are hit, the sled and driver absorb the force of the bump. If everything is stiff, then even a slight bump can unbalance a fast traveling sled. Such bumps are instantly transmitted to the team through the lines.

CENTERS OF GRAVITY

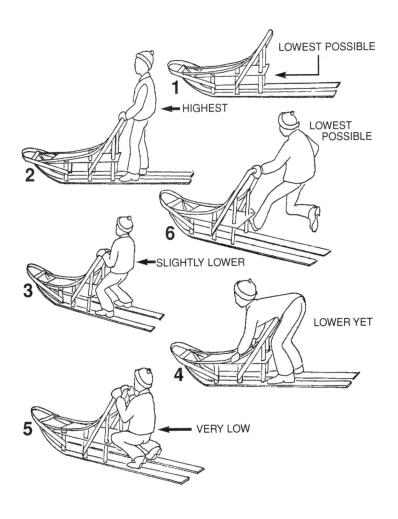

All sleds handle differently. Materials used and the way the bridle is connected can effect sled handling as well as the center of gravity.

When holding on (or is it hanging on?) keep your fingers, wrist and arm muscles flexible. Keep your knees slightly bent and flexible. Use your legs like shock absorbers. Relax on the runners. Feel your sled glide. Don't be a "white-knuckle" driver. All that will get you is tired and sore muscles.

BRAKING

There is an art of effective braking. When stopping a team using the sled brake, it should be as smooth a backward pull on the line as possible. By putting slow, continuous, downward push on the brake with the command, *Whoa,* being given near the start of the braking process. This puts the least strain possible on the team.

Raising a foot off the runner and putting it on the brake shifts the driver's center of gravity toward the side with the foot still on the runner. Moving the upper body in the other direction should counteract this. If the trail slopes to one side, keep your foot on the high side runner and let the low side foot work the brake. Being able to use either foot on the brake takes practice if you happen to be strongly right or left footed.

Braking can also be accomplished by dragging a foot. More accurately dragging a heel. Putting the heel into the snow just inside a runner does this. The ball of the foot rests on, or if your foot is small, against the side of the runner for stability. The ball of the foot should be pushed against the rear stanchion if great pressure on a firm trail is required.

Both heels can be used as brakes if necessary. But never with both heels digging in. There is usually not enough pressure to stop a briskly moving team. Heel dragging is normally used when the driver wishes only to slow the team when approaching a section of rough trail, an intersection, on down hill stretches, or when going around corners. Toe dragging is not done as the toe can catch on hard snow or other trail imperfections, which can lead to wrenched knees to broken bones. Drag your heel if you are going to drag anything.

Slight braking action can be accomplished by simply skimming the entire foot along the snow with light pressure. Have care to not let your toes catch.

Some sort of braking action is required whenever the gangline in front of you goes slack for any reason. Always watch for this and be prepared to act instantly. You may not want to lose even a second in a race, but braking until the line tightens will lose you a lot less time than letting it stay slack and getting a tangle.

Riding what is called a drag brake, brakes or slows the team. Early drag brakes were a piece of snowmobile track (with or without some form of a stud/cleats). The section of snowmobile track was connected to the stanchions of the sled and was placed on the snow between the runners, instead of applying pressure to the claw brake to slow the team down. Simply stand on the piece of track that is narrower than the space between the runners of the sled. Your weight causes extra drag. A bonus is the drag brake does not plow a furrow in the trail. Drag brakes have become much more high tech. They now have drag brakes that are spring loaded and will stay out of the way if you flip them up.

HILLS

Going down hills can be traumatic to the beginner because the sled wants to go faster than the team. Use heel dragging, as much pressure on the sled brake or stand on the drag brake with the necessary pressure to keep the gangline not just tight, but with a slight backward pull.

Why keep the gangline this tight? If the hill is steep enough the dogs running can get going too fast. A simple misstep and they are hurt. Injuries happen particularly in the shoulders. The feeling of being out of control or being drug too fast can scare an insecure or green dog. It could scare them to the point they won't ever run well downhill again.

By putting a bit of backward pull on the tuglines, it slows the dogs down, keeping them from running out of control and stabilizes your team. If they feel secure, they will all run. An insecure dog may "put on the brakes" and be pulled, scaring the dog even more because it is being drug. And it could be injured. For yourself, would you prefer to run downhill at top

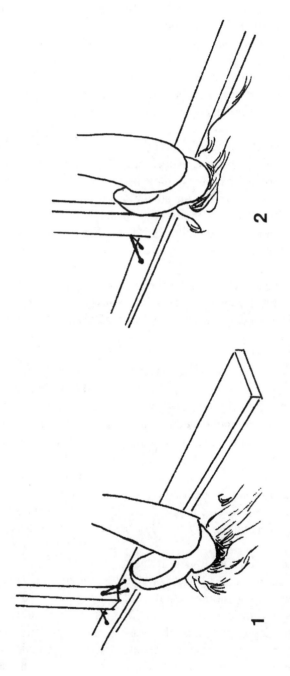

BRAKING

speed without any support, or would you prefer to run just a little slower with a supporting backward pull on a harness?

If going downhill scares you as a driver, SLOW DOWN until you feel you are once again under control. It's far better to go slower for a short distance than to get yourself upset, crashing or run the risk of capsizing.

CHAINS

There are times when the hill is too steep to safely go down. Some may unhook the tug line and have the dogs connected by neckline alone as they ride the brake. But the working teams of the Arctic with heavily loaded sleds came up with something when they faced hills that cannot be gone down safely with the sled brake alone.

The goal is to increase friction while using the weight of the sled. To increase friction, the driver stops at the top of the hill and wraps either rope or chain around his runners. The rope or chain is removed after safely reaching the bottom of the hill. Tuck this little fact in the back of your mind. You, too, may need it one day. That extra neckline you have in your ditty bag can work quite well.

STEERING THE SLED

On a straight trail the pull by the dogs on the gangline keeps the sled on the trail. It helps if you can keep the sled traveling directly behind your team. On occasion you may wish to maneuver the sled to miss an obstacle like rocks, pine cones, bare patches, etc.

Weight shifting

Shifting your weight to one runner or the other will steer the sled to a limited degree. The drag point of the sled tends to follow directly behind the team's centerline. Therefore changing the drag point from two runners to just one runner, the sled will pivot, with the drag point moving to the center line and the brush bow turning in the direction of the weight shift. The sled then tracks slightly off course. However, it will not go far off course, unless the trail slopes down in this direction.

Dragging a heel has a similar, though more pronounced

STEERING THE SLED

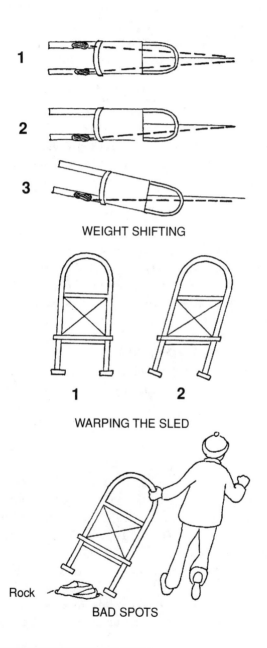

1

2

3

WEIGHT SHIFTING

1   **2**

WARPING THE SLED

Rock

BAD SPOTS

effect. It also slows the team down more than just shifting weight.

Warping the sled, or twisting it, will also turn or steer the sled. Standing with both feet on the runners, you hold the handle bar with one or both hands. The process involves physically bending the sled with the arms and legs so that each runner remains on the ground but becomes tilted. As the runner edges begin to bite into the snow, the sled starts turning in the direction of the low side of the runner.

Bad spots in the trail should be avoided. Running over a bare spot in the trail or a rock will slow down your team if you are standing on the runner as it goes over the spot. Not to mention the damage it can do to the runner itself.

With a bit of finesse you can avoid their effect on the team by: a) lifting your weight off the runner about to hit a small object or small area of poorer trail b) running behind or, as experienced drivers prefer, alongside the sled through larger areas of poor trail surface c) tilting the sled onto one runner edge while running alongside to reduce drag on the sled and wear on the runners.

CURVES AND CORNERS

The most common way to turn over a sled or capsizing is going around sharp turns too fast for the snow conditions or your driving ability. Centrifugal force comes to play as the sled slides toward the outside edge of the trail. If there is an edge to the trail, as soon as the outside runner hits the edge of the trail, it stops sliding outward. The next thing that happens is the driver goes flying because they were still moving outward. If the driver counteracts the outward movement by leaning to the inside of the curve, their weight can prevent the sled's tipping over to the outside. However, if they overdo it, an inside capsize can result.

Superior to just leaning alone is a combination of leaning and warping the sled to cause the sled runners to bite into the trail surface to carve the surface much like a snow ski. This biting reduces or can eliminate the sideways slide of the sled. Also, the warping and weight shift to the inside runner both act to turn the sled in the direction the team is going. Net result, the sled tracks

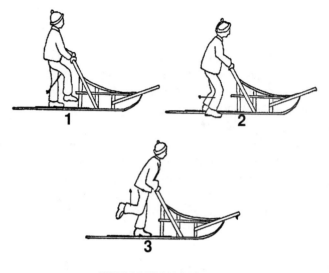

JERKY PEDALLING

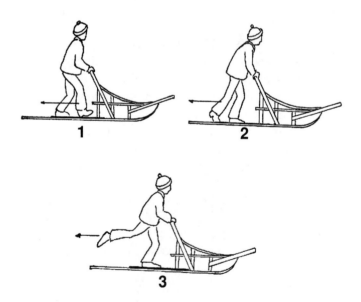

SMOOTH PEDALLING WITH FOLLOW THROUGH

right behind the team and you stay on the runners.

Now to some fine tuning

Braking and turning by dragging the inside runner heel works well on downhill curves, even if the curve is sharp, the team fast and the trail slick. By dragging a heel, crouching down or leaning over the handle bar, the center of gravity is lowered as well. A person with big feet can accomplish heel braking and turning more effectively than someone with little feet. Boots work better than running shoes.

Braking by using the sled brake on curves and corners may get you in trouble. It will reduce your stability and on a sharp curve can actually pull the sled too close into the inside corner if the brake grabs, making the sled pivot.

Braking when cornering is still recommended. The thing you need to do is to get your timing right. Like driving a car, you want to brake as you go INTO the corner. If you still want to use your sled brake at a sharp or fast corner such as on a downhill, use it *before* the corner to slow your team down. Have your feet back on the runner well before your wheel dogs reach the corner. Then lean inside and warp the sled only as much as required to have the sled follow the team and not slide to the outside. Don't overdo it.

If you still have too much trouble getting around corners, check how your bridle and gangline are fastened to the sled and the length of gangline between the sled and your wheel dogs. If there is too much play, the sled won't corner well.

Steering the sled with a passenger (human or canine), or with a heavy load, is more difficult than steering an empty sled. If your passenger is a human, ask them to lean into the turns. And unless the sled was built for a passenger, they may need to absorb some of the bumps with their arms on a sturdier part of the sled so that they won't break the basket.

PEDALING

Pedaling is very much like what you think it is. Much like you propel a scooter. You pedal or push the trail surface with one foot while keeping the other foot on a runner of your sled. Unfortunately it is not nearly as easy as it sounds. Pedaling is

POOR SLED HANDLING: BRAKING AROUND SHARP CORNER

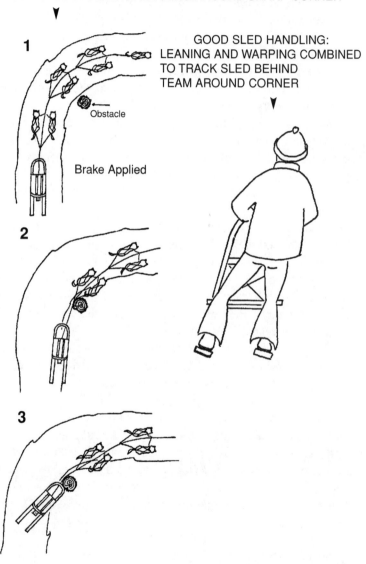

1

Obstacle

Brake Applied

GOOD SLED HANDLING:
LEANING AND WARPING COMBINED
TO TRACK SLED BEHIND
TEAM AROUND CORNER

2

3

actually quite difficult to master and do effectively. Why? Because the forward push to the sled causes the tugline to go slack. The sled then decreases speed to slower than it was going before the pedal and, as the dogs pull, the tugline jerks taut before the next pedal can be started. This jerking is hard on the team, and many times the team is better off without your pedaling "help". That is until you master the technique.

One solution is not to pedal fast with short leg strokes. The short strokes only cause more frequent jerking. Instead use a long pedal stroke with a long follow through. If you get the chance to see footage of a person that has this skill mastered, you will see the top drivers always have good follow through. As long as your foot is moving backwards, forward thrust is transferred to the sled. After your foot leaves the ground, the rate of the sled's acceleration decreases as the foot goes further back. Consequently the sled slows down gradually as the dogs slowly take up the slack in the line. By the time the sled slows down to the dogs' speed, the slack is completely taken up. Final result: no jerk.

BUMPS

A driver can assist the sled and his team through the bumps by shifting their body weight. This process basically consists of quickly pushing the knees and body weight down and forward just as the sled starts up over the bump. The driver rises back to their normal position as the sled goes down the other side of the bump. Many drivers do this without realizing it. This process of shifting weight back and forth is widely used in sailboat racing to help a boat get through the waves. In sailboat racing this is called "ooching".

Traversing bumps with no musher help results in a wide variation in sled's drag. This translates to jerking on the dogs. Pedaling may be particularly difficult to do on a bumpy or rough trail. If done effective and each pedal/push is individually placed just before each bump the pedal drives the sled forward and reduces the uphill strain or jerk on the gangline.

UPHILL

Your weight slows the team greatly on the uphill, so this is

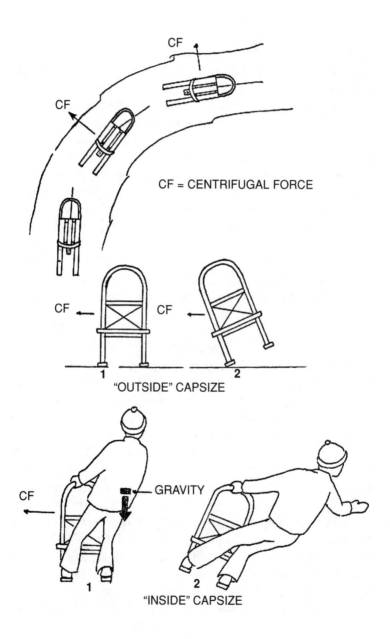

CF = CENTRIFUGAL FORCE

"OUTSIDE" CAPSIZE

GRAVITY

"INSIDE" CAPSIZE

when you should be doing most of your running and pedaling. You do not want to train your dogs to "expect" help on hills. But during races, you help on the steep parts to make the team go faster. Since your weight slows down the team, you may choose to get off the runners and run beside the sled. You may choose to push from between the runners or you may choose to stay on one runner and pedal. Whichever way you choose to help your team, pace yourself.

If the hill is long and you can't run all the way up, pick out the steeper parts for your assisting. Don't tire yourself out so much that you slip or fall. Don't get to a point you have no strength left for tangles or other emergencies.

TURNING OVER

It's going to happen. What you do is what will depend on if it's a big deal or not. If you turn over, *hang on tight to the handle bar. Don't lose your team.* Usually a small team will stop and turn around to look to see what has happened. Sometimes the dogs almost laugh!

I remember one race. The person's team took off like a shot from a cannon. The person disappeared from view because of the snow that was getting kicked up as their dogs were dragging the driver merrily along. The dogs finally stopped to see what the hold up was. No sooner was the person back up, the dogs took off again. Lesson learned, if you crash, get up as quickly as you can. Because you can't count on your dogs staying stopped for long. Get both feet on the runners as quickly as possible. Then check your surroundings.

If you are being dragged down the trail, try to right the sled and get one foot on one runner. You may only get a knee on at first, but that's a start to getting back on or righting the sled. If the sled is going fast, before it is righted, try to put a foot on the down runner. Then when you right the sled and the team goes even faster, you will already have contact with one runner. Pull yourself up and get the other foot on the other runner. Don't yell at your team to stop since yelling may only speed them up. A calm, low voiced *Whoa* might help.

Sometimes, if snow conditions are right, an overturned sled and a dragging driver will stop a small team better than a brake.

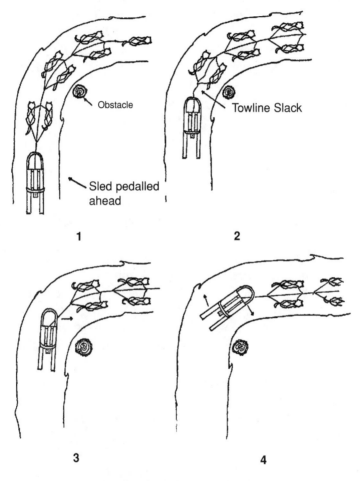

Obstacle

Towline Slack

Sled pedalled ahead

1

2

3

4

PEDALLING AROUND SHARP CORNER

If a driver is desperate to stop and the brake is ineffective, they may turn the sled over on purpose and sink the snow hook while they are still down. Many times all you need to do is get your sled to the side of the trail and tip it on its side.

Native Alaskans have a saying: "Lose your team, lose your life," since losing a team many miles from camp at far below freezing temperatures can be fatal. Your biggest problem is not freezing to death, but that letting your team run loose down the trail can cause the dogs serious injury. Your wheel dogs and others can easily overrun dogs in front of them since you aren't there to make sure the line stays tight. Tangles almost always occur, and sometimes dogs fall and are dragged for long distances. So the cardinal rule is: "Don't lose your team! Hang on for their sake!"

Of course there may be times when you are being dragged and can see that you are going to be slammed into a tree or rock. If you are going to be forcibly parted from the sled anyhow, let go and save yourself injury. When able, get up and run after the team.

PRACTICING RIDING THE SLED

You can actually practice riding the sled without a team. In a flat smooth trail, try pedaling. Feel how a smooth follow through helps and feels. Try to go straight. Work on your pedal and follow through until you can keep the sled gliding in a straight line. Ride down hills, particularly hills with curves.

If you want, preview a trail by getting a tow from a snowmobile. Use a long stout piece of rope and watch out for sudden stops by the machine.

As a beginning musher, you should also practice all aspects of riding the sled behind your team when you are having a good training run. Don't wait until you *must* use a maneuver: Try everything that has been mentioned so far until you feel at ease on the sled and gain confidence in your ability to control your team and the sled at the same time. Once you find it easier to relax, both you and the dogs will have more enjoyable runs.

EXPERIENCED DRIVER TIPS

While small-team drivers can help their teams by running at

the start, or after a trail stop, an experienced large-team driver rides the brake at the start. The leader may not have heard the command to go or may not be a fast starter. A tangle can happen very quickly. The race can be lost before the team has even gotten underway.

An actual case in point is the one of a not-too-experienced driver who came to the starting line of a major race with a long string of dogs. He didn't ride the brake out of the chute and a tangle soon developed. Before he could get up to the tangled dogs, he had a breeding – right in the middle of downtown Anchorage!

So large teams start with the brake partially on, giving the whole team a chance to get strung out and going smoothly.

Crouching down reduces the effect of a head wind, but experienced drivers don't do it since then they can't see what their front-end dogs are doing. Instead, they lean over their handle bar and hold onto the side rail by the basket.

To get around a very sharp corner, pedal just once as the wheel dogs make the turn. This shoots the sled straight ahead so that it doesn't cut the corner and hit a tree or bank. The sled will be spun abruptly around, so good sled control is necessary.

Some drivers go around sharp corners like this: Move the outside runner foot backwards to the rear of the runner and push down hard. Warp the sled to put the runners in bite position. The drag by the rear corner of the outside runner helps swing the front of the sled around.

Some drivers have been known to "jump-turn" their sleds like skiers. Jumping with the sled can also be used on a straight trail to get the runners in a different rut; or if the trail has a side slope and the sled has worked its way down, it can be jumped back up behind the team.

Practice will make you smooth in your movements. Smooth actions can add speed and fun to your runs.

The dogs we love and share our lives with all have feelings and emotions. And like people, they have their likes and dislikes. Dogs are basically honest. They don't know how to lie or deceive, unless you have inadvertently trained them not to show a behavior. Every movement they make is a form of communication, showing what they are thinking or how they feel at the time. While the position and parts of their body are viewed separately, every motion, twitch, duck, or grin means something.

The stance of their body, or the posture as a whole, must also be taken into consideration when interpreting what the dog is expressing. It is up to you to study your own dog(s) and learn to interpret what they are telling you with their body language.

As mentioned above, dogs are very honest creatures. If they don't like you, you know it, they do not lie. Dogs are not capable of feeling guilt in the human sense of the word. Frequently what we see is a dog being respectful or submissive based on either OUR body language or anxiety level. As we try to read them, they are reading us. And they have additional hints to read us, such as their fine sense of smell. They are masters at reading us.

For example, the dog that greets you with head/tail/ears down after chewing up the sofa is not feeling guilty (they didn't know it was bad to eat the sofa), but they are responding to either a physical (glare, stiffening, etc.) or some other cue from us (gasp, raised blood pressure, pheromones, etc.).

The following brief and far from complete snippets are intended to give you some idea what your dog might be feeling or thinking. The same reaction or a behavior can mean something completely different if they are at home or on the trail. You will need to closely observe your dog and learn which behavior at which time means different emotions. For example, a behavior such as teeth bearing could be is a warning or a grin.

EYES

Eyes are the first lines of communication. If you look into them carefully you can learn which expression means that the dog is happy, relaxed, excited, uncertain, determined, enraged, frightened, fearful, distracted, etc. Eyes that lack luster can mean that the dog is bored or not feeling well. Some dogs will look you straight in the eyes, defiantly.

When you have a new dog, you should not challenge the dog by staring them down. You need to make them feel comfortable. Work to gain their trust and admiration. Your goal is to see their adoration through their eyes.

HEAD

At home, a head held high can show attention, curiosity, or dominance. A head held low may show confusion or submission.

On the trail, a dog with their head up is not pulling and perhaps distracted. A head held low means the dog is focused on their work and pulling.

EARS

At home, ears held high show alertness. One ear twitching to the side can indicate some distraction, or sound which may cause the dog to turn their head in that direction. Ears held high and wide can indicate uncertainty, or curiosity. Ears laid back and low while the dog is being petted indicates contentment. Ears flattened on greeting can be respectful.

On the trail, ears held low and back while training indicates attentiveness to the driver. Ears that suddenly stand erect means something ahead of you has caught the dogs' attention.

One ear hanging to the side, particularly if the dog is also shaking their head, probably means that something is in the dog's ear. A tipped head can also mean an ear problem. Look to see if you can see something. If there is no change, it may be a good time to schedule a visit to your Veterinarian.

MOUTH

Both on the trail and at home some dogs' lips curl into a grin or smile. They smile when they are happy, playful, or when they are embarrassed. Some will give you a sheepish grin, while other happy dogs actually smile. However, curling of the dog's lips when cornered or when pushed too far, can mean trouble.

VOICE

At home, barking can mean boredom, play, feeding time or aggression. Whining can mean insecurity or being submissive. Whining can mean anticipation and excitement as well. Some growls mean play; other growls mean trouble. Listen to your dog and learn what they are saying with each of their noises.

In the starting chute, barking means impatience. On the trail, your dog should not be using their voice when pulling. When stopped they may tell you they think its time to continue.

TAIL

At home a briskly wagging tail indicates happiness, but that can also mean that you are being challenged. Be careful, it may be followed with a bite. Some dogs enjoy biting people. They will wag their tail the entire time they are biting. A slow moving tail may mean they feel unsure about something they have done, or think they may have done. Slow moving, low tail can indicate uncertainty or concentration.

On the trail: they should have what is normally a happy tail. A dog that usually carries their tail straight back and then suddenly raises it, means that they are not applying themselves. It can also mean they are about to relieve themselves. The tail carriage can also let you know your dog is tiring.

Depending on the breed, the carriage of their tail can be quite different. Learn the position in which your dog carries their tail naturally. Then be alert to changes in that position. Usually a tail carried low indicates placidness or rest. A tail carried high indicates attention and excitement. A tail slightly between the legs means uncertainty. A tail all the way between the legs or tucked up against the belly means extreme fright and confusion.

Any time a tail is erect and rigid, with slight movements; this means trouble, and possibly a fight, because high, stiff, quick wag can be extreme arousal.

HACKLES

Hackles are the hairs over the withers, top-line and croup. At home or on the trail, raised hackles indicate insecurity and that trouble is brewing.

BODY

At home, a dog that crawls or slumps low to the ground is lacking confidence. They may feel overwhelmed or simply do not understand a situation. A dog that rolls over on their back may be showing confusion, submission, or just wants a belly rub. On the trail the body is relaxed when resting, and indicates excitement when they are ready to go.

PEEING/URINATION

At home a dog may pee a small amount of urine as you approach. This is submissive urination. It indicates insecurity. This same dog may pee when other dogs approach, indicating its insecurity and desire not to challenge the other. Many puppies will urinate submissively to show the adult they are not challenging their position. In addition to submissive urination there is also excitement urination.

On the trail, hopefully your dog will have peed before you take off down the trail. Males and many dominant females will use their urine to mark. Sometimes marking is to set a boundary, other times it is to announce "I WAS HERE!" If you have an intact bitch that squats and urinates a small amount, and does this often, you might want to check your calendar. You may have a bitch coming in heat. If this happened outside of the heat cycle, watch her water intake and urination habits, this could indicate a Urinary Tract Infection (UTI). It is best to catch UTIs in their early stages.

COMBINATIONS

Combinations of the above should be looked at as well. For example: a head held low with fixed gaze could be stalking behavior.

An up and forward (tall, head up, ears erect, tail up) stance can indicate dominance or confidence. Body, head, ears, tail low and leaning back and away (not relaxed) indicate fear and an aggressive response may be forthcoming if this dog is pushed or cornered.

In Closing

It is essential you remember every dog is different. Behavior that may indicate a happy dog on one dog could be the opposite in another. Learn to read your dogs, and try to understand what makes them happy. It is important to remember that your dogs will react on INSTINCT. Instincts such as prey drive can override the best training in any given situation. For example, the obedience trained dog that chases a squirrel in front of a car is not making a conscious or emotional decision to disobey, they are reacting on instinct.

213   MUSH!

DOG FIGHTS

Dog fights happen. How you chose to deal with dogfights is a personal choice, but dogfights should not be tolerated, EVER. Having an aggressive dog on your team can be cause for you to be disqualified from a race.

How you deal with a fight can depend on what caused the fight in the first place. Sometimes the fight is a misunderstanding, a dominance issue, or simply two dogs that hate each other. Sometimes with two dogs that just won't get along, it can be best to place one of them in another home. Just because one dog is aggressive with another, does not always mean the dog will be aggressive in a different living environment.

With work a dog aggressive dog can be trained out of challenging other dogs (making eye contact), biting and/or fighting.

On your team you do not want a dog that loves fighting above running. There have been many a sled dog that was a scrapper and could hold their own in a fight. But they also did not fight when in harness.

There are people with large kennels that own items for emergency use at home, such as cattle prods, stun guns and electronic training collars. These things can be used when trying to break up a fight when air horns, spray hoses, banging pots and pans are ineffective. Chairs, doors, gates, garbage cans have all been used as tools to get between two dogs. Most people in their lifetime will never have to go to extreme measures breaking up a dogfight. But used correctly, the above items can be used to save lives. And these items are best left at home.

If you have a ZERO tolerance policy when it comes to fights in your yard, chances are the dogs will know with a stern "NO!" that you mean business and you will discover that many fights stop as quickly as they start. Still whenever you have two or more dogs, there will be the chance of a fight.

Putting some physical distance between you and the fighting

dogs when you are breaking up a fight will cut down on the chance of you accidentally getting bitten. The cardinal rule is to NEVER reach your hands into a fight towards the biting end of a dog. This is a sure way to get bitten. Even an accidental dog bite can mean broken bones, infection and permanent damage.

The following was written for and was published in an earlier edition of *MUSH!*. What worked then still works today:

The writer of the following section, Thom Ainsworth, was for many years a licensed instructor at Guide Dogs for the Blind, Inc. in San Rafael, California. Prior to this, he was an Air Police Sentry Dog Handler in the United States Air Force. Almost daily he works with up to 38 dogs at a time loose in an exercise yard. He is also a sled dog driver.

What do you do to prevent your dogs from fighting? First learn what situations are apt to provoke a fight and take precautions to prevent those situations from occurring. Get to know each of your dogs' personalities and how each dog reacts to other dogs. Recognize when a fight is coming and stop it before it starts. An ounce of prevention is worth a pound of cure.

If the worst comes, you must break up the fight whether it is between just two dogs or your whole team. This chapter will tell you how.

SITUATIONS THAT ARE APT TO PROVOKE A FIGHT
Bitch in Season

The odor of the bitch in season arouses the mature males and causes excitement and jealousy. Males in large kennels who are continually exposed to the odor do not seem to be as affected as males in a small kennel who smell it only once in awhile. Keep males separate from each other.

Bitches in season often do not like to be pestered by either males or other bitches. If the bitch in season snaps at a male, this is considered acceptable behavior and will not cause a fight because he won't snap back. But if one bitch snaps at another bitch, a glorious fight may follow.

Play

Play is fine; but when it gets too rough, a fight may develop.

Any object such as a toy, ball or piece of wood may start out being something to play with and end up being something to fight over. Never throw a ball into a group of dogs.

Weaker Dogs

Dogs have a tendency to gang up on a weaker dog. If he tries to get away from them, they give chase. When the weaker dog becomes cornered, he may snap and start a fight.

Hurt Dog

Whenever a dog yelps from pain, or even fright, the other dogs are apt to jump him.

Older Dogs

As dogs get along in years, they become weaker. Old, dominant males are often challenged by young, aggressive males. If a fight starts, all the young males may gang up on the old leader.

New Dogs

New dogs are greeted with curiosity and suspicion. Introduce the new dog to your team slowly and carefully.

Pecking Order

Dogs housed loose together work out among themselves who is superior to whom. Sometimes, but not always, a fight is part of the process.

Excitement and Tension

Tension and excitement will build up when a strange dog appears either near the dog yard or on the trail, when any dog is loose and the others are tied, when teams gather at a training or race area, when a wild animal or cat is sighted, and many other times. When not calmed down, your own dogs may jump each other.

Territory

Any dog that invades another's territory, whether on purpose or by mistake, may be attacked.

ADDITIONAL PRECAUTIONS

On the Trail

If two dogs on your team have had a recent fight, separate them as far as possible in the hook-up. At the first sign of interest in each other, call their names and tell them *No!* Dog fights between teams are rare even when teams are tangled together during a pass.

Group Running

An exercise yard 50' x 150' is large enough for ample exercise and yet small enough to maintain good control. Don't exercise too many loose dogs by yourself. Take care when letting the dogs out, as the most critical time is the first few minutes when the dogs are highly excited.

Housing

House together or next to each other only dogs that are compatible.

Feeding

Keep all dogs chained or otherwise separated.

PERSONALITY

Dogs, like people, are individuals, each with their own personality. But this personality can change with age and with each situation. If a fight starts, be warned that a normally shy and docile dog can turn instantly into an aggressive maniac.

While dogs are apt to fight dogs and bitches to fight bitches, the two sexes will fight each other in a general free-for-all. Likewise, members of the same family are less likely to fight each other than they are to fight non-members, but don't count on it.

Knowing your dogs will enable you to anticipate and stop possible fights. As you work with your dogs, think about what they are doing and why they are doing it. Always be alert.

THE CHALLENGE

Sometimes male dogs will go through a preliminary routine indicating that a fight is about to take place. The two dogs will approach each other with rigid bodies and short, stiff steps.

Stares are exchanged. Tails are held erect and almost motionless. Getting closer, the hackles begin to rise first about the shoulder and then along the top line. When the dogs are almost close enough to touch, they may circle slightly or stand cheek to cheek waiting for the first move. Though all these actions may take place in only a few seconds, they give you time to recognize the challenge and stop the fight before it gets started.

When bitches fight, their challenge sequence seems to be just a curled lip and a growl.

BREAKING UP A FIGHT
There are several ways to break up a fight, but in all of them it is important that you maintain complete control of yourself.

Yelling
Yell and scream as you run toward the skirmish. This extraordinary noise from you will often startle the dogs enough so that they forget the whole thing.

Water
If you happen to have a water hose that is long enough to reach the dogs or a full bucket of water close at hand, a dousing will often be sufficient to stop the fight.

Throw Chain
A throw chain is about eight links of medium weight chain or a slip collar. The chain amounts to an extension of your arm and is often called an "equalizer". When you see a challenge, roughhousing, or other form of misbehavior, throw the chain at or near the problem. As the chain hits, give a loud *No!* Dogs conditioned to a throw chain will soon respond to the jingle of the chain in your hand accompanied by your scolding tone of voice.

Sticks
Broom sticks, 3/4-inch plastic pipe, or any similar type implement slapped against a flat surface will often make a loud enough pop to stop a fight before it begins or to get the dogs' attention if the fight has not progressed too far. A stick can be used to strike fighting dogs across their muzzles with a short,

sharp rap. Dogs respect a stick, and any stick just held in the hand of the owner is a great deterrent.

Hands

If you have no implement except your hands, be careful where you grab, as even your own dogs will bite you. Go after the dog that is the aggressor or has the advantage. Yank his tail sharply and lift his hindquarters into the air as you pull him away from the fight. Scold and shake him. When all is quiet, lower him to his feet and separate him from the other dogs involved.

Grabbing and pulling the sensitive, loose flesh in the flank area can make one dog let loose of another.

Choking

Should one dog lock on another with such a hold that you can't pry its jaws open, then it becomes necessary to choke the dog. Squeeze his windpipe by hand or by twisting his collar from behind his head. Be careful that you don't use so much force that you collapse his windpipe. You will know that enough force has been applied when you hear his labored breathing. As soon as the dog releases his hold, lift his front feet off the ground so that he can't get back into the fight.

Bunting

You can use your feet either to break up a fight or to bunt other dogs away from one you have lifted up. Use your instep, not your toe.

GROUP FIGHTING

In a group fight, most of the dogs will go for the one on the bottom, although smaller fights may break out among dogs on the fringes. Usually one dog is the major aggressor while the others just want to get in on the action. Go for the worst aggressor first and get him separated or chained. Then go back to the fight and separate one aggressor after another until no dogs are left fighting.

FIGHTS ON THE TRAIL

If two dogs in a single team start fighting, pulling on one dog's harness may free them. If it doesn't, apply the methods described above. Keep yelling *No!* to the other dogs to keep them out of the fight. If two teams are fighting, both drivers must work together to break it up.

TEACHING A DOG NOT TO FIGHT

Some dogs are natural fighters. Try to socialize this type on a leash with a properly placed slip collar. Put the dog in a situation where he can show aggression but cannot reach another dog. When he goes for the other dog, jerk the leash sharply and give a harsh verbal correction.

If the dog seems insensitive to the leash correction, slide the collar high up on the neck and just behind the ears to give the collar more bite. This type of dog may have to be jerked off his front feet and given a good shake while up in the air. Scold him at the same time. Then slowly let him down and walk him around the other dog. If he starts in again, repeat the correction. If this still doesn't work, try giving him a solid and sudden upward slap on the lower jaw while he is being jerked off his feet. Be sure to praise him for any good behavior.

If your dog cannot be broken of fighting, remove him from your team. It is not fair to your own team or to others to have a fighter in the holding area or on the trail. You can be disqualified if you have trouble. Even worse, you may have a lawsuit on your hands.

"SCOTTY" ALLAN'S DOG FIGHT

This fight is reported in Allan's book (op..cit. pp. 264-267).

In late 1915, "Scotty" Allan arrived in France from Nome with 440 Eskimo dogs which had been purchased by the French government to help in the war effort, and thereby set the stage for what has to be the biggest dog fight in history.

After training sessions with the 50 new French drivers (Chasseurs), Allan was in the habit of letting half the dogs loose at a time in an enclosure. He always stood in the middle of the enclosure watching for, and ready to nip in the bud, any sign of trouble. Here is his version of what happened: "One afternoon just before entraining for the front, I drove into town to purchase some extra snaps, chains and rope. I didn't get back as soon as expected. With good intentions, and never expecting any trouble, the boys turned the dogs out as usual. I was on my way back. When I got about a block from the abattoir I heard a terrible noise. I knew what that meant; a good, old-fashioned dog fight!...I told my driver to step on it. He did, after he understood what I wanted. Long before the car stopped I had hit the ground a-running.

I'll never forget the sight I saw on getting through the gate. There were about five or six piles of snarling, fighting malamutes having the time of their life; that is the ones on top were. Those on the bottom of the piles were getting smothered.

"The piles were higher than a man's head; in fact, so high that a dog would have to take a running jump to get on top of it! Once on top he would fasten his teeth in the one he landed on and start shaking and hauling him for all he was worth. When a dog broke loose from the one he was worrying about, he would roll to the ground, only to jump back on top of the pile or some other pile ... it was a typical, Irish scrap such as I had seen at Stops Fair when I was a youngster. And such earsplitting howls and snarls from every animal that had breath enough to yelp, I have never heard."

"No dog had it in for any one dog in particular. It was a case of whoever was nearest. And every dog was having a grand time! If they could have talked afterwards I am sure they would have said it was the greatest scrap of the whole war. I have seen hundreds of dogfights, and some big ones, but never one that was deuce high to this!"

"The 50 Chasseurs were showing more action, if possible, than the dogs. . .Their hands, feet, and tongues were all working hard, as each man was whaling away with a big whip at the various piles of dogs, every blow an urge to more bitter battling. In fact, I suspect that the dogs thought they were taking part in the fight, rather than trying to stop it."

"The Chasseurs had completely lost control. The dogs knew it and were acting accordingly. They were amuck; indeed, if it hadn't been that they were so intent on fighting among themselves they might have tackled the men. That sometimes hap-

---

pens with inexperienced drivers."

"I took in the situation at a glance. At once I made a decision. If it worked it would be a good lesson to the boys in the discipline and control of dogs. So far I had had a hard time getting them to understand the necessity for handling dogs in a humane way."

"If I could only make myself heard above the tumult I thought I could quell the riot. I couldn't talk French but there were a few of the boys who could understand some English. I ran to them and begged them to get the rest of the Chasseurs and go inside the building."

"'When dog comes in, tie him up!' I shouted. I tried so hard to make them understand that I began talking pidgin English."

"Moving the Frenchmen turned out to be harder than stopping the dogs. I thought we'd never get the excited soldiers to quit pounding them. Finally I had to run in and drag some away by main strength."

"At last when the Frenchmen were all inside the door of the building I stepped to the center of the enclosure and during the first lull gave the familiar 'Yeah Yon!' and popped my long black, snake whip. The dogs heard and instantly recognized my voice. Those on the edges scurried away."

"On the first crack the main scrimmage broke. Joy, I had them! Quickly I followed up my advantage. For action during the next few minutes I had even the Frenchmen faded! Only, I wasn't laying my whip along the full length of the dog's back. I'd pop it to them at long range when they flew for their kennels. But every time the buckskin went out it brought a yelp of pain that threw fear and dismay into the other villains with an effect that was amazing."

"The piles of struggling dogs melted like snow on a hot stove. In a few minutes it was all over. Between 20 and 30 dogs were left lying on the field; but they all gradually came to life except four, which I thought were dead. However, some of the Chasseurs kept working on these and brought them back to life."

"I felt we'd got out of the jam very luckily. Quite a few of the dogs had skin cuts or gashes, but nothing to incapacitate them from work. The ones I thought were dead didn't have a scratch on them! They had been smothered in the bottom of the piles."

223   MUSH!

People that compete in obedience trials are another group of people that appreciate the bond between dog and human. The formal one-on-one obedience activities are no longer limited to the standard classes offered at obedience trials. The sport is progressing. There are now activities called rally and agility, herding and tracking, to name a few. Sports where communication and team work between human and canine are also key.

Still many obedience trainers become attracted to the sport of running sled dogs. It is an activity that requires an advanced level of communication, because to do it successfully is a challenge to their training ability. Sledding is vigorous outdoor exercise, and if they happen to have one of the northern breeds, it's a bonus to see if their dog can do what it was bred to do. However once bitten by the obedience bug, you usually don't want to give up an obedience role with a competitive dog.

If you are one of these people and your dog has been working toward an obedience degree that you wish to continue to the next level, there is no reason to abandon your hard work. Almost any dog that you feel had potential to be a top notch obedience dog will have the intelligence to distinguish between a show lead, an obedience collar, and the different types of harnesses.

A racing harness is quite different from a tracking harness, a carting harness or a weight pull harness. Many utility dogs take only once or twice in the tracking harness to become eager pullers after the trail. Running in a team has even a greater motivation to keep up with the other dog. Your obedience trained dog will quickly learn to lean into their harness with the best of them. The differences between sled dog training and advanced obedience work are so great that you can practice for one in the morning and the other in the afternoon without confusing the trained obedience dog. Even with the activities and training being quite different, you might not want to start both at the same time.

SOME DIFFERENCES BETWEEN OBEDIENCE AND SLED DOG TRAINING

The most obvious difference between basic obedience and basic sled dog training is the expectation of pulling. An obedience dog is corrected if they pull at all. A sled dog is corrected if they don't pull. The obedience dog is corrected with a pop to the collar to remind the dog to stay with the trainer, while a sled dog is coaxed to move away from the trainer. This coaxing is typically verbal in nature.

When working/training an obedience dog, it is standard practice to go over the same exercise over and over. You are teaching with repetition the behavior you are looking for. Make corrections to get that sit perfectly square, to not lag in the figure eights or work on a steady recall. Work on having the dog watch your face and gaze into your eyes eagerly anticipating the next move, waiting for the next signal. You may also train all year for obedience trials, which are held year round. Trials are held both inside and out.

Working with a sled dog is one trip around the training trail. The only dogs that may get additional repetition of the same exercise on the same day might be for special lead dog training. The trainer/driver must get their message across during only one trip around the course. Teams in training go out at most few times a week for only part of the year. Depending on the part of the world you are in, the actual racing season can be quite short. And in some parts of the country your season will depend on weather conditions if you even have a local racing season.

Obedience people train with food and lots of praise. They give verbal cues as well as physical cues. From a stand they will tell their dog to *heel* and *step out*. Or they will tell their dog to *stay* and *step out* with the other foot. The dog will listen to the command and see the foot the person starts out on. When they make that perfect square sit during the recall, there could even be a piece of food if they look into your face. Food is not used during competition; it is just one of the rewards given when a behavior or exercise is performed correctly in training.

---

225   MUSH!

Verbal communication is less frequent in sled dog training than in obedience. Talking is done only to give a command or a quick word of praise or encouragement to a specific dog or the team. Because of the distance on the trail (miles) versus a dozen feet in the obedience ring, there will be long periods of silence. When talking to your dogs on the trail, your voice is much quieter than in obedience practice or at a trial. There is no reason to yell. There is very little if any noise or confusion compared to a training class or at an obedience trial. There is a lot of noise all around you with other dogs in adjacent rings or the PA system making announcements.

With distance, there is silence on the trail. You can hear the dogs breathing; you can hear their foot falls. Your dogs can hear the slightest noise; there is no confusion, just a wonderful sense of tranquility. Even racing, once you and the team are a distance from the starting chute the dogs settle down and just enjoy the run.

When you are working with your team, close attention is paid to the attitude of each individual dog. They are coaxed to doing what you wish. Their teammates may reassure them they have it right because they are doing the same thing with much joy. When you first start working with an obedience prospect, the dog does the exercise because you tell them to, and then, if necessary, you reinforce the command with a correction. This command may be verbal, physical or a combination of the two. Your dog is within reach for most obedience exercises. So you may simply bend slightly, push a foot into place or give a stern look with a repeat of the command.

Sled dogs run for the sheer joy of running. The driver can't make the dog run; they can only attempt to control speed and direction. "You can't push a rope" is true when running dogs. Running a team is controlled chaos. If they refuse to run, you aren't going anywhere.

Obedience trainers could find it a challenge to train sled dogs because they are not close to their dog. This intricacy is magnified in sled dog racing because there is at least eight feet separating the driver from the nearest dog. Additionally when running, the dogs are looking away from and never towards you. From the first time the team is hooked up, control is at a distance and by voice only. Therefore, most obedience-trainers-turned-sled-dog-drivers find it more difficult to train an accurate, dependable sled dog than an accurate, dependable obedience dog.

As a general observation sled dogs have a bit more of an independent nature. You may tell your lead dog to go out onto thin ice. A good leader will refuse, where an obedience dog may lead the team out onto the thin ice. This is not to say that all highly trained obedience dogs that are command leaders would follow the command. It's just more likely that they would. For those people that do both sports, frequently the dog most do both racing and obedience with is their lead dog And this can be for many reasons. Frequently it is because their lead dog is more receptive to listening for direction and there is a mutual respect between the trainer/driver and their leader.

Chapter Thirty

SHOW DOGS
AND SLED DOGS

A show dog can be a sled dog but not all sled dogs can be show dogs. BUT just because it is a show dog that does not mean it will make a good sled dog. Show dogs must be registered with a registry before they can enter shows. At dog shows they are measured against a written standard for their breed. Most of this written standard is a visual standard, with some mention as to breed behavior. Their pedigrees are well documented. Sled dogs to be racing dogs do not have to be registered with any organization. Yet, most racing dogs have well known pedigrees, just not documented with an official organization.

Siberian Husky team at Shaver Lake race. *Photo by John Harshman.*

When you enter a dog show, the dog is entered. When you enter a sled dog race, the driver is entered. And unless you are entering a purebred or registered breed class, there is no information on your dogs that is requested.

Some races have classes for registered dogs. In SNDD our class is a sub class. All of the same number (three-dog class, four-dog class etc) run the same trail at the same time. But we have an additional offering if your team is 100% the same breed and 100% of the dogs are registered with a registry such as the American Kennel Club (AKC) or the Canadian Kennel Club (CKC). We do not allow dogs with special registration, like an ILP number, to compete as a purebred. The term purebred is a simpler way to say a dog registered with a registry as being of a specific breed and only of that one specific breed. Purebred is one of those grey terms that is not quite accurate, but accepted.

Dogs need not qualify to run in most races. Generally the

only requirement for a sled dog is they have a desire to run, the ability to do so and that they be healthy enough to run. Any combination of breeds can be run on a single team as long as they make the numerical maximum and/or minimum for the class.

There are a few races that are only for specific breeds. But most allow any breed to run. Your teams of ten dogs can be ten different breeds if you so desire. Unless there are special circumstances, any breed is welcome.

Steve LaBelle with a pair of AKC/International Champion Alaskan Malamutes at a race in Chemult, Oregon. *Photo by Paul Martin.*

Classes in racing are not based on breed but rather on the maximum number of dogs on a team. Races can have a three-dog, four-dog, six-dog, eight-dog, ten-dog maximum, and/or an unlimited class, which has set maximum or no maximum number of dogs. Distances vary with the class. The three-dog class minimum distance each day is three miles; four-dog class, four miles; six-dog class, six miles; eight-dog class, eight miles; and the ten-dog class, ten miles. The unlimited class minimums are different depending on the time in the season. Early in the season the mileage minimum is less than the minimum mileage mid-season. This minimum remains until the end of the season. The mid-distance classes and distance classes have different minimum daily mileage as well.

Generally speaking, a show dog can be entered in multiple classes at a dog show. And a racing dog can only be entered in one class per race/event. This is one of the reasons dogs are marked if the event takes multiple days. If there is a short "children's" class (sometimes called a pee wee race), dogs can run in it as well as their normal racing class. This way some musher's children get the chance to have fun too. Other than the child's class, one dog can not run in multiple races at the same event.

If a race is a multi-day event, one heat will be run each day. Only dogs and drivers that have run the first day may run the second day. And if the race is three days, they must have run day #1, and day #2 to run in the heat on day #3.

Entry fees for sled dog races range from $15.00 to over $1,000.00. The entry fee will depend on the class. Many times the larger the entry fee the larger the prize money involved. At dog shows, you pay an entry fee for each dog and class you enter (typically $25 per class per day). There rarely is purse money at dog shows. And prize money is usually only for special classes, like puppy sweeps, and you get a percent of the fees collected. For all intents and purposes, there is no purse money at dog shows.

Because the qualifications for a show dog and a sled dog are very different, a champion in the show ring may not make a good sled dog. On the flip side, a top sled dog of the season might not do well in the show ring; if they qualified to be shown (need to be registered as a specific breed, from registered parents of the same breed). There are some dogs that do compete in both shows and races and do well at both.

The Race Marshal/Chief Judge may give your dogs a look over. But they are only looking to make sure they are fit to run. How they place is up to you and how well they run for you.

In the show ring, winning is based on the opinion of a judge and their interpretation of the breed standard. The real judge in racing is the clock. The fastest time wins. Literally the winning team is determined by combining all the times of the heats. The team having the smallest total wins.

Glen Laughton with some of his Siberian Husky show dogs. *Photo by John Harshman from a race at Shaver Lake.*

231   MUSH!

Chapter
Thirty-One
JUNIOR MUSHER

So what is a Junior Musher? Junior mushers come in all ages, sizes and levels of competence. When people use the term junior, it's an issue of age and not their level of training. I have enjoyed watching a pee wee that can barely see over the handle bar, standing proudly on the runners while going for a 100 yard dash or even a one mile run (with checkers within eye sight of each other). It's pretty cool seeing a five-year-old driving dogs that are older than they are.

I have had the pleasure of watching children start young and by the time they are 17 (or younger) give their parents a run for the money. I have even offered to give one young man a ride home when his father jokingly told him if he beat Dad's "A team" with the son's six-dog "B team", he would need to find a ride home. Or the young lady that talked her grandma into buying her a sled and now has her Dad driving her to the races. These are junior mushers.

Some mushers' families are multi-generations. Some of these children were in the basket of the sled before they could walk or in a pack on Mommy or Daddy's back for a training run or dog yard chores. Other children read a book in school and have worked hard to get a couple dogs together and run.

For this section of *MUSH!* let's call our junior musher a ten-year-old beginner. You will need to adjust the instructions to fit the capabilities of your own child.

The first thing to determine is the degree of involvement your child really wants. Some children are willing to do pretty much anything if they think it will help in their quest to run dogs. But if it is you who talks the child into a commitment, the results may not quite turn out as you hoped. Be prepared for considerable commitment of your own, including time and money.

If you already have dogs, then those are the dogs you will be working with. But if your dogs are not interested, too old, or just plain wrong for sledding you may end up buying a dog or more. If the dog you try to use turns out to be too active, snappy, lazy, or just too strong for your child, you might consider finding another dog to start with. If you are buying your first dog for the child it is advisable to procure an older, reliable lead dog. An older dog can usually be found at a reasonable cost, particularly if it is going to a good home. Many times the price tag is simply a wonderful home.

There are many advantages to an older trained dog. Older mellower dogs tend to keep out of trouble and most will be patient while your child is learning. In time, this same older dog can be used to train a younger dog. And this older dog will probably do a much better job of

Pair of "Pee Wee" Mushers at the 2006 Lake Davis Race. *Photo by Bruce T. Smith.*

training the younger dog than you or your child can. Most important of all, this older dog can be depended upon to bring your child home safely.

Having gotten the new dog, or having carefully selected one of your own for your child to learn with, give your child as many responsibilities for caring for their dog as they are capable of assuming. Do not let the dog suffer because of the child's lack of maturity and the adult's lack of supervision. If you have multiple dogs, let your child share in the care and feeding of all of them. Practice makes perfect and good habits. The more animal handling experience the child has, the better their relationship with the dogs becomes and their understanding of their own dog will develop.

If at all possible, let your junior musher observe a team in action. This can be accomplished by having them riding on a snowmobile, in the basket of the sled, on the runners beside you or on a sled of their own if you are double sledding. It is quite helpful if an adult or another more experienced junior can explain to your child everything that is happening and answer the questions they may have.

Before their first run by themselves, they should know how to use all their equipment. This includes putting a harness on a dog and setting a snow hook so it will hold their team AND being able to pull the hook to release the team after clearing a tangle. They should know which dogs are the ones they can run and how to get them on and off the dog truck.

They should be able to select the right harnesses for their dogs and hook up the ganglines to the sled. Then they must put each dog in the right place in their team. Should they have a tangle, they should be able to move the dogs to clear the tangle. Don't play nursemaid, because when your child is on the trail, they will be on their own. On the other hand, give them enough instruction and encouragement so that they remain enthusiastic and do not become discouraged.

Start with a properly outfitted child. A cold child is not a happy child. If you will be working in the cold, get a parka, hat and gloves that fit. Also, get a pair of warm boots that are snug but not tight. Don't overdress your child. Dress them in layers if that is what is needed.

No matter how and where you train, many parents have their children wear a helmet and eye protection. Ski racers and snow-boarders now have lightweight, warm helmets at prices that will not break the bank. These same helmets will protect your child's head should they come in sudden contact with a hard object. If training on dirt and it's not cold, the bicycle helmet your child already has will work just fine. This same bicycle helmet can be worn in the cold, but be sure that your child's head is also pro-tected from the cold. It should not be able to slip. The helmet should not obstruct their peripheral view.

If your child is starting with an untrained dog, you may need to assist in the training. This may mean working with the child and dog until you have some comfort level in your child's ability to control the dog AND the equipment they are using. This may mean you riding the cart or sled until the dog is more under control (not quite so fresh) with your child watching and helping where they can. When your child first gets on the sled or cart, hook a leash to the dog's collar for added control. It is vital that the dog not be allowed to bolt. Retractable leashes work well IF you are familiar with their operation.

One dog is quite enough for a child to handle until they have become somewhat proficient. If you have a pair of compatible dogs, eventually you will try dogs in double lead. Do not attempt too much at one time. Keep the runs short and successful so as not to tire either dog or child. Watch the weight your dog has to pull. By keeping the weight to a minimum, your child does not have to run too much. It's important to keep training light at this point, it can all be over if your child or dog becomes discouraged at this early stage. If they have a tough day, give encouragement to your child and their dog. This is in the hopes that both of them will look forward to the next try.

If your child can hook down and clear a tangle with no help, they may be ready for their first race. Please don't give your child more dogs than they can handle and expect them to do well in a race. Do your part. Do all that you can to set your child and their dogs up for success!

SNDD Junior musher Alyssa Antonucci running a pair of rescued Siberian Huskies in a Junior race. *Photo by Bruce T. Smith.*

Chapter Thirty-Two
TRAVELING

Traveling anywhere with your dogs means advance preparation. Dogs are not inanimate objects. It's not like adding an extra suitcase. Preparation and forethought is required for their welfare and for the protection of your property and the property of others.

HOUSING

Some beginning mushers take their dogs loose in the family van or SUV, or in the back of a covered pickup truck, but this is not necessarily the ideal arrangement. Dogs need to have their own space, an area where they can enjoy the trip in comfort. It is much more convenient for you to carry your dogs in their own personal space because dogs like the security of their own den. Not to mention it is safer for the dogs and you.

If you use a crate or a dog box, the sides act like a seat belt in case of a sudden stop. If the compartment is nice and snug, they can brace themselves on bumpy rides and stay nice and warm. Another benefit is that if you need to be away from the vehicle, there are no chances of a fight, or a seat belt being eaten or damage being done to the interior. In the case of an accident, a loose dog in a vehicle can also slow down emergency treatment for fear of the dog getting loose on the highway.

For these reasons, almost all mushers transport their dogs in individual boxes. Some are interior opening boxes anchored or built into a box van, trailer or RV. Others are exterior opening boxes mounted on the bed of a truck or a trailer. Some have rigs that have both interior and exterior access.

If you use crates, compartments or dog boxes make sure it has enough bedding to keep the dog warm. There are many products on the market you can use for bedding. Some are better than others are. Straw has excellent insulating qualities and is inexpensive. A combination of shavings and straw works also. I like to add a handful of cedar shavings to the mix because I like the smell and it will keep many insects at bay.

In case of a potty accident, make sure that with whatever type of bedding you choose, water can seep to the bottom of the box while the top layer remains dry. Most dogs love to make a nest in nice dry bedding material so make sure to put in plenty of bedding at the start of a trip, and even try and carry some extra in an empty dog box. That way you can remove any wet layers as you travel, and replenish it if you need too. Damp or wet bedding is not only caused by potty accidents. Your dog's breathing can cause moisture buildup as well as blowing rain or snow.

It is not uncommon to see dog trucks with a bale of straw on top of their truck next to a sled or two. Some national forests and race locations will not allow grass or straw in dog boxes for fear of introducing a seed to their area.

Waiting between classes at Shaver Lake, CA. Safety cones are placed so that people don't run into the outriggers the dogs are connected to. *Photo by John Harshman.*

Your boxes will need the right amount of ventilation. If you have a nice sized opening in the doors the dogs are fine in warm weather. Some mushers have louvers they can close, or pieces they can bolt on to make the opening smaller in very cold weather. You need to watch the ventilation holes of the boxes as you travel. Blowing snow can block small holes. Or on a cold night they can ice over from the dogs' breath. In a bind, duct tape can be used to make a large opening smaller.

ON THE ROAD

On any road trip you can assume that you will want to stop,

stretch your legs, and relieve yourself. The same goes for your dogs. But you have control over when and where you will be stopping for them. Chances are you will not want to be stopping for them in the same place as you stop for your own breaks. For the dogs the best place is an isolated but safe roadside turnout. Use common sense about when to make your stops, they may not wish to "get on with business" if you are on the side of the highway with trucks zipping by.

There is a simple formula that many mushers use to determine when to make your stops to best fit your dogs' biological schedule. The formula is as follows: After giving food or water, you can drive one hour before you have to stop and let them out to potty (do not water at the stop). After that stop, you can then go two hours before letting them out (again, do not water). Then you can go four hours without letting them out (again, no water), and then finally, eight hours.

If you have planned the day right, that gets you to your hotel where you can have eight hours of sleep before waking up and starting the day over again. In order to arrive at the hotel at the right interval, you need to feed your dogs while on the road, sometime in the afternoon.

To work the formula, if you fed the dogs at 3:00 PM, then you would drive until 4 PM and then drop ("drop" is the act of stopping and attaching the dogs to your vehicle for a rest) them. Then you would drive until 6 PM, drop them, then at 10 PM hopefully you are at your hotel. At the hotel, drop the dogs to pee, do not water, and go to sleep for eight hours. At 6 AM they will need to be dropped, watered (probably baited water with a little food in it to make sure they stay hydrated during the trip) and the pattern starts again.

The idea to remember is that if any point (especially if driving in warm weather) you decide to water them significantly, you will also then need to stop more often. Having a pattern to follow also helps if you are traveling with other mushers because then you all know about when you are going to have to stop and can time your meals and your needs to those of your dogs. Planning ahead can make for a potty-accident-free trip!

Remember while you are traveling to ALWAYS clean up your area including raking up any loose straw and of course scooping poop. A couple items experienced mushers will always have in their truck are a rake, a dog poop bucket with plenty of extra plastic bags and a pooper scooper!

Whenever you stop for any length of time on the road, turn off your motor. Many people with dog trucks have modified the exhaust systems on their vehicles to vent the exhaust up and away from the dogs. In your own car, turn off the motor because you don't want your dogs to breathe the fumes from the exhaust. It is acceptable to ask someone parked near you to turn off their motor IF their exhaust is blowing in your dogs' faces.

It's no fun traveling with a dog that gets carsick or that drools excessively. Feeding a few ginger snap cookies (the ones with ginger in them) have helped settle the tummy of many dogs. Acclimation is still the best method to cure carsickness. If nerves cause carsickness, make short trips to fun places. Even errands around town can help to accustom them to traveling. In the meantime, carry plenty of towels.

A Siberian Husky looking out the door of a dog box.
Photo by John Harshman.

During your travels, your dogs will have to be secured at one point in time, as they can't spend all their time in the car, a box or crate. You will need to feed and potty your dogs. There are various time proven methods to keep several dogs secure and out of harms way.

DOG TRUCK CHAINS OR DROP CHAINS

Drop chains are short pieces of sturdy chain with a swivel snap at each end. The length of the chain will depend on how or to where you are hooking up the dogs. The chains need to be long enough so that the dog can eat from food or water dishes on the ground and lie down, but short enough so that two playful adjacent dogs cannot tangle their chains. Chains should also be short enough so that dogs cannot lunge out at passing children or dogs. It is better that the chains be a little on the short side, rather than too long. The drop chains need to be of sufficient strength to secure your dogs.

I take a bit of leg pulling because with my Malamutes, I have really hefty drop chains. But then again, I have had my dogs break drop chains when they were just happy to see me.

Few vehicles come with sufficient connection points for your dogs so you may need to add additional connection points to your car/truck/trailer/SUV for the appropriate number of chains you need. Most people accommodate this by using eyebolts. You can drill through your bumper, the bumper supports, and/or a suitable place along the side of the vehicle to provide a secure anchor/connection point. You can also replace some existing bolts with eyebolts. Space the eyebolts far enough apart so that the chains don't meet. Make sure the snaps on the chains will clip over the eye of the eyebolts.

Some people have "outriggers" added to their trucks. Basically an outrigger is a piece of steel that fits inside another piece of steel (or some other sturdy metal). The inner piece can slide out and will have a pin or other means of keeping it in place. A cable or chain is then stretched between the ends of the metal. Outriggers make the width of your vehicle greater and give the dogs more room. They also keep the dogs away from the vehicle body. If they can not reach the vehicle, they will pee on it less and they will not have access to chew on body parts of the vehicle. Brake lines, trailer lights, mud flaps and the connection for trailers all have been chewed on when someone turned their back on a dog or two for a little too long.

Jolene, an Alaskan Malamute, relaxes on her drop chain connected to the truck.
Photo by John Harshman.

Despite the name, drop chains need not be made only of chain. Plastic coated aircraft cable with a swivel snap attached at each end work very well as well. Be sure there are NO sharp edges if you make your own. The end of the cable needs to be incased in something and the drops need to be checked frequently for signs of age and fraying.

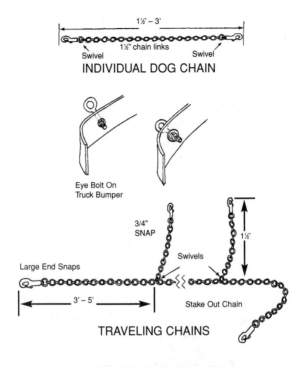

INDIVIDUAL DOG CHAIN

TRAVELING CHAINS

STAKE OUT CHAIN

As an alternate procedure to chaining your dogs to your vehicle, and as a necessity when you have more dogs than eyebolts, you can use a stake out chain. This is a long, heavy chain that is stretched tight between trees or any solid objects. Short dog chains are permanently attached to the main chain. The snaps of the dog chains should not be able to meet by about a foot when the main chain is tight.

The ends of the main chain are extra long to go around large trees and then snap back onto the main chain. The end bolt snaps are extra large and strong.

A variation to the stake out chain is a long piece of stout chain with a couple clips (double clips that have clips/snaps at both ends) and several drop chains. The long piece of chain is looped around a tire and the double clip is used to secure the chain. The other end of the chain is looped around another tire. You can then space your dogs out along the chain. When you are ready to leave, put all the dogs away and pull forward or backward so the long piece of chain is clear of the tires. Pick up and stow for the next time.

If you have a few chains and a large coffee can, this can work as well. One end of the long chain is clipped to the lip of the coffee can and clip one end of each drop chain to the lip of the can as well. Make a couple holes at the bottom of the can for the water to drain. This works well when you are not sure where you want to drill holes or you have a borrowed vehicle. Clipping an end to the lip of the can also makes it easy when you have to set-up. Remove the double clip and you have the long chain. The short chains are on swivel snaps and you will have no problems with tangling.

Drop chains can be stored in a variety of ways that won't get all your gear wet. Some leave them in the box with the dog. Some leave them in the box on the dog and others hang the drop chains on hooks screwed into the storage compartment area of the dog box itself. Most sledding outfitters carry different sized canvas bags that Velcro shut and are great for holding longer chains, picket lines and other miscellaneous gear.

Van and Shirley Austin-Peeke's dog truck with two sleds secured in the racks on top. *Photo by Shirley Austin Peeke.*

SNDD member Lucy Bettis with her dog truck. Note the hanging harnesses in the back storage area. *Photo by Bruce T. Smith.*

DOG BOXES

Trucks

The most common method you will see teams of dogs traveling in are dog boxes. Like everything else you can build your own or have a set of dog boxes fabricated to fit your needs. There are many new materials that can be used other than plywood with or without fiberglass. One company makes panels you snap together similar to a child's toy. But the material is a plastic and is waterproof along with the insulating factor and you can order it in the color you want.

The easiest design for building a set of dog boxes to be placed on the bed of a pickup truck involves a flat deck that spans across the pickup bed and projects on either side between four inches to eight inches. Allow for minimum inside box dimensions of 18 inches wide, 20 inches high and 30 inches deep. Variation of height dimensions is required if you have tall or big dogs, like Alaskan Malamutes. You do NOT want to make the boxes too tall or too wide. With the average racing dog you may wish to vary any dimensions, but not more than four inches.

Boxes should be small enough so that the dogs can keep the boxes warm with their body heat in cold weather. The size of your boxes will depend somewhat on your climate and the size of your dogs. The dimensions given will comfortably accommodate a dog of 24 inches at the shoulders in northern California weather which frequently gets down to 10 degrees Fahrenheit at night.

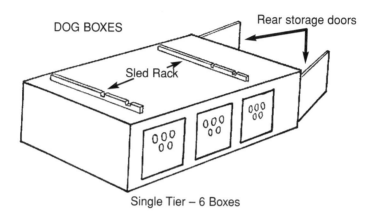

DOG BOXES

Rear storage doors

Sled Rack

Single Tier – 6 Boxes

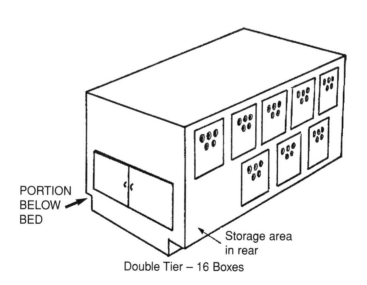

PORTION
BELOW
BED

Storage area
in rear

Double Tier – 16 Boxes

Some people will build boxes that are wider rather than tall. They may put a pair of dogs in each box. Having two dogs in a box has several advantages. Not only do they keep each other company; they can keep each other warm too. When doubling up dogs, you need to make sure the two you put together 1) get along, 2) are not male and female if the females is in heat unless you WANT puppies and 3) they both fit in the box (both can stand up, turn around and lie down).

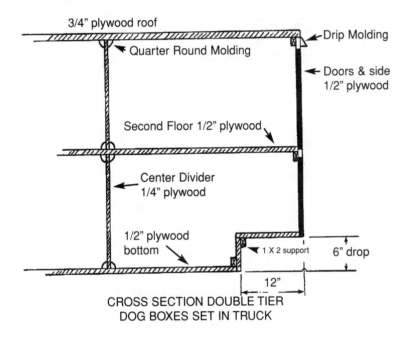

CROSS SECTION DOUBLE TIER
DOG BOXES SET IN TRUCK

Trailers

A trailer outfitted with either a single or double tier of boxes works very well for some people. A platform can be built (or space left) behind the boxes to accommodate snowmobiles, ATVs or a training cart. A trailer has the advantage that it can be parked when not in use. A trailer is also an answer for those using campers or motor homes. Or for times they want to bring more dogs than they can fit on the truck alone.

A two-axle trailer gives maximum stability. However, a single axle trailer is easier and lighter to maneuver when it must be detached from the vehicle so that it can be turned around in the small spaces that are often the only parking places available at a race site.

If you are going to buy a basic trailer and then convert it, a small utility or boat trailer with minimum wheels of 14 inches will provide a beginning. If you are going to build the trailer completely, it would be wise to have the advice of someone who is familiar with trailer construction and dog box construction give you some ideas. Electric brakes with a breakaway switch are highly recommended. Make sure you understand the laws in your travel area regarding when you need tire chains, and which tires need to be chained as some states require tire chains, even if towing with a 4 X 4. (For example, in California, at the time of this printing, chains are required on the trailer if you have electric brakes or the ability to have electric brakes.)

You will find that empty boxes are very convenient places to store gear, people food, water, and anything else that you might want to reach quickly on a stop. Once you have your outfit set up and your routine down pat, you will see how easy it is to travel with a dozen or more dogs and wonder why you didn't move to the dog box set-up sooner!

Dog trailer, shows sled and training cart. You can be creative with the vents in the doors. *Photo by Michael DeZelar.*

247   MUSH!

There are a lot of people involved with sled dog sports. There are the people that put on the race, people that sanction the race and people that help with whatever is needed to have a race. Plus the dog drivers and their support people.

RACE GIVING ORGANIZATIONS

From time to time you will hear the term RGO. RGO is much easier to say than Race Giving Organization. An RGO is normally a club or group of people that put on a race. In some communities, the people of the town itself play a major role in the event.

Races can be very beneficial for the community. Not only is a race an economic benefit, it can also be of historic interest and just plain something different to do. When a race comes to town there is something unique to do (in many parts of the world, running dogs is not a part of normal life). When a race comes to town, hotel rooms get filled up. The local watering holes or eateries get additional business. Racers spend money in the local shops. And there will be people from out of the area that may come to watch the event.

Some communities use a race weekend as a way to build town spirit. The local school children may make posters for the windows of the shops. The local organizers may do fundraising for the school or a town project. Many races are part of a town festival.

Some communities that wish to add a dog sled race to a festival or just to their winter activities will contact a local racing club and ask for assistance. By working together a race may come out of the contact.

The Sierra Nevada Dog Drivers (SNDD) is an RGO, we as a group sponsor multiple activities, including putting on races. Most of our races and classes are sanctioned with a sanctioning body. By sanctioning races, people that attend from out of the area can have set expectations regarding how the race will be run. They know that the rules will be the same and the formats will be similar.

SANCTIONING BODIES
The International Sled Dog Racing Association

The International Sled Dog Racing Association (ISDRA) was founded in 1966. It dedicates its activities to the sport of sled dog racing on a worldwide basis by standardizing race rules and race management procedures, by promoting public interest and driver education, and by encouraging cooperation among clubs.

Four officers, five at-large directors and thirteen regional directors govern ISDRA at this writing. All directors are elected biannually by the membership. Any individual or organization interested in the sport can become a member of ISDRA by payment of dues.

ISDRA rules were originally based on Alaskan rules. Many races either use ISDRA rules entirely or use these well-accepted rules as a basis for their own rules. ISDRA sanctions some, but not all, races that meet its standards. Sanctioning is optional with the race giving organization. If the event is ISDRA sanctioned there is a fee that is paid by the entrants as well as a sanctioning fee paid by the RGO. Sanctioned races earn points for the entrants that are ISDRA members toward medals and regional certificates.

The ISDRA Officials Handbook is a guide to procedures governing the duties of officials. Every serious driver would do well to study this handbook so that they will be prepared to serve in some official capacity at some time. This manual is available to ISDRA members from the ISDRA web site (http://www.isdra.org.)

The ISDRA Race Manual provides guidance to clubs on all aspects of racing, including trail making, trail marking, publicity, sanctioning, and media press releases before and after an event. Should you do well, ISDRA will send a press release to your local paper.

IFSS Nordic World Championships in 2001, Fairbanks Alaska, long (23 km) pulka gold medalist Ole Petter Engli from Norway. *Photo by Andrea Swingley.*

RACE GIVING ORGANIZATIONS

Countless hours of planning and hard work are required to put on a race. Members of the organizing club must find a suitable race site, put in and maintain a trail, obtain sponsorship, assign officials, arrange publicity, etc. The number of jobs that are carried out for a major race and the relationship of the officials doing those jobs can be learned by study of the charts in the ISDRA Officials Handbook.

RACE OFFICIALS

Every race, large or small, must have certain key officials in order to be a success. These are:

Race Marshal/Chief Judge: some races divide the job between two people. The Race Marshal is the person in complete charge of the entire race. They are appointed by the race giving organization and reports only to it. All other officials report to the Race Marshal (RM). The Race Marshal is available for consultation during all phases of planning a race, and any questionable areas should have the approval of the RM.

The starting times for all classes and events, charge of the officials' meeting, drivers' meeting and Protest Committee fall on the shoulders of the Race Marshal. They are the only people who can disqualify a team, and the Race Marshal also has the power to cancel or stop a race due to weather or trail conditions.

In short, the Race Marshal has final say on all matters, within the limits of the race rules.

Trail Boss: is responsible for the preparation and condition of the trail. They must know the requirements of a suitable trail and try to eliminate all hazards from the trail. Or clearly mark those that can not be moved. The Trail Boss and crew see to it that the trail is well packed, well marked, and that checkers and stewards are stationed at appropriate places.

Chief Timer: records and posts the time it takes each team to run the course. The Chief Timer may have several assistants to help time, but they alone call the countdown for each team leaving the starting chute.

Dog Marking Judge: marks each dog for identification so there can be no substitution of dogs. Different colors are used for the different classes. Markings are small, waterproof and harmless. Dogs are only marked on multi-day races. A one-day race need not mark dogs.

STEWARDING

In addition to the official race officials, the help of many other people is needed on the day of the race if the race is to run smoothly. These people can be the one that: ride snowmobiles to pack the trail; dog drivers not running in that class or that race and members of their families; and sometimes, in a pinch, even casual spectators who are interested in taking part. The jobs these people do can be included in the following categories:

Trail Checkers' main function is to check off on a list each team as it passes and note any irregularities.

The Race Marshall stations Trail Stewards at various places along the trail where drivers may need assistance.

Anyone on the trail may at some time find themselves in a place where a team needs help. Assisting a team usually involves holding the sled while the driver untangles lines, leads their team into a turn, or perhaps changes the position of a dog. Once a team has left the starting line, only the driver is allowed to handle the dogs themselves if there is no emergency. An emergency is when any dog or driver is in danger of being hurt. A team running loose down the trail is definitely an emergency and any official or spectator is encouraged to stop it.

In these emergency situations anyone may handle the dogs without the driver being penalized. In most cases the Trail Steward's job is to stand arms outstretched, quiet, motionless and appreciate the teams go streaking past. You need not answer the driver if they quietly say thank you as they pass you.

Sled Holders are two or more strong persons asked by the Race Marshall to hold each sled as it comes to the starting line so that the driver can go up to speak to their dogs. The Sled Holder uses the stanchions of the sled to hold the sled until the driver is ready to go. A third person may stand on the brake when the driver is going through the final check of their dogs before the start. The Sled Holders will release the sled and quickly step to the side at "1" in the countdown.

Club or Dog Handlers are those who help teams to the starting line. They can be officials appointed by the Race Marshall for the entire race, or they can be people who are not busy at the moment and are willing to help drivers who are short of handlers. It is always nice to offer the people in the dog truck adjacent to you if they need help if you are free. In turn you can ask them for help with your team when the time comes.

The job consists of asking drivers if they want help, then following their instructions. Usually the driver will want you to hold the main towline, keeping it at the level of the dogs' backs. Be alert for the driver's instructions; do not carry on loud conversations with friends. Watch the dogs for any chewing of lines. Sometimes the driver will ask you to carry the sled over a bare spot or to ride it while they take the lead dog. When the team reaches the starting line it will be taken over by the Sled Holders, and you will be free to go back to help another team.

In the noise made by teams waiting to go it can be difficult to hear. Some communication is non-verbal. A driver that puts their arm in the air means they are stopping. Most handlers will put their arm up as well to signal to the other helpers and the driver. Sometimes the person at the front will put their arm up first. This means for some reason they have to stop. The driver will apply their brake to slow and stop the team. This is to keep the team from balling up and getting tangled.

EUROPEAN SLED DOG RACING ASSOCIATION

The European Sled Dog Racing Association (ESDRA) is the counterpart in Europe to ISDRA. All its members are national sled dog racing organizations. It has rules for and sanctions two types of races: 1) the regular sled dog races held in North America, which they call Nome style racing, and 2) races where the driver is on skis, and weight is carried either in a sled or inside a closed toboggan-like carrier called a pulka, which they call Scandinavian style racing. ESDRA is responsible for the annual European Championship races held each year.

INTERNATIONAL FEDERATION
OF SLEDDOG SPORTS

When ISDRA and ESDRA attempted to jointly apply for Olympic recognition from the International Olympic Committee, they were advised that only a single organization could make the application, in its capacity as the over-seeing organization for the sport worldwide. This necessitated the formation of a new organization in 1986 which was named the International Federation of Sleddog Sports (IFSS), with both ISDRA and ESDRA as Associate Members. National sled racing organizations become regular members on application.

IFSS is responsible for an annual international invitational sled dog event held among Olympic lines and called the IFSS World Championship Sled Dog Race, or the IFSS WC. Each country member sends teams to compete in as many of the classes as it wishes. Both Nome style and Scandinavian class races are held. Currently, the classes being raced are Unlimited, eight-dog, six-dog and four-dog Nome style classes, skijor classes and Men's and Women's Pulka Scandinavian style classes. The Pulka classes have a three dog maximum and usually race the six-dog sprint trail.

ATTEND
AS A SPECTATOR

Races are held all over the world with and without snow. These days the Internet has made it much easier to find sled dog clubs and races.

A couple places to look on the Internet for races in your area are on the ISDRA (International Sled Dog Racing Association) web site http://www.isdra.org and another popular site is "sled dog central" http://www.sleddogcentral.com.

When looking up the information on a race, some questions may come to mind. For one there are a lot of classes or types of races. The following are VERY general and to not be taken as law.

RACES

Speed or sprint races

A speed or sprint race is a race that takes place in heats over multiple days. The heats are run on consecutive days. Most races are two days in a row. But there are races that are three consecutive days. There is one heat per day per class. Please note the term "sprint" is not exactly what the word implies. Sprint is a term that is commonly used for races that are shorter distances. The minimum daily mileage or distance depends on the number of dogs and the time of the year.

Mid-distance race

A mid-distance race is very much like a sprint race. But the length of the trail is longer. The trail can be 8-12 miles (or longer) per day with distance totaling 25 to 40 miles (or longer). There will be times the mileage is less if conditions demand. These classes too, will have minimum distances depending on the time of the year and the number of dogs run in the team.

Distance or long distance race

A long distance race is very much like a mid-distance race.

But the length of the trail is considerably longer. The Iditarod (listed as 1,049 miles) and the Yukon Quest are two of the better known long distance races. Distance races may be 40 or more miles a day. Most are 200 or more miles in length. These races are not run in heats. They are run from point A to point B. Which can be from point A out to point B and back to point A. Because of the distance there will be stops between points A and B (A is the start and B is the finish).

Freight Race

A freight race can be of varied distances, it can be held in stages, or like a sprint/mid-distance or even a long distance race. The defining feature that makes a freight race a freight race is the sled must carry weight. In freight race there is a set amount of weight that must be carried for the entire race. Some will have a set minimum amount of weight that must be carried in the basket of the sled. Other races will say X pounds per dog is to be carried in the basket of the sled. The material used for weight varies, but sand and cement bags work well. Dog food works as well.

You could say a freight race is a cross between a weight pull and a regular race.

Stage race

A stage race is very much like the other types of races. But instead of running the same trail on day two, they run a different trail. And day three can be different from days one and two. It can be a 100 or more miles run with daily mileage of 25 or 30 miles. The people putting on the race determine the length of the "stage". But each stage is determined prior to the first start. The maximum and minimum number of dogs per team is also factored into the distance.

Skijor

This is a race with a person that races without a sled, wearing skis. The dogs are hooked up the same way as you would if you had a sled. But instead of a sled, the dog driver wears a special belt or harness. The dogs are connected with a quick release to the person that is wearing cross-country skis. Skijoring is a wonderful sport that is done with one or more dogs. Please learn how to ski BEFORE trying to skijor with your own dogs! More on skijor in the skijor section.

Race Marshall looks over Dotty Dennis' sled prior to the start of a freight race.
Photo by Bruce T. Smith.

Gig or rig

It's a race that uses some sort of a wheeled sled. Some look like a chariot. Others look like a scooter or are a bicycle with no chain. Some carts/gigs/rigs have two, three or four wheels. And some gigs are very light and were built specifically for racing.

COMMON QUESTIONS
How is the winner determined?

The shortest over all time is the winner (fastest). In sprint racing, mid-distance racing and stage racing, all the heats are timed. The times from the heats are combined and the fastest combined time is the winner. A long distance race is the elapsed racing time minus any hold times.

**The teams are not started at the same time ...
how do you keep track?**

Each dog driver wears a bib. The number is their number only. If the teams go out one or two teams at a time, they leave at one, two or more minute intervals. The interval is subtracted from the elapsed time to determine the time they took to run the heat or the distance. Typically the first day of a race the starting order is determined by a drawing. The following day(s) the faster the time, the earlier in the order you go out in your class. The fastest team goes out first, and the slowest team goes out last -OR- some races go the other way around to make it more interesting. With the slower teams going out first there is more passing and the day is a bit shorter.

With races like the Iditarod, every fifth team goes out one minute later than the interval all the other teams go. This additional minute is for the local TV and radio stations to do their advertising or station identification without missing any of the live start.

How far do the sprint race dogs run each heat/day?

The length of the course depends on the number of dogs running. The lengths are not set in stone and can be shorter or longer depending on conditions. But the general rule for sprint classes is that the trail is one mile per dog on the team. The three-dog class goes three miles, the four-dog class goes four miles, six-dog class goes six miles and the eight-dog class goes eight miles...per day. These are the classes. From time to time you may see a team go out with less dogs than the class. But never more dogs. This may be due to a number of reasons, one could be the dogs are being trained for the distance and one dog is unable to run. For example in the eight-dog class, a team may go out with only seven dogs. There are set maximum and minimum numbers for each class.

Why do some of the dogs look like they have paint on them?

The first day of the race the musher or dog driver shows which dogs will be running which classes. Each class has a different mark. It may be a color or the location that is marked on the dog. The dogs can only run in one class/heat/race per day and the same dogs run on the same team each day. The dog driver can choose to not run a dog on the second day. But the dog driver cannot substitute dogs. Some races allow a pool of dogs for the racer to choose from. Other races let the driver leave dogs in the care of qualified people and continue on with fewer dogs.

You will also see colored zip ties on collars or an id tag. If the race is using ID tags, there is one tag per dog. There are many different ways to identify dogs.

How do the mushers know where to go on the trail?

There are several means of marking trails. Some trails have

formal markers. Other use colored pie plates (paper plates). There are different colors to warn the musher of obstacles or an upcoming turn. This low tech but efficient way for marking trails is to staple colored pie plates to stakes put in the snow. The mushers are made aware of which color means what. ISDRA even has rules that state which color or placement is to mean something specific.

Some of the dogs look so skinny!

Weight is mentioned in another chapter, but it is important to remember when you go to your first race that many of the dogs look skinny because they have hound in them. They may have thin coats and are lean. If you look closely you will see dogs have hard muscled bodies. They aren't malnourished. They simply are not carrying extra weight. Sprint dogs also tend to be much leaner than long distance dogs. But the addition of hound has made some of those dogs look skinny as well.

Are these racing dogs loved?

You BET they are!!! Some sleep in bed with their owners. While others may not sleep in bed, they live pampered lives with plenty of exercise, love, food, proper housing, veterinary care etc.

Miscellaneous things to make the experience.

One suggestion when attending your first race as a spectator... leave your unentered dogs at home. You can experience the event much more if you don't have to worry about your dog. It is much more difficult to meet mushers if you can't chat with them when they are at their dog trucks. Who knows, you might get to go out on the trail and watch a heat as a checker.

You might also use this time to walk in the dog truck parking area. Meet mushers; meet someone that may offer to mentor you. You might be asked to help get a team to the line. Who knows where attending your first race might lead you. When I attended my first race, I never thought I would become so involved with sled dog sports!

Now go enjoy your time at the races. Are you ready yet?

259   MUSH!

Chapter
Thirty-Five
GOING TO
YOUR FIRST RACE

If you have a race that is within an hour of your home you may wish to return home each night so you and your dogs can sleep in your own beds at night. If the race is really close to home you may wish to take your dogs home, feed them and return to spend time with the other mushers. Or you can hang out all day and head home when the out of towners retire to their hotel rooms. Still, there is something special staying in a motel and doing it all at your first race.

If you live close to a race site, you may wish to invite a fellow musher to stay with you. In return they should be happy to give you suggestions and additional hints that could make your first race less stressful. Even if all they do is reassure you that you are ready, it's worth it. Many will share stories of their first races or times they messed up. Some of those mistakes everyone makes, but hearing others might help you so that you don't make that mistake yourself.

If you live more than a four-hour drive from the race site, you will probably want to arrive at the area the day before. If you have the time off and the trails are public trails, you can even go a couple days early and run the trails. Just make sure to stay out of the way if there is any trail markings going on. If you are there, some groups will welcome your help in marking the trails.

Arriving the day before is advisable for several reasons. It is a more relaxed time and you may meet the other drivers, both to be friendly and to pick up useful tips. You and your dogs will be rested from the drive and will have more time to become used to any altitude changes as well as changed weather conditions. The change in conditions could be as drastic as there is snow on the ground and where you normally live, it doesn't snow. Altitude is something to take into consideration. Especially when going up in altitude.

Many races have a drivers' meeting the evening before a race. Or they may have a location you can pick up your race packet the evening before. Having your race packet in hand is one less thing for you to do on race morning. And in the race packet there could be a detailed trail map. You can familiarize yourself with the trail via the trail map and have a better understanding of what the trail will be like. And you will not be trying to absorb as much at the driver's meeting if the trail boss has comments to share about the trail.

Make sure to be there in time for the drivers' meeting (sometimes it's held the night before the race), at which you will be briefed on the trail and other aspects of the race. Check your information sheet for time and place of this meeting.

On race day arrive at the race site early, even if your class is not scheduled to go out until later in the day. There may be an updating of driver information (change in the trail due to varying weather conditions). At some races you might be needed to serve as trail checker for other classes or to help other drivers get to the starting chute. If you can leave your dogs, being a checker on the trail is another way to see what the trail will look like. Being a checker is not a tough job, but it is important. Who knows, you may want their help when your turn comes.

You will want to have your team available to the dog markers. Dog marking typically takes place before the first teams go out and just after the drivers' meeting. You will be asked to present each dog you will be running for each class you entered. Dog marking can be done in many methods. Some use colored livestock markers and use color AND location for the class. Some use colored tags, paint, zip ties. (Hint: baby wipes will get livestock marker off your dog. If you have a show dog, let the dog marker know if you will be showing within a week or two. I learned this lesson the hard way. One year I ended up showing a dog with a green dot on his white face. A green dot between his eyes...nothing but time got that off.)

As your race time approaches you will mentally check off last minute details. If you feel the need, make up a check off sheet at home and refer to it to make sure you have remembered everything necessary. By now you should have studied the trail map; your dogs have been watered, pottied and marked; and you have your race number in a safe place if you have not already attached to the outerwear you will race in. Triple check your equipment and make sure you have your gloves, dog bag, hat, snowhook, extra double-lead neckline, etc.

If you are parked any distance from the starting line, you will want help getting your fresh, excited team to the line. If you have been helping others get their teams to the line, you can ask them for help with your team and you won't have to run around frantically looking for assistance at the last minute.

Once in the holding lineup, your sled will be inspected by an official to see that you are carrying the required equipment. The dogs will be checked for the right color, tag or whatever was used for dog marking. Be sure to firmly anchor your team (with brake and/or snowhook) and HANG on as the team before you heads out.

In the chute there will be someone to hold your sled. You should leave your sled to give each individual dog a few final words of encouragement. While you are talking to your dogs, check collars, necklines and tug line connections. Keep one ear open; don't forget to listen to the Starter/Chief Timer.

Be on the runners of your sled for the final 30 seconds of the countdown to the start. 5-4-3-2-1-GO! You are off. Many dogs have learned the countdown and are ready at 1. Hang on and enjoy the ride.

Whether the trail runs across a frozen lake, on a narrow trail through pine woods, or up (and down) a snowed-over trail, there is nothing quite like your first race. Enjoy the ride, but don't forget to be thinking too. Try to remember the trail map, anticipate turns and possible problem areas you were told of at the drivers' meeting. Watch for other teams. If the trail is a loop trail, then you will not need to worry about head on passing. But you need to listen for teams coming up behind you. Remind yourself of the right of way rules on overtaking and passing. Try not to mix up *Gee* and *Haw* and be sure to familiarize yourself with all trail markers. Above all, watch your dogs and enjoy yourself.

It will feel like all too soon, and you will be across the finish line. In your excitement that should still be there, don't forget to tend to your dogs. Plenty of praise for your dogs is in order after you are well beyond the line.

Back at your vehicle, unhook each dog. Give water and a snack. If the weather is favorable leave them on their tie out chains. A rub down might be welcome and check each foot. After you have cared for your dogs, you will want to check your time on the posting board. Talk to other drivers and exchange your trail experiences with them. Don't relax too much; there may be other classes that need your assistance.

If parking was not assigned, pay close attention where you parked the first day. Tomorrow you should make every attempt to park in the same place. This cuts down on your dogs being exposed to anything the team next to you might carry. Their dogs may be completely healthy, but their dogs have developed tolerances to something your dogs do not. And you do not want to share with their dogs.

After the day's entire racing is over and people are packing up to leave, you may want to take some additional time to unwind. It could be to massage each dog and give an extra treat or take turns giving your dogs short walks on a leash. Or you may prefer to go back to the motel to feed and water your dogs and enjoy a hot shower and beverage of your choice before the mushers' banquet that evening. At the banquet there will be more talk and tale swapping, some eating and drinking, and lots of socializing. Some banquets are more formal than others are. Some may simply be a group that all decide to meet at a local watering hole.

For most 10 PM is a magic hour. 10 PM is time for the final dog drop, giving the dogs a last chance to relieve themselves and give them a last drink of water. This is a chance for you to take one last look at any dog you worried about before heading to bed.

The next morning you are back for another day of racing. Look for and park in the same place as the day before. Go through all the same steps as the day before.

By the time this day is over, perhaps a trophy or prize money will be one of your rewards. Don't leave before the awards are given out, its part of this memorable event. For most, this first race will always be a special memory, cherish the time. The exhilaration of an active weekend and getting to know new friends, as well as yourself and your dogs in a new context should be a reward in its own.

The issue of safety equipment should be something you are aware of. Sled dog sports can be quite dangerous if you are going all out. Head protection is something you might wish to always wear, in both training and racing. There are clubs that recommend that you wear a helmet at their races. If the race requires any equipment, that will be listed on the entry form or race info. There are many commercial helmets that work quite well when running dogs. Check local ski and snowboard shops for helmets.

If you have problems with a specific dog or simply worry about your dogs backing out of harnesses, there are steps you can take. One is to use an extra neckline (the one with a snap at each end, not the ones connected to the gangline). You can clip the neckline to each side of the back of the harness and run it under the belly. This is now called a bellyband. I added straps to my racing harnesses because I worry that we could have a dog back out of a harness during a race. When training, time is not of the essence, but for added insurance we have bellybands so that we don't worry about any of our dogs backing out of their harness and costing us time at races.

Children are welcome at races. If you have children with you, you will need to keep a close eye on them so that they don't accidentally get hurt. At home your children may be great with your dogs. But you never know how the dogs in the dog truck next to you will react to your children. Your children will be used to your dogs and may approach other dogs with a lack of caution. Many sled dogs are kennel dogs and are not used to strangers. Do not be surprised if your mellow dogs are high-strung at a race.

For your children's safety keep your children away from other dogs. Explain the situation to them, and then provide for their amusement elsewhere. Bring along toys suitable for their ages and local conditions. You may even see mothers and fathers with children in chest or backpacks tending to their dogs. Some dog clubs are made up of many families. One club used to have bags of kids clothes and boots they used to pass from family to family as their kids outgrew the apparel.

SNDD member Dotty Dennis sorts gear at her dog truck. This rig has a center isle you can walk down. *Photo by Bruce T. Smith.*

Some local papers will have photos and articles letting people know of upcoming events. The publicity may add more spectators. The race you enter may be well attended by spectators and the media. If people are asking you questions, keep your eye on the clock. It's OK to politely let someone know that you are unable to visit with them or answer questions because you are working on preparations for your race. It's not uncommon for there to be color photos on the front page of the local newspaper complete with multi-page articles the second day of an event. Many times rookie drivers are pointed out and get added attention.

So far this chapter has been all about attending your first race on snow. Your first race need not be on snow. And for some they may never have a race on snow. If you don't have the chance to run on snow, all of the above will still come into play. The activities, parking, excitement, all of it, but it just might not be quite so cold. Have fun while you and your dogs enjoy it all!

It's not quite over. The actual race portion may be over. You've attended the awards ceremony. But there are still a few things to do before you leave. You will want to clean up your parking site, fill out your race report, return your bib (if they have cloth bibs, they may need them back). Care for your dogs; load your dogs into your vehicle, making sure any external latches are secure. Verify your sleds or gigs are securely anchored. As you pull away, look back to make sure your space is clean, tidy and that you have not left anything behind as you pull out of your parking space. Once you finally start for home, re-live your race as you drive and plan for the next one.

Many times
your local paper will
run articles on you or an event.
These mention ISDRA medal winner Will
Wanless. *Photos courtesy Will Wanless.*

Chapter Thirty-Six

WEIGHT PULLING

Weight pulling is a hobby for the person with a small kennel or people with as few as one dog. Weight pulling can also be for that big wheel dog you have or the dog that is too big or slow to fit on the race team but just loves to pull.

Weight pulling is a competition where the dog that pulls the most weight in the fastest time is the over all winner. Some weight pulls also give awards for the dog that pulls the highest percentage of their body weight the required 16 feet. But the big prize normally goes to the dog that pulls the most. If two or more dogs pull the same weight, the fastest dog is the winner.

TYPES OF DOGS

Any breed may compete at a weight pull, unless the pull is for a specific breed. At pulls today the common breeds are Malamutes, Huskies, Rottweilers and Pit Bulls (and other Pit Bull type breeds). I have been to pulls with French Bulldogs, Saint Bernards and Mastiffs. The smaller dogs tend to pull larger percentages of their weight than the bigger dogs. Pit Bulls do very well in the percent and the most weight. They hunker down and don't seem to know when to quit. While many of the northern breeds can be stubborn and will stop long before their capability. Some dogs will let the time run out, then walk like there is nothing behind them, which can be quite frustrating for the handler.

In weight pulling the dog's conformation is very important. The dog should be well balanced with strong hindquarters in which to push their body forward, pulling the cart/sled. This too is an event where training and proper nutrition are important factors. Aggressive dogs are not welcome at weight pulls. Neither are bitches in heat.

EQUIPMENT

Harness

A correctly fitted harness is very important. It is so important that people like me can have two or three harnesses for the same dog. The different harnesses are for different times of the year depending on the amount of coat the dog has.

The harness used in weight pulling is similar to a racing harness except for one key factor. With a racing harness the back of the harness is hooked up on the back of the dog, above the tail. A weight pull harness is hooked up below the tail. The tail goes between harness pieces because the harness is lower and is on both sides of the dogs rear legs. A spreader bar or single tree is a dowel made of wood that goes between the sides of

Weight pulls are held all over the world. Here is a photo of an Alaskan Malamute, owned by Hideto Murahashi, at a weight pull in Japan. *Photo courtesy of Yasuko Nojima.*

the harness. The wooden dowel, webbing and the ring that the dog is hooked up to make a triangle when pulling.

This spreader bar is very important. And the higher the weight, the more it is needed. The term spreader bar is also the function. It keeps the harness spread so that the dog is not encumbered when pulling.

Wearing a correctly fitted harness, the dog pulls from the chest. Which is the reason there is extra padding on the chest area of the harness.

The rules are pretty basic when it comes to the way you treat your dog. Any abuse toward your dog will disqualify you, and you are asked to leave. Any situations deemed dangerous for the dog will be corrected (a tangle) or the dog will be disqualified. You cannot coerce your dog to pull. It is up to their willingness and just between you and them. No food (other than water) may be awarded during their class – not even between turns. You may only coax with voice and gestures, no implements. No double handling with a plant in the audience. And if your dog gets into a dogfight, ALL parties are asked to leave. No matter how it started.

Carts or sledges

In competition there will be some sort of apparatus the weight is put on. If the pull is on mat, carpet, dirt or other natural surfaces other than snow or ice, a wheel rig may be used. The wheeled rig or cart must be able to hold a minimum of two tons for most pulls.

When pulling on snow or ice, a sledge or sled is used. A weight pull sledge may not look like more than some plywood with runners. But it too needs to be able to support two tons as well.

Material used for weight

Most pulls will have 4,000 pounds of material for putting on the cart. Dog food works. So do bags of sand. Cement block, tires and kitty litter all work well. I know of a club that has sections of train track cut to specific weight. Another club uses plastic buckets. They haul their empty plastic buckets to the weight pull and then proceed to fill them up with water. They have a mark on the bucket to fill to and then weigh the filled bucket to verify the weight. They can add or remove water to adjust the weight.

Whatever you use for weight, you need to be able to stack it safely without it shifting and you need to know the exact weight.

WHEN TO START TRAINING

You will want to start your weight pull training or exposure to the equipment as early as possible. This in NOT to say you have your young pup pulling a hundred pounds. This training will be so that your pup or young dog gets comfortable with the equipment and does not have an issue with something being drug behind them. Most groups that put on weight pulls will not let dogs under the age of twelve months enter. They also do not let bitches in heat in the area.

WHERE DO YOU STAND WHEN IT'S YOUR DOGS TURN TO PULL?

There are two places you can stand when your dog is in the

chute for its turn to pull. The most common is at the front across the finish line. When you stand in front you can call your dog. You can make gestures, pretty much anything but crossing the line or touching the dog or chute. You can not use bait of any kind to coax your dog to pull. They must come to you because they want to.

The other place you stand is behind the front of the cart. If you are standing behind the dog, most call this driving the dog. You can not touch any equipment when you are driving your dog from behind.

AKC Alaskan Malamute *Timber* (Ch Tanunka's Majestic Red Knight CGC, WPD, WWPD, WWPDX) weight pulling in California. *Photo courtesy of Debbie Hunyada.*

WEIGHT PULLING CONTESTS

At any weight pull you enter, there will be multiple weight classes. Some breed clubs have three or four weight classes. The weight class is a weight range. Normally any fraction of a pound is rounded DOWN to the lower pound. ISDRA has a set of weight pull rules. So does the IWPA (International Weight Pull Association), another of the weight pull contest-sanctioning bodies. IWPA has eight different weight classes.

IWPA WEIGHT CLASSES
   20 pounds - dogs weighing 20 lbs. or less
   40 pounds - dogs weighing 21-40 lbs.
   60 pounds - dogs weighing 41-60 lbs.
   80 pounds - dogs weighing 61-80 lbs.
   100 pounds - dogs weighing 81-100 lbs.
   125 pounds - dogs weighing 101-125 lbs.
   150 pounds - dogs weighing 126-150 lbs.
   Unlimited - dogs weighing more than 151 lbs.

Both ISDRA (www.ISDRA.org) and IWPA (www.IWPA.net) have weight pull rules as well as many individual breed specific dog clubs like the Alaskan Malamute Club of America.

The simple rule is pull the most weight the fastest. Different rules have different amounts of time to complete the pull. Some rules are 45 seconds, others are 60 seconds. If the cart is stopped and not across the line at the time, the pull is incomplete.

READY TO TRY A WEIGHT PULL?

If you feel your dog is ready, then find a pull and go. But before you do, make sure to familiarize yourself with the rules that will be used. Many pulls offer a novice class. This may be a class you can use a leash to coax your dog. Or it could be a pull you get to try three times. If you want to enter, check out the rules that will be used.

I have not gone much in the way of detail on weight pulling. Weight pulling could be a book of its own. This section is just another option for something you and your dog may enjoy together.

I can tell you it's pretty awesome when you are standing in front of your dog and they are coming slowly towards you and you know the cart has over 2,300 pounds of dog food on it. I start my dogs with the command *PULL!* And having a Malamute, we did win the most weight pull a few times.

273   MUSH!

Hiking and/or backpacking has become more and more common for the average dog owner. Hiking and/or backpacking are a great way to spend quality time with your dog during the snowless seasons.

THE DOG

For carrying a pack, your dog should be medium to large in size and must be in good physical condition.

Obedience training is not a requirement but your dog must understand that when wearing a pack, pulling is not the goal. Commands such as *easy, whoa* and *come* can be most helpful. Charlene G. LaBelle, the author of *A Guide to Backpacking with Your Dog,* strongly suggests that your dog be leashed at all times because you never know what you will encounter. It is asking a lot of even the most well trained dog to cease chasing a deer on verbal command alone.

THE PACK

These days there are a variety of commercially made packs available for purchase. Some manufactures make packs that are better suited for some breeds than others. There are some fancy options.

The basic dog pack consists of two compartments, or panniers, one for each side of the dog, fastened together at the top. The material at the top will distribute the load and allow the panniers to be on the sides of the dog. Some panniers were held together by straps. This is fine IF the amount of weight is minimal.

The pack should be constructed so that it is placed comfortably over the shoulders and upper back where the muscular and skeletal structure of the dog is the strongest. They are called backpacks, but the majority of the weight is not on the center of the dog's back.

The panniers should be packed with even weight so the pack stays balanced.

DOG PACK

Dog packs are made with a variety of materials. The material should have sufficient weight so that it keeps its shape when packed and it does not easily tear. There should also be some sort of padding on the top of the saddle as well as around the buckles on the straps that hold the pack on the dog.

Buddy, a multi-champion Alaskan Malamute owned and bred by the author is wearing a Wolf Pack Banzai™ dog pack.
Photo by Charlene G. LaBelle.

The number of straps on the pack differs somewhat with the construction of the individual pack. The pack should have one strap that goes across the front of the chest to hold the panniers in and forward and one that goes just behind the front legs. A third strap that is towards the belly works well. Buckles are often padded for extra protection.

Packs can be made with one or two-piece construction. A two-piece pack may have a pad or saddle the dog wears and the panniers are attached to the pad/saddle. Either one or two-piece packs can have extra pouches that can be attached to the outside of the pack. Some have a pouch that fits on the top and is a great place for a map or a snack.

TRAINING

Your dog should be introduced to the backpack. It should be shown the pack so that the pack is not something they fear.

I put crumpled up newspaper and a box of some dried goods like Mac-n-cheese in the packs to make a gentle noise as they walk. I gradually add more weight. My dogs love hiking and get very excited when they see a dog pack.

Your first trip with a pack on should be around the house, neighborhood or simply on a familiar walk.

Please don't expect your dog to hike with a full/heavy pack if you have never taken them hiking or had the pack on them before you get to the trail head.

WEIGHT

You do not want to overload your dog. A physically mature dog that is in condition will have no problem with 30% (1/3) of their body weight in their packs. I have hiked with dogs carrying close to 50% of their body weight in their packs and the dog was not stressed or overloaded.

For introduction or training, start with 20-25% or less of the dog's body weight in a material that is well balanced and will not poke or shift. Young dogs should carry less than a physically mature dog to not put undue stress on their growing joints. This is not to say you have to leave your young dogs at home. Just be careful with their developing joints if they are under 12 months or 24 months of age. Different breeds and dogs develop at different rates. Conditioning is key.

When you are packing the panniers, adjust the weight your dog carries to their age, strength and experience.

BALANCE

One of the most important things is to balance the load. I tend to pack an item of like bulk and weight in each side. I also hook a metal pail to the outside to be used at rest stops. This pail can be used to fine tune the balancing.

CONTENTS

If the item can be damaged by water, you need to protect it by putting it in a plastic bag (hint: use the heaviest or thickest bags you can find. These are usually sold as freezer bags.) Plastic bags that can be sealed work best.

We pack cook stoves, cook kits, sturdy food, water, dog food, trail mix, dried fruit etc. in the dog's packs. Pretty much anything that can not be easily broken or punctured. I do not put freeze dried backpacker's food in a dog's pack. I do not like food that is a fine powder when I open the package. If you pack a sandwich, make sure it's in a squish proof container or you will be eating flattened food.

Always carry some emergency supplies. You want items pro-tected that can be damaged if they get wet because your dog WILL find puddles to lay in or creeks to cross. Letting them relax in the water is a great way to cool them off.

We carry first aid supplies in both the dog's packs and our own. There are emergency items you should always carry and there are additional items you will want to add depending on where you are hiking.

Don't put all your survival gear in the dog's pack, there is always a chance that you will become separated from your dog. Or your dog will lose their pack. Matches are something you should have in multiple places.

If we are planning to be out overnight I pack a section of chain for each dog. This chain is a means of securing them in camp. I will frequently use a piece of rope around a tree and secure the chain to the rope. I try to do little, if any, damage to the bark of the tree.

FEEDING

I feed my dogs a light meal at the trail head prior to getting ready to leave. This way they eat and relax while I am busy preparing all our gear. I like to feed food with more calories when we hike. Once we reach camp, my dogs normally go to sleep while we set up camp. I feed them after I prepare my own dinner.

I feed a morning meal in camp before I tear down and pack up our camp. This is usually before I eat my own breakfast or while the coffee is perking.

TRAIL MANNERS

This is a BIGGIE for me. It's the irresponsible owner that has ruined it for all the dog lovers and made it that so many places are closed to dogs. Do all that you can to make your dog an asset to the back county or on the trail. This could be packing out other people's trash. This is how my dog's pack got to be almost 50% of his weight.

1. ALWAYS remove poop from the trail.

2. Be respectful of others. Always treat fellow hikers with respect, many can be afraid of dogs. Let fellow hikers have their space.

3. Do not camp next to a water source. Get your water and set up camp so that water is easily accessible to other hikers and the wildlife whose home you are visiting.
4. Do not let your dog chase wildlife or other animals.
5. When you leave, leave the area in the same shape or in better shape than when you arrived. Leave only your footprints. Good sense is still your best guide.

Much of the National Forest is still used for open range (grazing). Range cattle-chasing or sheep-chasing dogs can be shot with no warning. An irate range cow can wipe out a dog with a head butt, horn or hoof.

REGULATIONS

The National Park Service has rules about dogs in National Parks. Basically none may be taken on trails – anywhere. At this time I know of only one National Park that allows dogs on the trails. So, if you are planning on hiking in a National Park with a dog, it's best if you check ahead. You might find out dogs are not allowed.

The U.S. Forest Service has individual restrictions here and there, but generally dogs under control are welcome. MOST have leash laws. The U.S. Bureau of Land Management (BLM) share the Forest Service's attitude about dogs. If there is any question about dogs being permitted in an area, check before you start.

A Guide to Backpacking With Your Dog (LaBelle) has a lot more details for people that are interested in pursuing more of the back country experience. This section is to help you become aware of yet another activity you and your dog(s) can enjoy together.

Happy trails!

Dogs can be quite helpful to the wilderness camper. The family pet that has been trained to pull a load on a sled will be a great addition to your snow country outing.

Any breed of dog that is in sufficient shape and willing to pull your belongings will do. Breeds such as the Alaskan Malamutes are particularly suited to this form of recreation. The breed has a natural willingness to work and the strength to pull a load. Most Malamutes rarely get frustrated if they must go slowly and they like to spend the night curled up in the snow.

For a harness a weight pull harness works quite well for a single dog pulling a sled or toboggan. A racing harness (X-back) or a recreational harness (no X in the back) will also work for this purpose.

Use a sturdily constructed sled, one that will hold all your gear, without getting too tall. Many sleds not much heavier than racing sleds have traveled the thousand mile Iditarod race trail from Anchorage to Nome. The main point about the sled is that it should have a long enough basket to stow all of your gear without getting top heavy.

A hardwood toboggan can be used as a freighting sled for the purpose of hauling gear. Most toboggans weigh approximately 40 pounds and are easy for a large dog to pull. Of course, it would be suitable for only certain trails and the musher would have to be on skis or snowshoes.

Pack your gear in a bag or with a tarp to hold everything together. The tarp or bag is also to keep snow from getting into everything. Tie the load down securely so that you won't lose anything should the sled or toboggan overturn. Pack heavy items as low in the sled as you can. By keeping the weight low, you will have less chance of overturning the load.

Carefully pick the area and trails you wish to travel. Do not plan a long trek the first day on your first trip. Set your trip up with plenty of time. Go slow and easy to avoid sweating or overheating yourself.

If you are planning an overnight trip, make sure to have plenty of time build a camp or arrive in camp before the temperatures drop.

Be prepared for drastic weather changes. Have extra supplies for emergencies, especially extra matches and food. And don't forget safety rules and safety equipment. Go out there. Have fun. Enjoy quality time with your dog.

Happy camping!

Sally Meyner and *Poppy* on a snow camping trip. *Photo by Gus Meyner.*

Chapter Thirty-Nine
SKIJORING

Ski·jor·ing (sk jôr ng, -jr-) n. [modif. of Norw skikjøring, fr. ski + kjøring driving]: A sport in which a person wearing skis is drawn over snow by one or more dogs.

Skijoring started with the Fins, Laplanders, Norwegians and Swedes. Skijoring can been done using horses and reindeer as well as dogs. Currently when someone uses the term skijor, it's a skier pulled over snow by one or more dogs.

You can think of skijoring as dog sledding without a sled. It is a sport that the person with a single dog can take up. Still there are a few important things to be aware of. It is very important that you are a competent skier prior to taking up the sport.

At one time skijoring was slapping on a pair of skis and holding the end of the leash. Actually that will work, but to have a really good time and to reduce the risk of injury, you need to have some training and the right equipment.

EQUIPMENT
You will want a harness for your dog, skis (with boots and poles) and a means of connecting you and your dog.

Harness
The style of harness you use will depend on your dog, but a x-back or a recreational harness work best. This way the tow line is not under the tail of the dog, like it would be with a freight harness.

Skis
Most people use cross country skis and it is highly recommended to use skis that do NOT have metal edges. Many races require the skis NOT have metal edges. This is for the safety of you and your dog(s). The thought behind this ruling is a safety

issue. Metal edges can cut flesh.

There are many types of skis on the market these days. You can purchase skis with bases you need to wax and skis with bases that are waxless. There are skating skis and mountaineering skis. Skis have become a specialized piece of equipment. Become familiar with the use of your equipment before you think of hooking up to your dog.

Skijor Belt

There are many commercial skijor belts on the market these days. In the early days people simply held the tow line. This progressed to attaching a line to you. Thick belts, rock climbing harnesses and even a "diaper" made with webbing were used.

The skijor belt is worn low and around your hips. The dog or dogs are connected with a tow line to a point in the front and center of the belt. Most people use some form of a quick release between the tow line and the skijor belt. This way they can let the dog free if they are about to take a tumble or the dog goes on one side of a tree and they ski on the other.

Skijor belts, like all other equipment, are constantly changing to improve the feel and performance.

Tow Line

If you are running a single dog, you connect your line from the loop at the back of the dog's harness to the skijor belt. If you are hooking up to two dogs you can use a two dog or double leader section (or you can hook them one behind the other in single file). If you use a double leader section, you will need to lengthen the distance from the dog to you. Think of it as adding a tail to the section, making it a "Y". The back of the closest dog should be nine to ten feet in front of you. A line that is too short may have you too close to your dog. If you are too close you don't have time to react to a sudden stop or change of direction. Basically the added distance allows for reaction time.

These days, most commercially purchased skijor towlines have a piece of shock cord (*Bungee* cord™) incorporated inside the tow line. This shock cord is in the last couple feet closest to the person. This keeps the jolt easier on both the dogs and the skier.

COMMANDS

When you first start out, basic obedience commands will work. But as you gain experience, you will want to refine the commands you use. There are sections on Training a Leader as well as Commands that you will want to review to help with training.

One of the hardest things when starting may be to get your dog to stay out in front of you, keeping the line taunt. Keeping the line taunt without pulling you over is something else you will want to teach them.

Your dog should understand some sort of a *whoa* command. The command *easy* is also quite helpful. *Come!* when called is also something your dog should do.

Additional or added training is advised. Especially for hook-up and clearing tangles. With work, your dogs should be reasonably calm for starting (not lunging) and stopping, as well as patience while you clear tangles. This is important because you are attached to the dog the entire time.

NUMBER OF DOGS

Skijoring is usually done with one to three dogs. There are people that are more talented (or some say crazy) that will hook up more than three dogs. If you have more than one dog, you can run the dogs in a single file or you can connect them like you would a team (side by side). It's best if you don't take more dogs than you can safely handle.

There are people that have dogs they train specifically for skijoring and only enter skijor classes. There are other people that will take dogs right from their racing sled team, put on skis and skijor.

BONUS

With dog power you and your dogs can get farther away from the trail head than most people with only snow shoes and cross country skis. You and your dog can enjoy the time well spent together, working as a team. Both of you getting exercise while spending quality time together.

ADDITIONAL READING

The Internet is a wealth of articles. There are several fine books on the market dedicated to skijoring such as *Skijor With Your Dog* by Mari Hoe-Raitto and Carol Kaynor.

Have fun, take your time. Be careful and patient. If you are starting with an untrained dog, the first couple hook ups may be difficult for your dog to understand it's okay to pull. But once they learn it is okay to pull when wearing a harness you are ready to head for the trail. Then once they get the hang of it ... HANG ON and enjoy the tow!

Mike Callahan, the first ever ISDRA gold Medallist in Skijor (first and second years). *Photo by Bruce T. Smith.*

Chapter Fourty 40
BIKEJORING

Basically bikejoring is skijoring using a bicycle. Your dogs are hooked to the bicycle and they pull you along the trail. This is a very simplistic definition and there is equipment you need to have.

Photo by Filip Chludil – www.fchfoto.cz

BICYCLE

Most people will bikejor with a mountain bike. But any sturdy bicycle with an excellent breaking system will do. Chain off or on is up to you. But with the chain on, you can help on the uphill or crossing streams.

During the learning process, if you don't have the coordination, you may want to devise a means to keep the towline from getting tangled in the bicycle wheel until the time you do have the coordination. Some people bend wire to make something to hold the lines clear, others use a ski pole and run the line through the basket of the pole (the pole is attached to the bicycle).

Another inexpensive method can be accomplished by slipping the towline through a short ridged hollow tube. A piece of

PVC (plastic pipe used for garden sprinkler systems) works quite well. A small hole at the end closest to your bicycle with a string run through it, tying it to the bicycle, can be used to keep the pipe from being able to slide down the line towards the dogs. The plastic pipe should not be so long that it could reach the ground when connected to your bicycle. This piece of plastic pipe is simply to help keep the lines out of your front bicycle tire while you and your dog are figuring out what to do.

Once you and your dog have a bit of trail sense or you get the hang of holding your line out of the way, remove the piece of pipe (or whatever you were using during the learning process) and try it without the pipe.

Please be careful. Wear protective clothing and gear. Eye wear and helmets are also good to wear. You will be surprised how much dirt your dog can kick up while running full speed ahead.

Chapter Forty-One

CANICROSS

The term canicross is of European origin. Canicross is cross-country hiking or running with your dog. Canicross is not simply walking a dog wearing a harness. Running with your dog on a leash is not canicross either. In canicross the dog is pulling you as you keep up behind them.

Canicross uses equipment similar or even the same equipment you use for skijoring.

Many people that canicross use ski poles since their hands are free. Using ski poles when canicrossing will give your upper body muscles a work out as well. If you move the pole as you do when skijoring (poling), you will help maintain the muscles you use while skijoring.

Photo by Filip Chludil –
www.fchfoto.cz

289   MUSH!

PULKA

This has not yet caught on in the USA, but pulka driving (or Nordic-style dog mushing) involves skijoring with a small sled (pulk) attached either between skijorer and dog or with the skijorer between the dog and the pulk.

A pulk is an efficient option for carrying supplies over a distance as opposed to wearing a backpack. Many backwoods skijorers and distance racers frequently include pulks in their varied pieces of equipment they own and use.

In Scandinavia, pulka driving is very popular. This includes racing. There are pulks specifically designed to give children rides or to carry them while Mom and Dad drive the dogs.

A pulk can be pulled behind a skijorer instead of between the dog and skier. This is done by attaching longer shafts to the pulk, which are connected to a modified skijoring belt.

When the pulk is between the skier and the dog, the dog is hooked to the pulk with ridged shafts. When the skier is between the pulk and the dog, the ridged shafts for the pulk are attached to the skier.

2001 IFSS Nordic World Championships in Alaska, short (13 km) pulka silver medalist Olivier Traulie from France. Olivier also took the silver in the long pulka.
Photo by Andrea Swingley - www.outdoor-exposures.com.

291   MUSH!

Chapter Fourty-Three

NUTRITION

Proper nutrition is very important for any athlete. Our working dogs are athletes in every way. Sled dogs are unique animals in regard to feeding since they expend a great deal of energy in a relatively short period of time. This energy must be replaced daily to assure good performance.

There are many options for the modern dog driver as to what they choose to feed. Whatever they feed, the goal is to supply a balanced diet for their dogs.

Many people have dogs that are outstanding athletes and are fed a quality commercial made kibble with little or no supplementation. Others purchase nutritionally balanced food, most are predominantly meat, which is bought frozen and then fed thawed, but still raw. Still others will mix their own raw food (commonly called a B.A.R.F. diet).

Most competitive mushers feed a combination of quality commercial kibble and some form of finely ground raw meat. Fine ground chicken is one of the most common meats, but beef, beaver, fish, moose, and just about anything else you can think of has been used depending on what is available or common in your region.

Part of the feeding process is to soak the meat and kibble with water. Soaking can be from a half hour to overnight. The meals are fed as an easily digestible mush to their dogs. This style of feeding has the added benefit of making sure your dog is getting enough water into their system daily. The downside is you will lose any benefit your dog may gain to its teeth from crunching up hard kibble and tartar may build up. To remedy this, if you notice build up, is give your dog something to chew on such as a raw bone.

There are now some manufacturers that are making commercial kibble that needs no additional raw meat or other supplementation to maintain top performance at the advanced level.

Feeding is an individual choice based largely on what is available in your region and what your dog enjoys eating. New and experienced mushers alike should constantly read bag labels and ask questions from as many mushers as they can.

The bottom line is you need to feed whatever YOUR dogs do well on. Minimally you want to maintain body weight and muscle mass. It is very important to feed something your dog will eat and that you can handle safely. If you feed anything raw, make sure to practice safe handling of raw meat, especially in warm weather or while traveling when there is no refrigeration.

Some breeds of dog need more to eat than others do. The Hound crosses that are popular need more calories to maintain body weight than big dogs like an Alaskan Malamute who has a slower metabolism. Several years ago, a team of Bob and Nancy Russell's AKC Malamutes ran part of the Iditarod with Jaime Nelson. The dogs weighed twice what most of the other team's dogs weighed. But the Malamute team packed in just over half the food. Those dogs maintained body weight on the smaller ration.

To determine if your dog's diet is adequate, several things must be watched. They must generally look healthy. Check weekly to make sure that their weight is maintained and they are not getting fat or thin. You should always be able to feel ribs. You may have to feel through their coat, but you should be able to feel ribs.

HYDRATION

Hydration is something that many people overlook. It's just as important for you as it is for your dogs. And it is more important than feeding, as you and your dog can last much longer without food than you can without water.

Hydration doesn't happen in one day. To keep your dogs properly hydrated you can think of it as a puzzle. If you get all the pieces right, you have a dog that performs at its best.

At home most people have dogs with water available to them all day long. When traveling this may not be so easy to do. It's your job to make sure your dog gets plenty of water. There will be times you will need to trick your dog into drinking more water that they want. This is done by a means referred to as baiting the water or giving them baited water.

Baited water can be cool clear fluid with a few pieces of kibble floating in the water. Kind of like bobbing for apples, but your dog will drink the water going after the kibble. If kibble is not a high enough value item, then you can add meat.

Baited water can be a couple spoons full of canned food added to a bucket of water. Canned fish works well as does canned cat food. And canned cat food can be purchased in little pouches you tear to open. Whatever you use, your goal is to make a flavored light broth.

For a dog in the 50-pound range you will be trying to get four to eight cups of liquid into your dog approximately two hours before you train. You will give approximately the same amount after you run. And if you have a long training run, you may want to give baited water on the trail as well. If your dog has access to water all day long, the baited water should do the trick to get the additional fluids into them.

If you feed soaked food, this is another way to get fluids into your dog. Many mushers will feed a soupy meal. Some will make a soupy snack on the trail and heat it. They will ladle warm liquid onto fresh snow in front of each dog. Their dogs will eat the soup and a bit of extra snow (moisture) trying to get every morsel.

Take care of yourself too! You need to make sure you are eating and drinking enough. If you are not taking care of yourself, you can't adequately care for your dogs.

By now you should be thinking: How do I tell if they are getting enough water? One way to tell if your dog is getting sufficient fluids is to look at their urine. A well-hydrated dog will have almost clear urine. If their urine is dark yellow in color, then that is a sign that you should be trying to get them to drink additional liquids.

Another way to check hydration is by a skin test. This test is not scientific but it does work without needing any supplies. Try this at home so you know what is normal for your dog. You will gently grab some skin along the backbone (close to the collar/neck works well). Lift the skin and then let go. With a dog that is NOT dehydrated, the skin will snap back into place. You are not lifting a lot of skin and you are not lifting very far.

You lift just enough to be able to tell if the skin rapidly returns to normal. If the skin seems sticky or is slow to return to normal, your dog is dehydrated and it's time to make sure your dog drinks some water... NOW.

Dark pee... give water. Skin does not bounce back rapidly... give water. Hydrate yourself as well. If you don't take care of yourself, you can't take care of your dogs.

If your dog becomes dehydrated, it can take several days to bring them back to normal. Keep in mind that overheating a dog (which can be caused by being dehydrated) is a serious and potentially life-threatening condition for a dog. While running your team, ALWAYS monitor each dog constantly for any change to their mental attitude or signs of stress such as tripping, lagging, wide-open-mouth breathing or anything else that is unusual for that dog. Remember, an ounce of prevention is the best cure!

Drink up!

Chapter Fourty-Four

SAFETY ON THE TRAIL

Whenever you hook up your dogs, it is your responsibility to watch out for their well being. Their safety is on your shoulders alone. You are responsible for their feeding, veterinary care, transport and training. It is solely your responsibility to determine if your dogs are ready to enter a race. If you feel conditions are not right for your dogs, pull your entry. Don't risk their health or safety. There will always be another race.

THE IMPORTANCE OF SANCTIONING

When you enter a race that is sanctioned by a sanctioning body, there are expectations that are set. You will be able to access the rules that will be used. You will have ideas of what to expect for the trail.

As you watch team after team leave the starting chute at a race, it normally looks quite organized and you might think it looks pretty simple. But it's not all that simple. There are a group of well trained volunteers that follow rules set by a sanctioning body. By following the rules and written procedures, what looks like a chaotic scene in the staging area and dog truck area become a safe race.

This all begins with some sanctioning body and their rules, regulations, guidelines and other miscellaneous printed matter. Many clubs sanction with the International Sled Dog Racing Association (ISDRA) and use their race rules. Clubs that don't sanction with ISDRA may use rules that are quite similar to ISDRA rules.

Race rules were designed to promote animal welfare and safe conditions for both dog and driver. Rules have always been part of any competition, including sled dog racing.

In 1909, The All Alaska Sweepstakes in Nome, Alaska was one of the first, if not the first, major sled dog race. Before the race, a full set of rules was drafted. These race rules were implemented to safeguard dogs and mushers alike.

ISDRA sanctioned races must comply with ISDRA's rules and regulations that dictate everything from trail length and layout to mandatory safety equipment to canine fitness.

In order to become an ISDRA sanctioned race, an application process is followed, a notification process, as well as detailed trail requirements, etc. The race course must comply with ISDRA rules. The basic premises governing all, including the trail design, is a concern for safety. For example, for trail design:

The trail must not endanger dog teams or drivers.

All avoidable hazards must be avoided.

Difficult passages should never be accepted when an easier passage is possible.

Distances should be both sensible for conditions and accurately described in publicity.

All hazards that can not be avoided must be clearly marked.

Even the turns are clearly marked with an ISDRA designated marking system that forewarns the driver of an upcoming turn.

ISDRA's trail design rules insure that even a musher who has traveled across the country or around the globe to run a race will know what to expect on the trail. These rules also enable the musher and the dogs to train for the conditions they will encounter.

ISDRA race rules are designed to safeguard sled dogs on and off the trail. For example: Abuse of dogs is strictly prohibited. Anyone who is convicted of animal abuse or neglect shall be barred from racing.

The race officials have many duties to perform to insure that the rules are followed and insure a race is fun and safe for all. If the Race Marshall feels a team is unfit or incapable of safely running the race they can call for a veterinarian. If both feel the team is unfit or incapable of running a safe race, they must disqualify the team. Many races have a veterinarian at the site. If not, a veterinarian must be on call for all races. To prevent the spread of disease, the race veterinarian shall disqualify any team that includes a dog with a contagious disease.

ISDRA has strict doping or drug rules. Use of any substance (from steroids to aspirin) that may affect the performance of a dog is strictly prohibited. ISDRA rules provide for drug testing and disqualification.

The musher's equipment must comply with race rules. For example, the sled must be equipped with a basket and sled bag capable of safely carrying any dog that is too tired to complete the race. The use of choke collars, muzzles and other equipment that might be dangerous to the dogs are prohibited.

A driver may not leave a dog on the trail for someone else to pick up, nor may a driver replace a dog on the second day of the race with a new dog. This rule is intended to ensure that each dog team is well treated throughout the race.

While on the race course, the team must stay on the marked trail. Shortcuts are not only cheating, they pose unknown hazards to the teams. The rules also provide rules of the road including right of way requirements and passing rules to prevent collisions, as well as unnecessary tangles.

ISDRA race rules and sanctioning standards are designed and intended to ensure the health and safety of the canine athletes.

One of the jobs you can volunteer to do at a race is to be a checker. A checker is help on the trail and has simple ISDRA rules in which to follow.

INSTRUCTIONS FOR CHECKERS

Checking can be one of the most fun things you can do at a race... if you are not racing that is! You will be recruited by a race official, usually the Chief Checker, sometimes it's the Trail Boss.

Transportation to your assigned station will be arranged by the either the Chief Checker or the Trail Boss. It can be in a snow cat or on the back of a snow mobile.

Some corners will be within walking distance and you may walk out to them. When walking on the trail, try to not make holes in the trail. If the snow seems soft, walk beside the trail if possible.

If you have cross country skis or snow shoes, wear them to your corner. Remove them before the first team arrives, but you can stand on them while you wait between teams. Just do not have snowshoes or skis on while the teams are coming by. If your assistance is needed, you will need to unencumbered by either. Normally you are only out on the trail checking for one heat/class or distance.

Trail checker Charlene LaBelle in position as racer Paul Martin passes intersection with his Samoyeds. *Photo by Bruce T. Smith.*

As a checker and volunteer, you have a very important job for the success of a race. You will be standing at an intersection blocking the trail teams are NOT to take. If you rode out on a snowmobile, it may also be used to help block a trail. You may have a physical barrier the trail help may have set up. Your job is to be there if needed.

At your assigned intersection, teams may go out one way and come in another. If this is the case be prepared to go back and forth depending on whether teams are coming or going. The person that assigned you to the corner will let you know from which direction the teams will be coming and the direction they will be going. If you are a novice checker, it is unlikely that you will be assigned to a corner that is more than a turn onto or off of the main trail. Checkers at "gates" (places teams go multiple directions) are normally people familiar with racing.

TRAIL CHECKER DUTIES
As a checker you will find you have the best seats in the house. The duties are simple.
- Once assigned a corner or place on the trail, please stand

quietly and motionless as each teams passes. Your job is to discourage teams from taking the wrong trail. You may want to squat down and put your arms out to the sides as far as you can go, making yourself as wide as possible. You should get into position well before teams arrive. It's okay to move about as long as a team is not in view. If you see a team coming, it's time to "play statue."

- Please do not say anything to the dogs or the driver (or some teams may want to come say Hi!).
- Pick a place to stand and try to stand motionless as each team goes by. Stand in the same place for each team.
- Should a driver ASK or need help... you can hold the sled. Put your foot firmly on the brake and do not let off until told to do so. Do NOT touch any dogs or lines unless there is danger of injury to dog or driver.
- If a loose team comes your way, please do anything you can to stop them. Tip sled to side, tangle them in a tree, set the snow hook, stand on the brake... this rarely happens, but if you hear "LOOSE TEAM"...do everything in your power to catch them.
- You may be given a checker sheet listing the teams and their starting order, many times this is for your use. It will give you an idea how many more teams are left in the class. The info on the sheet MAY NOT be complete or accurate, since teams may have been added since this info was collected or teams may have chosen not to run. No new teams will be added on second or third days. If you have an official check off sheet you will be turning in, fill in the blanks and turn in when you return to the starting chute area. Do not leave your post until instructed to do so, which is normally when your ride comes for you.
- If something happens or you witness something while you are out on the trail and you are not sure if you should report it, quietly report it to an official and let them decide if action needs to be taken.
- IMPORTANT: IF YOU DIRECT A TEAM DOWN THE WRONG TRAIL, THE WHOLE CLASS RACE MAY HAVE TO BE DECLARED NULL AND VOID! This is different from a team taking the wrong trail. Should a team

take the wrong trail, make every effort to let the driver know they are on the wrong trail and help them to get on the right trail.

ASSISTANCE IN AN EMERGENCY

An emergency is defined as when a dog or person is hurt or in danger of being hurt.

In an emergency, you are encouraged to grab dogs, lines, untangle dogs or do anything in your power to stop or prevent dogs and drivers from injury or further injury.

An injured or frightened dog may bite so always approach cautiously. If you see a driver in trouble down the trail, go to their assistance. The driver will not be penalized for emergency assistance.

ABUSE OF DOGS AND INTERFERENCE

Drivers are not allowed to deliberately strike a dog, no matter how gently. They are allowed to cuss out their own dogs, but not the trail help!

Drivers are not allowed to interfere with another team.

ANY abuse of dogs or deliberate interference that you see anywhere on the trail should be noted and reported to the Race Marshal and/or the Chief Checker when you come in. Dog abuse is not tolerated. Quietly make what you witness known to a race official.

CHECK OFF DRIVERS WHICH PASS YOUR STATION

Some intersections will have an official check-off sheet that you will need to turn in. Other times you may be given a sheet for your own use. You will be told if you need to turn in your sheet. If you are filling out an official sheet, simply fill in the blanks. Identify each driver by the number they are wearing. Check off or list each one as they pass. All teams must cover the ENTIRE TRAIL.

When all teams have gone by in the last class, both coming and going, OR when you have been informed that the remaining teams have scratched or turned back, come on in by foot or snowmobile.

If you had an "official" vest, PLEASE return your vest to the Chief Checker. If you have not heard it enough... THANK YOU

FOR YOUR HELP!
ISDRA is mainly geared to the racer. They do welcome the
non-racer. There are groups such as Mush with P.R.I.D.E. that
welcome ANYONE interested in sled dogs.

MUSH WITH P.R.I.D.E.

P.R.I.D.E. stands for Providing Responsible Information on a
Dog's Environment.

The relationship between sled dogs and humans is one of the
oldest bonds of its kind. Modern sled dog owners are proud of
their dogs as canine athletes that are bred and trained to do what
they love: run as part of a team.

Mush with P.R.I.D.E. supports the responsible care and
humane treatment of all dogs and is dedicated to enhancing the
care and treatment of sled dogs in their traditional and modern
uses. Specifically, Mush with P.R.I.D.E. was founded to:

- Establish guidelines for proper sled dog care and treatment.
- Facilitate communication among dog mushers about the
  treatment and care of sled dogs.
- Educate young people about sled dogs and mushing
  through existing youth groups and schools.
- Enhance the care of sled dogs by the development of
  improved husbandry and veterinary practices.
- Promote public understanding about the care, treatment,
  and traditional and modern uses of sled dogs.
- Welcome and assist beginning mushers.

P.R.I.D.E as an organization includes a wide variety of mushers, including recreational and professionals, long-distance and
sprint racers, weight pullers, skijorers, and freight haulers, as
well as sled dog veterinarians and other concerned citizens.
Mush with P.R.I.D.E was formed for people to work together
toward common goals.

P.R.I.D.E. publishes sled dog care guidelines and a first aid manual. They promote a kennel inspection and certification program.

To join Mush with P.R.I.D.E., go to their web site:
http://www.mushwithpride.org or just send your name,
address, phone number, and membership dues to:

Mush with P.R.I.D.E.
P.O. Box 84915
Fairbanks, AK 99708-4915 USA

ISDRA and P.R.I.D.E. have and welcome members from anywhere on the globe.

For additional information on ISDRA, go to their website: http://www.isdra.org or write to:

ISDRA
22702 Rebel Road
Merrifield, MN 56465 USA

Chapter Fourty-Five

THE DOG YARD

Many people say that sled dogs are like potato chips. You can't stop at one. The following was contributed by SNDD member Rob Loveman. It will give you some idea what you have to look forward to as you get more and more dogs.

SETTING UP A DOG YARD

The overwhelming majority of your dogs' lives will be spent in the dog yard. As a musher, you'll spend about as much time in the dog yard taking care of the dogs as you will on the trail. Even if you allow your entire team in the house (some mushers do this, some don't), the dogs are going to need a place to eat, sleep, play and relieve themselves. At least some of these are going to occur in the dog yard.

Designing a dog yard that is safe, comfortable for you and your dogs, and allows you to efficiently take care of the dogs is clearly important. Safety is a requirement. Comfort for you and your dogs may not be a requirement in the same sense as safety, but it makes pursuing the sport of mushing that much more fun. Finally, even small differences in efficiency are very worthwhile. Saving ten minutes every feeding is an extra hour a week, and during mid-mushing season when time is extremely limited, this is absolutely critical.

DESIGN CONSIDERATIONS

Safety is one if not the most important consideration in designing a dog yard. First and foremost is keeping the dogs from wandering off. Inevitably, chains and other hardware fail. The only way to avoid this is to both buy high quality hardware and to replace pieces regularly so that they aren't worn to the point of failure. Even with this regimen, occasional failure will take place. If the yard is unfenced, this gives the dogs the opportunity to wander. If the yard is fenced, but there is no separation between intact males and females, unwanted matings are a likely consequence. Conversely, any fencing is at least a significant initial cost in setting up a kennel.

Among the sled dogs are Siberian Huskies. These dogs are certainly considered by their owners to be the kings and queens of the art of escape. For Siberians or other sled dogs that don't jump fences, a six-foot fence is a minimum. For Siberians and sleddogs that do jump fences, put up a seven-foot fence and hope that it works. Additionally, these dogs are particularly adept at digging out. Usually what happens here is that a dog digs a "nest" adjacent to a fence and discovers that this hole is a ticket to freedom. A lot of grief can be eliminated by making sure no nests give the dog an opportunity to learn that they can dig their way to the promised land. Once a dog learns this, it certainly will never be unlearned.

Even in fenced dog yards, the dogs are often tethered. There are a number of advantages for this. The first separation is going to be between males and females. If that is the only fencing to separate dogs, all the dogs of a single sex will be in a single yard together. Fights will be likely.

In larger kennels, it is inevitable that some of the dogs will simply not like each other. When the dogs are not being supervised, the ones that don't get along must be kept separated, or they will fight. Even in smaller kennels where a single pack structure will keep the dogs from fighting too often, there is a lot of efficiency gained by having dogs tethered. All sleddogs like to pull, but a lot of them do not like being harnessed. Even if a dog has no objections to being harnessed, he can decide that a good game of chase is a great idea right before a run. Even in a small yard, a dog can keep a person from catching them as long as they want to.

Finally, tethering the dogs means that the musher knows whose feces is whose. This is one of the quick ways that mushers know if their dogs are healthy or not, and which dogs are having problems.

Among the key considerations for designing a dog yard is the ability to do the chores necessary to take care of the dogs. The primary daily chores are watering the dogs, feeding the dogs, and cleaning the yard.

Dogs need a considerable amount of water for their well being. Like people, the onset of severe dehydration can occur quickly (less than one day) and is quite dangerous. In a temperate climate, clean water can simply be left out for the dogs to drink whenever they feel like it. Sometimes, the musher may want to pull the water one to several hours before a training run. If the weather is below freezing, the water cannot be left out and the dogs have to drink it when it's placed in front of them. Under these conditions, the water is usually baited so that the dogs drink it all.

The ease with which the water can be given to the dogs is a significant consideration in designing a dog yard, particularly its location and layout. In a moderate climate, a faucet in the yard may be the most convenient way to do this. Any hoses in the yard should be kept out of reach of the dogs; many dogs eat hoses. In colder climates, the water will be coming from indoors where the temperature is above freezing. Bathtubs or any other faucet with clearance enough for a big bucket are likely to be the source.

A hose can be attached to a faucet that doesn't have good clearance, and this can be used to fill buckets or other large containers so that water can be given to the dogs. In a pinch, the spray tool on a kitchen sink can also be used, but this has two drawbacks. The first is that the overall water flow is low. The second is that somebody has to hold the switch on the spray tool, though a band of some sort that slips over the switch could be fashioned to accomplish this.

The location and layout considerations for feeding are similar to those for watering. Among other things, many mushers mix water with food and/or use feeding as an additional watering. The one difference between feeding and watering is where the food is stored. If the primary food is kibble, storage is generally pretty easy. The two concerns regarding kibble are keeping the food dry and keeping animals, primarily rodents, out of the food.

If meat is included in the diet, food storage is more complicated. In general, the meat is kept frozen until a day or two before the dogs are to eat it. At that time, the meat is thawed. At feeding time, the thawed food is mixed with whatever the musher wants to mix it with; dried dog food, supplements, water, etc., and then given to the dogs. The locations for the freezer, thawing the food, and mixing the food should all be considered while laying out the dog yard. Finally, making sure the dogs can eat their food without getting into fights is an important safety consideration.

The cleanliness of a musher's dog yard is a good measure of how well he takes care of his dogs. Because they have a limited area to relieve themselves, dogs living on tethers should have their yards cleaned at least once a day. Depending on the size of the confinement area for untethered dogs, cleaning may be required frequently or very infrequently.

In snow country, cleaning the yard is rather time consuming as the feces tends to freeze into the snow and ice. Shovels and/or other metal digging tools are necessary. Actually digging out and picking up the excrement takes the overwhelming majority of the time. When there isn't snow, most of the time in cleaning the yard is taken up by moving around rather than the action of picking up the excrement. For winter cleaning, the layout should allow easy access to shovels and other tools. For summer cleaning, the layout should allow the musher to move through the entire yard quickly and easily.

The surface of the dog yard is important for a number of reasons. The ease with which the yard can be cleaned is key among them. Drainage is also a key. Other important considerations are that it should be healthy for the dogs' pads and that if ingested, it won't hurt the dogs.

Most mushers prefer gravel or sand because they clean relatively easily and they drain very well. Arguably, turf in a sandy soil would work well. Depending on your dogs' digestion systems and how much they like to eat grass, having grass available all the time may be a plus or a minus. The primary difficulty with turf is that it needs a fair amount of work to maintain.

One final consideration regarding yard cleanliness is how the excrement is to be disposed. If the musher owns a significant amount of land, there will always be a place to simply dump and let it decay. If the musher has a small kennel, the excrement can be included in the trash. Regardless of how the waste is to be disposed, it is going to have to be transported either frequently or as a significant load, and this is a consideration for dog yard location.

The ideal location for a musher's yard allows the dogs to be hooked up nearby to train. During late summer and/or fall, mushers typically use some sort of gig or ATV for training. During late fall and winter, this means a sled. The further the hook-up area is from where the dogs live, the more time each and every hook-up takes.

If the musher has to truck his dogs to run them, it is absolutely critical that the truck can be brought near the yard. Again, the further the yard is from where the truck can be parked, the longer it takes to load and unload dogs. This is a particularly critical consideration as it affects both loading and unloading of dogs and any inefficiency is doubled.

If the hook-up and/or loading area can be part of a fenced-in area that includes the kennels, tremendous efficiency can be gained. In a fenced-in area, even the escape artists in a kennel can be taught to head to their spots. If none of the dogs are likely to wander, there is no need for fencing.

The gain in efficiency comes because handling the dogs, for example with a leash, isn't necessary. This allows several dogs to be moved at once. A lot of the time it takes to hook-up or unhook the team is taken simply by the musher moving back and forth from the hook-up spot to the kennel. If the number of trips is dropped, this time can be shortened considerably.

Many mushers swear by the advantages gained by letting their dogs run freely without tethers or lines. For dogs intent on exploring new worlds, this will require a fenced-in area. For dogs that will stay with the pack, this can be done as a group walk or run.

Mushers and dogs interested in the pack walk may face significant legal restrictions. There are few urban and suburban areas in the country that do not require dogs to be leashed. In rural areas, it is generally legal for a farmer to protect his or her animals against a dog attack by shooting an attacking dog. This having been said, there are areas that are sufficiently remote and whole kennels of dogs that are sufficiently bound to the pack that free running is easy either by walking the dogs or riding slowly in a vehicle such as an ATV. If the group walk/run is useable, there is little to consider in the yard design.

If the dogs are to be let free in a fenced-in area, there are several important considerations. A separate yard from the living area is usually quite desirable. The primary advantage of separate play and living areas is that the musher can choose which dogs play together as a group. Fights and unplanned matings can be prevented this way.

If there is a separate play yard, it is convenient to have it connected to the living area so that dogs do not have to be leashed and walked for significant distances between the two areas. This saves a lot of time. Ultimately, using the yard the dogs live in as a play yard as well is faster, but as noted above it means that all of the dogs will be in contact with each other, and this may not be desirable.

Another consideration is the proximity of the dog yard to the musher's house. Certainly, many mushers' kennels are separate from where they live and this works out fine. However yards even a couple of minutes from a musher's house are less efficient than those adjacent to the house. Between the time it takes to get from the house to the dog yard and the time it takes to set everything up to minimize the number of trips between the house and the yard, even a short distance between the dog yard and the house can end up costing half an hour a day or more.

Each dog living outside should have a sheltered area in which it can sleep. Depending on the dogs' personalities, this may mean an area it can call its own or it may not. Many dogs will choose to sleep with buddies given the opportunity. If the dogs are tethered, each dog must have its own house. Sharing is no longer an option as the tethers will likely become tangled. If the dogs are free in kennels, enough houses or sheltered area should be available for the dogs to either bunk together or separately, depending on their taste and for that matter their mood at the time.

The main requirement for the sheltered area is that it be dry under any and all weather conditions. If there is no natural shade, there should be constructed sheltered areas that provide this as well. Finally, it should be noted that most dogs like cramped shelters. Many dog owners have been astounded when they give their dogs big, beautiful doghouses only to find that the dogs have crammed themselves in some nook under the porch.

Legal considerations are also important. Laws pertinent to owning a kennel vary from almost non-existent to very stringent. While many mushers ignore laws regarding the number of dogs allowed on a piece of property and have no problems, they are certainly more vulnerable to legal problems. Inevitably, these become an issue when there is a neighbor who doesn't like dogs. Consideration for how the sound travels from the yard may be a legal requirement and certainly can prevent neighborhood disagreements. Additionally, if the musher wishes to obtain a kennel permit, there may be legal requirements for the yard such as for its surface or for a fence.

The last consideration is cost. Good fencing is never inexpensive. Cheaper mediocre fencing may prevent a quick mad rush from the dog yard, but certainly won't keep a determined dog from breaking out. The larger the area, the more it is going to cost. By comparison tethers are quite inexpensive.

DESIGN VARIATIONS

The least expensive yard has no fencing and consists of tethers and houses for each of the dogs. A platform for the doghouse to sit on is a nice addition and not very expensive. It is usually desirable for the platform to be between one and two feet off of the ground. Several drop lines, including one near the hook up area, are desirable if not necessary.

Tethers should be at least four to five feet long. They should be arranged so the dogs don't get themselves tangled either with each other or with posts and so forth. Either the dogs have to be savvy about keeping from being tangled in the legs of any platform, or boards have to be nailed between pairs of legs so that the dogs cannot wrap themselves around a leg (two boards on opposite sides of the platform are all that are needed).

Finally, tethers can easily be arranged so dogs can touch each other and yet so that they cannot be tangled. As long as the tips of the snaps at the end of tethers cannot touch, the dogs hooked on those tethers cannot get tangled. A side note, depending on the spacing, adjacent dogs can still mate.

While fencing seems like a very high cost, because it is a

one-time expense, the cost will end up being only a small portion of taking care of your dogs. As pointed out earlier, it is inevitable that hardware on tethers fails. Males realizing that there's a female in heat certainly will test the hardware. Without fencing, failures can result in unwanted matings, fights, and missing dogs.

Ideal fenced dog yards have multiple interconnected yards. How the yards are arranged and which ones are where is certainly a matter of taste. The primary considerations to remember are 1.) that the closer to the house everything is, the faster it is to do everything, 2.) interconnecting all yards almost always results in a significant time savings and 3.) if the dogs are being run from the dog yard, one of the yards should be for hook-up. It should be noted that if the dogs can be trained to stay with the pack, interconnecting the yards is not necessary and a closed yard isn't necessary for hook-up.

Finally, using the musher's house as a part of the fencing has several plusses. First, it saves money on fencing material. Second, it means that the dog yard is adjacent to the house. This saves time and assuming there is adequate space in the house, means that water and food storage are easily available. Finally, given the right arrangement, the dog yard may be visible from the inside of the house. This has the advantage of allowing the musher to quickly check on the dogs and has the aesthetic of letting the musher spend time just watching the dogs as they interact.

Chapter Fourty-Six

ISDRA
MEDALISTS

Here is a list of ISDRA medals that SNDD members have won.

Member	Year	Event	Medal
Dottie Dennis	2004	Mid-distance (6-dog)	Bronze
Dottie Dennis	2005	Mid-distance (6-dog)	Bronze
Karen Gardella	1999	3-dog	Silver
Rick Meyer	1992	8-dog	Silver
Rick Meyer	1993	8-dog	Bronze
Kathy Miyoshi PB	2002	Mid-distance (6-dog)	Bronze
Lisa Sato	1999	3-dog	Gold
Barbara Schaefer PB	2002	Mid-distance (6-dog)	Gold
Barbara Schaefer PB	2003	Mid-distance (6-dog)	Silver
Barbara Schaefer PB	2005	Mid-distance (6-dog)	Gold
Gary Slattengren	1985	6-dog	Gold
Gary Slattengren	1986	6-dog	Silver
Gary Slattengren	1989	6-dog	Gold
Will Wanless	1980	3-dog	Bronze
Will Wanless	1998	3-dog	Gold
Lauren Wells	1998	3-dog	Bronze
Ralph Whitten	1993	8-dog	Silver
Ralph Whitten	1994	3-dog	Bronze
Ralph Whitten	1995	8-dog	Gold
Steve Whitten	1998	3-dog	Silver
Steve Whitten	1999	3-dog	Bronze

ISDRA gold medalist Barbara "Dog Drop" Schaefer with a pair of her Siberian Huskies. *Photo courtesy Barbara "Dog Drop" Schaefer.*

Rick Meyer with Tom, 1981, when Rick won SNDD's 5-dog championship. *Photo by Bob Levorsen.*

SNDD member Laura Crocker, 2002 ISDRA bronze medal winner. *Photo by Jane Smith.*

Rick Meyer (left) and Bob Levorsen (right). Rick is pictured with his Region 8 8-dog trophy made by Ginger Dunlap. *Photo submitted by Virginia Meyer.*

LEFT - SNDD member Kathy Miyoshi and her team, at the 2002 Snow Dog Super Mush in Conconcully, WA - the year Kathy won the ISDRA Bronze.

ABOVE - ISDRA medalist Steve Whitten with a 4-dog team.

LEFT - ISDRA gold medalist Ralph Whitten with an 8-dog team. *Photos by Bruce T. Smith.*

315   MUSH!

Adanac Sleds & Equipment
Jack Beckstrom
Address: PO Box 76, Olney, MT 59927
Phone: (406) 881-2909
Comments: Skijoring equipment, custom and pre-sized belts, harnesses, and lines.

Alpine Outfitters
Address: P.O. Box 1728, Marysville, WA 98270
Phone: (360) 659-3800
Email: sales@AlpineOutfitters.NET
Web Site: www.alpineoutfitters.net
Comments: Stock and custom harnesses, modular cable lines, skijoring, sleds, carts, etc.

A Wilderness Haven Inc.
Address: 9293 N Cty Rd E, Hayward WI 54843
Phone: (715) 634-1060
Email: wldhvn@cheqnet.net
Web Site: www.wildernesshaven.com
Comments: Classes in wilderness survival, driving dog teams, snowshoes and dogsled building. Build full size sleds and custom sleds, plus custom trophy sleds (hand tied with no nuts or bolts made of select Ash). * The John Bear Grease marathon race buys the custom sleds for their trophies every year.

Black Ice Inc
Address: 3620 Yancy Ave., New Germany, MN 55367-9311
Phone: (320) 485-4825
Fax: (320) 485-3352
Email: shilon@tds.net
Web Site: www.blackicedogsledding.com
Comments: Complete selection of sledding, skijoring, scooter-

ing, carting, and backpacking equipment, specialize in helping
beginners.

Black Star Kennels
Address: P.O. Box 22333, Minneapolis MN 55422-0333
Email: tom@blackstars.biz
Web Site: www.blackstars.biz
Comments: Supplies for all your needs.

Coldspot Feeds
Address: 910 Old Steese Hwy #A., Fairbanks, AK 99701
Phone: (907) 457-8555
Fax: (907) 457-8556
Email: info@coldspotfeeds.com
Web Site: www.coldspotfeeds.com
Comments: This is a really fun store to visit if you happen to be
in Fairbanks. They carry just about anything you could want for
skijoring or mushing.

Cudos Rigs Limited
Address: Bee Farm, Nuthampstead, Royston, Herts, SG8 8NB,
United Kingdom
Phone: +44 (0) 1763 848052
Web Site: www.cudosrigs.co.uk
Comments: Dry land racing, training rigs, scooters, spares, har-
nesses and rig bags. There are also second hand rigs available
occasionally.

Dogscooter
Address: 2524 S. 317th Street #201, Federal Way, WA 98003
Phone: (253) 839-1502
Email: daphne@dogscooter.com
Web Site: www.dogscooter.com
Comments: Scooters, sulkies, harnesses, dog scooter book.

Frank Hall Sleds
Address: 5875 McCrum Rd. Jackson, MI 49201
Phone: (517) 782-1786
Comment: Dog sleds (beginner to professional) and rigs, har-

nesses, ganglines, videos, books, etc.

Ikon Outfitters LTD
Address: 7597 Latham Road, Lodi, Wisconsin 53555-9526
Phone: (608) 592-4397
Web Site: www.ikonoutfitters.com
Comments: Supplies for all your needs.

Lost Creek General Services (Sometimes abbreviated to: LCGS)
Address: 96519 Kiska Lane, Coos Bay, OR 97420
Phone: (541) 267-6556
Email: mjflcgs@harborside.com
Web Site: www.trainingcarts.com
Comments: Builds and sells some of the toughest training carts
and scooters around.

Mushing Boot Camp
Jamie Nelson & Ann Stead
Address: 3033 Roberg Road, Duluth, MN. 55804-9611
Phone: (218) 525-2139
Web Site: www.mushingbootcamp.com
Comments: They train you to train your own dogs with your
equipment. They offer both one-day pull training clinics as well
as three-day boot camps. Classes are held all over the American
continent, see web page for locations and dates.

Never Summer Sled Dog Equipment
Leslie Fields
Address: 5623 West US HWY 34, Loveland, CO 80538
Phone: (970) 622-8658
Comments: Stock and custom harnesses, collars, anti-shock
neckline, shock cord, snow hooks, dog bags, booties, snaps, per-
formance dog foods, modular cable lines, skijoring, sleds, carts,
etc.

New Moon Ski Shop
Address: P.O Box 591 Hwy 63 North, Haywared, WI 54843
Phone: (715) 634-8685 (help)
Fax: (715) 634-2711

Orders: (800)754-8685
Comments: They still sell waxable backcountry skis.

Nooksak Racing Supply
Grey & Kathy Pickett
Address: 202 Mechanic Falls Road, Oxford, ME 04270
Phone: (207) 539-4324
Fax: (207) 539-9681
Email: info@nooksackracing.com
Web Site: www.nooksackracing.com
Comments: Harnesses, skijor, sled accessories, snow hooks, brakes, sled bags, lines, etc.

Nordkyn Outfitters
Address: P.O. Box 1023, Graham, WA 98338-1023
Phone: (253) 847-4128
Fax: (253) 847-4108
Orders (800) 326-4128
Email: nordkyn@nordkyn.com
Web Site: www.nordkyn.com
Comments: Nordkyn harnesses, collars, leads, sled bags, lines, *Kema* sleds, *Wenaha* and *Wolfpacks* (dog packs).

Perry Greene Kennel & Outfitters
Address: 449 Atlantic Highway, Route 1, Waldoboro, ME 04572
Phone: (207) 832-5227
Email: info@mainely-dogs.com
Web Site: www.mainely-dogs.com
Comments: Specializes in equipping the working pet with dog sledding equipment, skijor supplies and dog backpacks.

Powderhound
Address: W2892 Hess Lane, Jefferson, WI 53549
Email: powderhoundmals@dogmail.com
Comments: Weight pull and sledding harnesses for adults and puppies (with and without spreaders), ganglines and other sled lines (snow hook lines, necklines, snublines, shock cords).

Prairie Bilt Sleds
Address: 720 119th. Ave SE, Luverne, ND 58056

Phone: (701) 769-2620
Fax: (701) 769-2797 (24-hour)
Email: prairiebilt@ictc.com
Web Site: www.prairiebiltsleds.com
Comments: Sleds, bags, *NEOS* overshoes and accessories.

Ruff Wear Packs
Address: P.O. Box 1363, Bend, OR 97709
Phone: (888) 783-3932
Email: luckydog@ruffwear.com
Web Site: www.ruffwear.com
Comments: Hiking supplies.

Raven's Watch
Sue Moss
Address: 416 Sandhill Rd., P.O. Box 133, Sundridge, Ontario
CANADA P0A 1Z0
Phone: (705) 386-2524
Email: info@ravenswatch.on.ca
Web Site: www.working-dog-equipment.com
Web Site: www.ravenswatch.on.ca
Comments: Customize and ready-made Working-Dog
Equipment: harness, standard and custom, h-back, x-back, collared harness, walking, tracking, flyball harness. Collars: mushers collars, semi slip, flyball collars. Backpacks. Leads/leashes.
Booties, mushers booties, polar fleece lined pet booties.
Sled/ladder bags, customized bags for racing, day trips, or trip operators. Contact us with your ideas. We will design to your needs.

Risdon Rigs
Clyde Risdon
Address: PO Box 127, Laingsburg, MI 48848.
Phone: (517) 651-6960
Fax: 517-651-6970
Web Site: www.risdonrigs.com
Comments: Sleds, wheeled rigs, harnesses, snow hooks, dog bags.

Schusski Outfitters (Australia)
Wayne and Diane Baker

Email: schusski@gil.com.au
Web Site: http://assa.flix.com.au/P/schusskiprice.html
Comment: Harnesses, ganglines, collars, rigs, sleds, fids, repairs etc.

Skijoring Outfitters
Dina McClure
Address: 89970 Ben Bunch Road, Florence, OR 97439
Phone and Fax: (541) 997-3764
Email: info@skijoringoutfitters.com
Web Site: www.skijoringoutfitters.com
Comments: Information, equipment and personalized advice.
They cater to the beginner.

Snopeak (Scotland U.K.)
Address: 1 Sedgebank, Ladywell, Livingston, West Lothian,
EH54 6HE, Scotland, U.K.
Phone: +44 1506 499243
Email: supplies@snopeak.com
Web Site: www.snopeak.com
Comments: They are the UK's distributor for *ManMat*. Selling collars, harnesses, lines for canicross, scootering, bikejoring and rigs/sleds. Can also supply scooters, dryland rigs and sleds.

Timberpak
Ken Roggow
Address: 8459 Hawk Dr., Eaton Rapids, MI 48827
Email: timberpak2003@yahoo.com.
Comments: Ken invented and sells *Timberpak's Swivel-Matic* tangle-free dog stake out system. It is a swivel with a sealed ball-bearing which allows it to revolve so freely that the chain doesn't become tangled around post. For more information and pricing, contact Ken.

Trailhound Gearshop
Address: 63 Brook Street, Asheville, NC 28803
Phone: 1-866-DOG-PACK (1-866-364-7225)
Local: 828-274-3335
Email: jay@trailhound.com

Web Site: www.trailhound.com
Comments: Trail dog supplies.

Tumnatki Siberians
Karen Yeargain
Address: 8066 SW George Millican Rd, Prineville, OR 97754
Phone: (541) 447-1253
Email: tumnatki@earthlink.net
Web Site: www.tumnatkisiberians.com
Comments: Distributor for *TAIGA* harnesses and collars, *K-Collars* team (circle and semi-slip) and obedience (half-check) collars, *National Dog Food* products, *Champaine* race diet, *Tin Man* pooper scoopers.

Tun-Dra Outfitters
Address: 16438 96th Ave., Nunica, MI 49448
Phone: (616) 837-9726
Fax: (616) 837-9517
Comments: Books, sleds, harnesses, outer gear, Iditarod collectibles, etc.

Wenaha Dog Packs
Address: 5274 State Route 9, Sedro Woolley, WA 98284
Phone: (800) 917-0707
Email: wenahadp@aol.com
Comments: Manufacture dog packs, joggers pack for your dog.

White Pine Outfitters
Address: 62245 Delta Lake Road, Iron River, WI 54847
Phone: (715) 372-5627
Fax: (715) 372-5628
Email: info@WhitePineOutfitters.com
Web Site: www.whitepineoutfitters.com
Comments: Hiking/skijoring belts; tracking harnesses; collars; fly-ball collars; leashes

Windchill Dog Gear (Australia)
Ralph and Sandy Kosh
Address: PO Box 41, Hurstbridge VIC 3099, Australia
Phone: (613) 9714 8540
Fax (613) 9714 8303
Email: windchill@bigpond.com.au
Web Site: www.windchill.com.au
Comments: Collars, harnesses, leads, backpacks, scooters, sleds,

water bowls, ganglines, walking accessories, stakes and tie-outs, booties, walking belts etc.

Windigo Kennels and Outfitters
Address: 8685 Lavin Road, Iron River, WI 54847
Phone: (715) 372-8889
Fax: (715) 372-8686
Web Site: www.windigooutfitters.com
Comments: Manufacturers three different x-back racing styles, weight pulls, h-backs, carting, tracking, and side pull harnesses. Cable and rope lines, collars, leads, sled bags.

Wolf Packs, Inc
Address: PO Box 3195, Ashland, OR 97520
Phone: (541) 482-7669
Web Site: www.wolfpacks.com
Comments: Manufacture dog packs and supplies.

Xpress Outfitters (Australia)
Craig and Melissa Turner
Address: 320 Wilton Park Rd Wilton NSW 2571
Phone & Fax: +612 46772177
Email: ionamal@cyber.net.au
Web Site: www.xpressoutfitters.com
Comments: Harnesses, leads, collars, dog stakes, lines, shock cord, booties, sleds etc.

For general information on the web:
Sleddog Central has more info than you can ever use, it's a great resource. **www.sleddogcentral.com**

I N D E X

329   MUSH!

Charlene G. LaBelle

Charlene, and her husband, Steve LaBelle, are lifetime members of the *Sierra Nevada Dog Drivers* (SNDD). They have been active with sled dogs sports for well over twenty years. Charlene and Steve own and breed champion Alaskan Malamutes. Their dogs are run in harness as well as show. They also backpack, weight pull and do a variety of other activities.

Charlene spent several years on the SNDD Board of Directors as the Treasurer. She also has held every job associated with putting on an ISDRA sanctioned race. She worked with local communities to put on successful races.

Charlene and her dogs have visited many schools and enjoy doing public education on responsible dog ownership, the Iditarod and sled dog sports.

Charlene at the time of this writing is currently in her second term as a Director at Large on the Alaskan Malamute Club of America board of directors.

Charlene is the author of *A Guide To Backpacking With Your Dog* and had articles published in magazines such as *Dog Fancy* and is frequently quoted in publications.

Charlene is a member in good standing in many clubs. Some of which are: *The Dog Writers Association of America* (DWAA), the AMCA, a lifetime member of the *Sierra Nevada Dog Drivers* (SNDD), and the *Northern California Alaskan Malamute Association* (NCAMA – of which she held several offices including President).

Charlene was profiled in Hoflin Publication's *Alaskan Malamute Annual* for 2006.

Other Great Books From Barkleigh Productions

Partners in Independence
A Success Story of Dogs and the Disabled
By Ed and Toni Eames

Partners in Independence is about dogs and those whose lives they enhance. This is the story of visionary people who recognized the potential and made possibilities into realities. Thanks to the dogs and people you will meet in this book, thousands enjoy more enriched lives. They pursue careers, attend school, make friends and cope with the normal situations each day brings. Their dogs are their best friends in the truest sense of the word.

#5041 – Partners in Independence – **$19.95**

Other Great Books From Barkleigh Productions

Scent and the Scenting Dog

By William G. Syrotuck

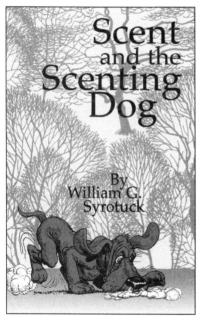

#5024
Tracking Dog – **$19.95**

Unveil the mysteries of Scent! Now you can understand how and why a dog can work scent. This fascinating book explains the composition of scent, how it works in the dog's nose, and what affects scent and much more!

- The Sense of Smell
- Anatomy and Physiology
- Theories and Odor
- The Human as a Scent Source
- Transmission
- Atmospheric Factors and Airborn Scent
- The Ground Scent Picture
- Working on Dog's Scent
- Snow Experiments

Barkleigh Productions, Inc.
970 W. Trindle Road • Mechanicsburg PA 17055
(717) 691-3388 • FAX (717) 691-3381 • Email: info@barkleigh.com

www.barkleigh.com